Travels in America

A LARGE PRINT ANTHOLOGY

Other Anthologies available in Large Print:

Best-loved Poems in Large Print
Favorite Short Stories in Large Print
Favorite Poems in Large Print
Famous Detective Stories in Large Print
A Treasury of Humor in Large Print
Favorite Animal Stories in Large Print
The Best of My Life: Autobiographies in Large Print
Great Ghost Stories in Large Print

TRAVELS IN AMERICA

A LARGE PRINT ANTHOLOGY

EDITED BY
ROY BONGARTZ

G.K. HALL &CO.
Boston, Massachusetts
1988

G.K. Hall Large Print Book Series.

Set in 16 pt Plantin.

Library of Congress Cataloging in Publication Data

Travels in America : a large print anthology / [compiled] by Roy Bongartz.
    p.   cm.—(G.K. Hall large print book series)
  ISBN 0-8161-4412-5 (lg. print)
  1. United States—Description and travel.   2. Travelers—United
States.   3. Large type books.   I. Bongartz, Roy.
[E161.5.T7 1988]
917.3'04—dc19   88-11934

ACKNOWLEDGMENTS

The editor gratefully acknowledges permission to reproduce the coyright material included in this volume. Selections not cited here are in the public domain. In the event of any error or omission, the publisher will be pleased to make the necessary correction in future editions of this work.

"Memories of a Day's Walk from Massachusetts to Maine," from *Spring Jaunts* by Anthony Bailey. © 1975, 1977, 1980, 1986 by Anthony Bailey. Originally appeared in *The New Yorker*. Reprinted by permission of Farrar, Straus and Giroux.

"Gettysburg, PA" by Philip Hamburger. From *An American Notebook* (Knopf). © 1964 Philip Hamburger. Originally appeared in *The New Yorker*. Reprinted by permission of *The New Yorker*.

"Fred King on the Allagash," from *Walking the Dead Diamond River* by Edward Hoagland. © 1985 by Edward Hoagland. Published by North Point Press and reprinted by permission. All rights reserved.

Excerpt from *Travels with Charley: In Search of America* by John Steinbeck. © 1961, 1962 by The Curtis Publishing Co., Inc. © 1962 by John Steinbeck. All rights reserved. Reprinted by permission of Viking Penguin Inc.

"Against the Sea" by Paul Theroux. © 1986 by Paul Theroux. Originally appeared in the *New York Times Magazine*. Reprinted by permission of Paul Theroux.

"Needles in the Dark," from *The Walk West: A Walk Across America* by Peter and Barbara Jenkins. © 1979 by Peter and Barbara Jenkins. Reprinted by permission of William Morrow & Co.

"South by Southeast," from *Blue Highways: A Journey into America* by William Least Heat Moon. © 1982 by William Least Heat Moon. Reprinted by permission of Little, Brown and Company.

"The River," from *Old Glory* by Jonathan Raban. © 1981 by Jonathan Raban. Reprinted by permission of Simon & Schuster, Inc.

"Stapleton, Nebraska" from *Special Places: In Search of Small Town America* by

TABLE OF CONTENTS

Introduction

Roy Bongartz

It is a mysterious fact that we all seem to believe in some magical insight in a stranger's view of us. It may indeed be the case that, knowing little about us, or of our well-established defenses (for the way we are, for the way life goes on around us), the visitor does see people more directly, more objectively—and with the sudden clarity of vision that comes with a new experience. In this collection of travel adventures the watching, probing, commenting mind is nearly always newly arrived on the scene.

These scenes range up, down, and across the United States, just as the writing about them reaches back and forth in time—back as far as the first days of the republic. Through all these dimensions come images—some fleetingly caught, others captured in great detail—that reflect the American spirit. Here we have Tony Bailey wondering just why he is trying to hitchhike on a highway on the Atlantic coast, or—a century and a half earlier—James Audubon's happy sense of a haven found, in the warmth of a rustic country cabin. We regale ourselves in the hit-or-miss quality of chance encounters with strangers, like those of Peter and Barbara Jenkins during their monumental hike across the whole continent. John Steinbeck sends his dog Charley out as his ambassador in meeting strangers along his way.

We discover in the novelist Charles Dickens a discriminating critic of American ways, perhaps disapproving yet participating in the experiences he tells about; we join in on the curiosity of Berton Roueché, who had wondered about the life of farm people in tiny hamlets isolated in an ocean of wheat fields, so spent a month in such a place just to find out. There are firsthand accounts from an emigrant woman heading west in a covered wagon, and from an itinerant peddler roving through the South with a one-hundred-and-twenty-pound pack of goods on his back. All the writers here are involved in some direct way that affects their view of the passing life around them. Often it is their presence that makes something happen, that makes the writing work for us.

The styles are hugely different, of course, from William Least Heat Moon's wonderfully happenstance wanderings on the back roads of the South, to Tom Huth's delightful but nerve-shattering account of the modern-day Los Angeles freeway. And we have a nature lover's hair-raising saga in Enos Mills's report of stumbling his way out of frozen mountain country because of snow blindness.

The writer on travel takes on many roles—sometimes as critic of food, art, music, architecture; he becomes an instant-powder sociologist, and a self-analyst as well, assiduously noting his least reactions to new stimuli. He becomes a historian, a folklorist, a political theorist—not to say a philosopher.

Above all he becomes an actor in a theater of his own devising, the interacting characters appearing unscheduled, pell-mell, according to the luck of the road. Here in this collection, consider Jonathan Raban on his little boat, riding brazenly down the vast Mississippi, the motley folk he meets ashore along the way amazed at his foolhardy venture (and his English accent). He becomes somebody else, somebody quite new, simply because of that trip he is taking. We can all feel the spark that animates the writers selected here, feel the sudden onset of a rare new character within our minds, somebody with an urgent new purpose; it can come with that very first moment of starting out on a trip. Every tiny event then looms large, important, recordable, unforgettable. As travel writer Paul Theroux notes at the beginning of a solitary boat trip across Cape Cod Bay: "Travel is an attitude . . . travel is mostly in the mind."

Travels in America

A LARGE PRINT ANTHOLOGY

EASTERN UNITED STATES

Memories of a Day's Walk

ANTHONY BAILEY

Anthony Bailey, born in England in 1933, has homes on both sides of the Atlantic and writes frequently about his travels afoot. Among a dozen books, including two novels, Bailey has devoted one to a boat he constructed himself, The Thousand Dollar Yacht. *This following selection, recounting a day's hike along the New Hampshire coast, illustrates well John Updike's recent description of Bailey as "the last great walker" and one who "writes as naturally as he walks."*

In the evening, hitchhiking back, I was quickly faced with the question of what I was doing there, a mile or so out of New Castle, New Hampshire, thumb pointing south, one foot supported by a yellow fire hydrant improbably stuck by the dusty rural roadside, and my green nylon knapsack propped where the late-in-the-day, late-August light might dwell on it as evidence of an honest traveler. But since with strangers, even those kind enough to give one a ride, one has the right to shorten one's explanations, I said simply, "I've just walked the New Hampshire coastline." There was also the fact that, just then, starting back down a road I had trudged along a few hours

3

before, I felt enveloped in a sort of concentricity, with time curled up on itself, my mind warm and swollen and in a blurry tingle, like my feet—I must have walked some twenty-two miles, counting the ins and outs and a few reverses—and I didn't feel like enlarging on my reasons why. There were various answers, or parts of answers, anyway, to questions of motive. I could borrow Mallory's response "Because it is there"—in New Hampshire's case not record height like Everest, but record brevity, the coast being eighteen miles long as a seagull might fly it, the shortest coastline of any state touching salt water; or I could give another answer, that I was born on the coast of old Hampshire, England, but now lived mostly in London and took whatever chance I could of walking in sight of the sea. Or I could say that I was visiting old friends who, since I'd last seen them, had separated. I had a day free between seeing them separately, one in one Massachusetts town, one in another. An appropriate time, and time enough, to go walking.

I set off northward along the New Hampshire beach at 7:50 a.m.—sand behind me, sand to my left, sand in front, and to my right the calm sea; small wavelets running in; sun low and very bright; a barely perceptible offshore breeze to be felt on my left ear. I had left my car on Route 1A, two hundred yards inland over the slight ridge of dunes, where the honky-tonk sprawl of Salisbury Beach, the last town in Massachusetts, petered out at a road junction with a few cottages, gas station, traffic lights, and restaurant signs. Just north of the junction, a big road sign said "Welcome to /

Bienvenue au New Hampshire." I failed to rouse any response in the house attached to a narrow roadside lot where all-day parking was advertised for one dollar (and offenders who failed to pay were threatened with being towed away). I walked, therefore, across 1A to a combination gas station and general store called Salisbury Building Supply (which also sold Frisbees, fishing gear, and newspapers). A mustachioed young man who stood behind the till took the dollar bill I proffered as a parking fee and handed me fifty cents. I asked him if he could tell me exactly where New Hampshire began. He said, "Out through the door, about four yards on your left." I parked my old Saab on what was as yet the shady side of the building, front wheels in Massachusetts, back wheels in New Hampshire. So far, the day was cloudless. I left my raincoat and shoes in the car, donning an elderly white cricket sweater, worn blue sailing sneakers, and a broad-brimmed olive-green ex-British Army bush hat—an item military historians might take into account when pondering Britain's success (compared with other nations conducting counter-insurgency operations) in quelling terrorists in the Malayan jungles. Wallet, spare socks, notebook, Texaco road map, geological survey map, and Coastal Chart 1206 (Portsmouth to Cape Ann) went into the knapsack. I popped back into the store to ask the man whether there was any public transport back down the coast I intended to walk—any trains, buses?

"Nope—not a thing."

"Then I guess I'll have to hitchhike back."

"Yep. Nothing like the good old thumb."

On the beach, I fell into an optimistic north-bound stride. The low light, sweeping in from the sea over the gently tilted expanse of sand, gave dramatic prominence to the people already there: four solitary joggers; a man slowly searching the beach with a metal detector, caressing it almost, as if polishing a floor; several dog owners being taken for exercise by their pets; and, in two ragged ranks to one side of the gap in the dunes through which I'd come, what in that light might have been taken for the larvae of a giant insect—long brown and green tubes which wriggled, opened, and released forms that stood up, stretched, yawned, and sometimes hugged one another. As I went by, one pair of teenagers who had spent the summer night thus in their sleeping bags ran to the water's edge and stuck their feet in an in-running wavelet and, to judge by their squeals, found it chilly.

The air, too, had a go-fast nip to it. The tide was roughly half up, and I walked midway between the water's edge and the high-tide line, following a strip of flat, hard, gravelly sand. On it, the footprints of joggers could be recognized by an abrupt ridge of pushed-back sand—the aft end of the mark made by the ball of a foot. There were also footprints of dogs, the trident marks of gulls' feet in the darker sand beside the tide pools, and—farther up the beach—the rippled tire tracks of a six-wheeled former army truck onto which debris from litter drums was being emptied. The sand was furrowed in some places into miniature ravines and deltas, where water ran off seaward. The asphalt-shingled roofs of modest summer bungalows peered over the fringe of dunes; the roofs thickened not far ahead into the community—municipally complete with water tower and at least two Stars and Stripes on flagstaffs—of Seabrook Beach. Beyond, the visible coast stretched northward as far as a promontory I identified on the chart as Great Boars Head, roughly four miles distant. Seaward, the horizon seemed higher than one expected: I felt as if I were walking in a valley banked with sand and water; both nearby rocks and far-off fishing boats sat high on the sea's surface. The onshore light, glinting off the sea, skipping off tide pools and sand and forming dark caves and slots under the cottage eaves and porches, had lost the hazy look of summer. It had an autumnal chiaroscuro, a specific New England property that is the effect of sunlight of a southern strength in a northern landscape. (Winslow Homer and Edward Hopper come to mind as painters who have captured it.) Meanwhile, my shadow, knapsacked and bush-hatted, progressed at right angles to me, uphill on my left.

At 8:25 I reached the first break in the coast—in fact, a breakwater composed of large granite blocks, forming the southern side of the entrance to Hampton Harbor, a marsh-backed estuary at the junction of the Hampton Falls River. Here, warmed up by now, I took off and stowed away my sweater. A party fishing boat, complete with party on deck, was bludgeoning its way out against the tide—whose incoming was announced by a black can buoy, C7, tilted inland. Less organized individuals, including a number of small boys, were already fishing off the end of the breakwater.

To the northeast, offshore six miles or so, could be made out the silhouetted humps and whalebacks of the Isles of Shoals; from that angle, which placed some islands in front of others, there appeared to be only two of them, rather than seven. Westward up the harbor entrance lay the bridge that carries Route 1A, the only way across the channel. But when I started toward it I ran up against a barrier of private gardens and fences belonging to a prosperous clump of houses at this corner of beach. Evidently, a lot of people were put in a similar quandary here, for in the otherwise inviting yard of a modern gray-cedar house stood a sign: "Exit to road 7 houses back." I therefore went back and found between two houses a sandy path lined with chain-link fencing, leading to the quiet streets of what might have been a year-round subdivision, unromantic except for the many Italian and French names outside the houses. At the Jolivets', an additional sign proclaimed that metal detectors could be bought within (I assume all the loose change that falls out of the pockets and purses of beachgoers is the lure.) Not a person was to be seen in the streets, though numerous cabbage butterflies were taking an 8:35 spin. The houses were eerily quiet. In one front yard, a pale woman in her late forties lay sleeping in an aluminum garden chair. Had she spent the night there? I'd gone past when the name Cedarburg jumped into my head. I spent a long summer college vacation in Wisconsin, and one of several jobs I had for sustenance and pocket money was assembling garden loungers. Several days a week, I came in from my digs in the outlying town of Cedarburg to work for a sweet couple called the Jungs. They lived in a pastoral suburb of Milwaukee with an apple orchard, a garden store, and a lissome seventeen-year-old daughter named Susie. I picked apples, read Yeats and MacNeice to Susie, chatted to the Jungs over lunch about the wild doings of Senator Joseph McCarthy, and in the afternoons bolted together the webbing-covered tubular frames that formed the light, stretched-open Z shape of the loungers. (I believe I still could—if handed the cardboard box in which the parts came—assemble one in three minutes, possibly while declaiming MacNeice's "The sunlight in the garden, / Hardens and grows cold, / We cannot cage the minute / Within its nets of gold. / When all is told / We cannot beg for pardon.") At summer's end, I hitchhiked to New York to get the boat back to England. Come to think of it, that, twenty-odd years ago, was my last serious venture in free road travel.

New Hampshire (1938), the WPA guide to the state, says that in 1657 a stone on the dunes near Hampton Harbor entrance was inscribed to mark the then boundary between Massachusetts and New Hampshire, but I didn't see it. In 1938, the bridge here was wooden and cars had to pay a fifteen-cent toll to make the crossing. Now it is steel, and free, with a bascule section that lifts for boats needing the headroom. I walked across it a few yards behind a barefoot girl in flared blue jeans. Perhaps we should note for future historians that some in our time went barefoot by choice or from fashion, and not out of necessity.

Hampton Beach is the town on the north side of

the span. It is also well placed at the seaward end of Route 101, a multi-lane highway that comes in at right angles to the shore from Manchester and other inland points and gives Hampton Beach good reason still for the WPA guide's description of it as "the mecca of hundreds of thousands of vacationists." Atlantic City rather than Mecca is the resort you would probably think of in Hampton Beach, though the scale of things is smaller. A wide, oceanfront boulevard aptly named Ocean Boulevard has amusement arcades, a state beach, and various hotels and motels with such names as Sea Breeze, Hollywood, Sea Den, Alecia, King Neptune, Blue Haven, and Sun 'n Surf. Suggestions are made that the Hampton Beach vacationing crowd is cosmopolitan—or at least French Canadian. *"Ici on parle français,"* a sign said outside one motel. *"Remorquage à vos frais,"* which means "Towed away at your expense," declared a placard in a private parking lot. Between the boulevard and the beach lay a long municipal parking area, with parking meters, and the green-and-white license plates of New Hampshire cars, each presenting the belligerent—but evidently rather wishful—state motto, "Live Free or Die."

At 9 a.m., Hampton Beach had the feeling of bustle building up: kids were arriving on the sand and getting their kites off the ground, flicking Frisbees, and laying the foundations for sand sculptures; bike and beach-umbrella rental stands were being opened for the day; elderly couples were parking their cars and getting out for a short stroll, quite a few of them speaking French. Other cars were moving remarkably slowly down the boulevard—partly perhaps because of the holiday atmosphere, partly because of frequent 10 m.p.h. speed-limit signs and cruising police cars. Drivers were politely yielding to cars parking or unparking, and were stopping to allow pedestrians to cross the roadway. I walked along the seafront promenade, noting but refusing to be ensnared by the restaurants and cafés on the other side of the boulevard. Advertisements begged passersby to sample their breakfast specials—"fried dough" being one that intrigued me, though not, then and there, to the point of actually wanting to sit down in front of a plate of it. (Other Hampton Beach fare, presumably for later in the day, including a bucket of spaghetti and eight meatballs for $4.50.) I took in the fact that the Bavarian Brauhaus Band was scheduled to play in the Sea Shell Stage from 7 to 8:30 p.m., while from the free copy of *Beach News*, picked up in the information booth next to the auditorium, I learned that the big movies showing on the shore that week were *Tidal Wave* and *Jaws*. I stored away the information that at 7 p.m. daily the Seabrook Greyhound bus left the Ashworth Hotel for the Seabrook dog track, offering, if all else failed, a possible partway trip back to my car. On Friday, the local Chamber of Commerce intended to "host" the weekly New Hampshire Sweeps drawing at the Sea Shell, with beach towels being awarded courtesy of the New Hampshire Sweepstakes Commission. Lotteries and sweepstakes have a long and useful past in no-state-tax New Hampshire: one institution that was given a boost by them is Dartmouth College.

Indeed, New Hampshire seems to have concluded some time back that man's baser instincts might as well be put to public use: not only betting but drinking, with grog shops run by the state government, and liquor sold comparatively cheap. But to make up for this largesse, numerous signs along the shore prohibit the consumption of alcoholic drinks on state beaches. And, perhaps to make up for *that*, other activities the Puritans might have frowned on were being countenanced as I walked through Hampton Beach: on the sand just past the Sea Shell Stage, I saw five swimsuited girls in a neat circle playing gin rummy; nearby, a boy and a girl on a beach towel were having a morning cuddle.

Walking, and especially walking on beaches, provides good exercise for one's memory. I passed a green notice board with the chalked information that high tide that day was 11:12 a.m., low tide 5:05 p.m. The water temperature was yet to be announced. Another notice told the public to "Contact Life Guard About Lost Children." I remember being lost on the beach at Sandown, Isle of Wight, when I was four or five—or rather (the truth doesn't turn up until one begins thinking about the occasion more intently), remembering being found, being hugged and kissed, "Nothing to worry about, it's all right," and recall how vast that tiny beach had seemed with nearly the whole population of the known world on it and no sign of my parents or my bucket and spade. And possibly because the water of the English Channel in those prewar British summers didn't strike me as hospitably warm, forcing me to take adventurous excursions on foot, I didn't learn to swim until I reached America the first time—was "evacuated" for the duration of the war in Europe, and found myself, with great good fortune, living with an Ohio family who spent the summer of 1941 on Cape Cod. In Chatham, aged eight, on the splendid beach which encloses Pleasant Bay, I discovered that the withdrawing tide left pools of various depths, which were soon heated by the sun. So I proceeded from shallow pool to deep, from feet on the bottom to strenuous dog paddle, and on Labor Day was awarded the cup for the dog-paddle stakes in the end-of-season swim meet of the local beach club. The cup still sits in a glass-fronted corner cupboard in my parents' house, my sole contribution of prize silverware among the many pieces won at country athletic meets by my father, a middle-distance runner.

I was forced to stay on Route 1A for the next mile or so, behind Great Boars Head and along North Beach. The beach, already narrow by natural circumstance, was made even more so by the rising tide. Rather than hop from rock to rock, I walked on the sidewalk, which was sheltered from the waves of storms by a four-foot-high green-painted steel seawall, a bit rusty in places. From this point, I could see the remainder of the New Hampshire coast stretching ahead—could see, in fact, across the mouth of the Piscataqua River, where the state ends, to Gerrish Island, Maine. From this angle, four of the Isles of Shoals were visible. At this point, too, it became palpable that my sailing sneakers weren't ideal road shoes, and at 10 a.m. I was happy to clamber down to the actual beach again. Here, at the north end of

North Beach, groins had been built of large granite blocks to preserve the sand, and seemed to be doing their job. But the beach thus formed was zigzag, the seaward edge of the sand between each groin slanting outward toward the northeast. From dry sand on one side of a groin, one climbed over the granite barrier and was met with water on the other side. This forced one to scramble inland a little along the groin before arriving over dry beach again that one could jump down to. Inland, behind a single row of houses spaced out on the inshore side of 1A, marshy meadows ran for a mile or so westward; then there was a range of low green hills. Along the road itself, a procession of cars streamed north, faster here, perhaps, because under the seawall drivers had no view of the sea. Unlike cars that notoriously flood into cities on weekday mornings with a single occupant, these cars were generally full to bursting with children, dogs, sleeping bags, suitcases, and sometimes bikes on the back, carried like lifeboats in davits.

Here I began to wonder about 1A's potential for south-bound hitchhikers. An unworthy thought at this time of the morning, no doubt. Would Scott have reached the South Pole if he'd worried about getting back? Ah, but Scott didn't get back. My hitchhiking life flashed before me. At one time or another, I had given plenty of rides to high-school students clearly stranded by later-than-usual school hours and no bus service, and to back-packing youngsters on the way from London to the cross-Channel ferries. But I'd also passed a lot of hitchhikers by in the years since I had last put myself out on that particular roadside limb, and I doubted

14

if my standing was good in the record of whatever god or goddess (Mercury? Iris?) looked after hitchhikers' interests. Drivers, of course, think of the risks to them, but as I remember it, the peril for the rider should also be considered. One wet Good Friday, hitchhiking from Dieppe to Paris, I was given a lift by a French angler, and driver, who as the car went round the bends of a slippery *route nationale* at numerous kilometers an hour kept taking his hands off the steering wheel to demonstrate to me, in the back among his rod and baskets, the length of a fish he had caught or was going to catch (the tenses were hard to make out), often turning round to grin amiably at me as he gestured. Coming east from Wisconsin, armed with cardboard and crayon for making destination signs, I had an apprehensive ride across part of Indiana with a man whose business card, produced with a snap of the fingers from a point in midair up near the rearview mirror, proclaimed him a vice-president of the International Society of Magicians. (I expected rabbits to pop from the cigar lighter. I neglected to ask how the lady was sawn in half.) And from Chillicothe, Ohio, to Charleston, West Virginia, on the great-circle route I took to New York City, I rode with a truck driver whose reminiscences consisted largely of the number of times he had overturned his tractor-trailer rig, skidding great distances and skittling Burma-Shave signs.

At the north end of North Beach, a small, unnamed promontory gave a measure of shelter from the north and west to a dozen boats moored there, bobbing. Two lads were joyfully rowing a pair of brightly painted dories in the gentle surf. I

15

made my way over the rocks that buttressed the headland, with its complement of unpretentious, well-built shingled summer houses. The rocks, interspersed with patches of mud and eel grass, ran out to an offshore ledge, and as I negotiated them, three small girls in swimsuits came by. One, also wearing purple bedroom slippers, said to her friends, "You guys going out on the rocks?" It was the sort of place where things are assembled by wind and tide. I saw a dead seagull; a single flip-flop; fragments of foam mattress; a crushed take-away coffee container; a plastic spoon; a frayed strand of polypropylene lobster-pot line. But very little driftwood. There were midges in the air, and a swooping band of swallows, presumably gobbling up midges. Friends had warned me of the possibility of "greenheads"—fearsome flies that torment beachgoers, at least in Massachusetts, forcing communities to set up expensive trap boxes to try to catch them. But so far no greenheads.

One difficulty with beach walking is that after a while you feel one leg is getting longer than the other. As I stepped out onto the sand again, I tried walking backward for a way to put things into balance. It may not have helped my muscles, but it certainly gave me more "visibility." Several people, turning their heads to look at me, said "Good morning," and an elderly man in sun hat, swimsuit, and sneakers called out, "How's it going there, young fella?" On the extensive porch of one beachfront house, a crowd of informally dressed people had gathered. I was wondering if it was a property owners' meeting, when I heard a boy call out to a woman coming down the steps from the porch, "Was he old?" Perhaps it was—albeit in bright Bermuda shorts and terry-cloth wraps—a wake.

For a change, the parking lot at this North Hampton beach (just south of Little Boars Head) was free. However, one had to pay if one wanted to use the little shingled bathhouses—fifty cents for a quick change, $3.00 daily rate, according to a sign. I crossed 1A behind the beach at this point in order to reach the Sand Dollar Sandwich Shoppe for what back home we call elevenses. I'd had a boiled egg and an English muffin for breakfast much earlier that morning, and now felt the need of some small thing to get me through to lunchtime. I found a place at the crowded counter, next to a woman eating a blueberry muffin, which looked scrumptious. When approached by one of the pair of somewhat sullen-looking girls—who wore the nurse-like uniform of white dress and white shoes that is apparently *de rigueur* for summer help along this coast—I said I would like a cup of coffee and a blueberry muffin, please. "We're fresh out of blueberry muffins," she said. "How about an English?"

I'm usually a pushover for English muffins. I sometimes take a large box of Thomas's back to England, since the English muffin as known in America is just about unobtainable there (Sainsbury's, a supermarket chain, sells a muffin that isn't a patch on Thomas's) and I've gone off a former love, the crumpet. But one muffin a day keeps desire at bay. I made do with a coffee while I tried to read that morning's Manchester (N.H.) *Union Leader* (a single-seat space at coffee shops

17

doesn't give much scope for page turning; I read what I could of the *Union Leader's* front page, folded up, on my lap). The paper goes in for blue headlines, a bouncy line in white stars on a blue band printed down the right-hand margin, and under the paper's name an epigraph from Daniel Webster: "There is nothing so powerful as truth." However, this particular edition seemed to support the belief that there is nothing as effective as tickling the reader's sense of *déjà vu*. I was carried back to the summer of 1953 and McCarthy country by the banner headline, SOVIETS GET U.S. WARNING, subheaded "Told to Keep 'Hands Off' of Portugal." Surely a redundant "of"? The front-page editorial began flatly and ungrammatically "The key to straightening out the mess that this country is to be found is in informing the people of the United States as to what is actually going on." The woman on my left, who had just finished the ultimate blueberry muffin, was saying to her female companion, "But if they're not living together anymore, why does she still get up at seven?"

The southwest breeze had bestirred itself while I was in the Sand Dollar. The flap of my knapsack blew against the back of my neck and had to be secured before I walked on. Offshore, darker patches of wind-ruffled water seemed to travel seaward, where a gray lobster boat was hauling and shooting traps off Little Boars Head. The road climbed the headland, which, despite its name, is a good deal more impressive than Great Boars Head. Beside an introductory bend of the road, a gardener was weeding a big cambered bank of flowers, including phlox and chrysanthemums, provided by the local residents' association. The local residents didn't have their names on their gates or mailboxes, but according to the WPA guide, which in these dynastic matters may still have some force, "from the south and rounding the curve in the road appear in order the Studebaker estate, and the Nutting, Fuller, Spaulding, Manning, and Studebaker mansions." The mansions were what people in Newport call cottages —big, well-built 1920s houses with (one imagined) butler's pantries, nurseries, and laundry chutes. Garden contractors were at work on the spacious lawns, their pickup trucks parked in the driveways, their mowers mowing, and their hedge clippers buzzing. There was actually a sidewalk here, and a trim grass verge on the sea side of the road, which was now a corniche thirty or forty feet above the rocks. Bushes and plants had a placed look about them, and several comfortable varnished pine benches had been set there for people who wanted to sit and admire the view. The additional height above sea level allowed one to see the whole sweep of the coast southward round Ipswich Bay to the tip of Cape Ann. To the north, off Portsmouth, New Hampshire, and the mouth of the Piscataqua, a huge black tanker rode at anchor.

Little Boars Head merges with Fox Hill Point, and the coast then makes a shallow concave dip to the town of Rye Beach. There were neither boars nor foxes to be seen, but plenty of birds. Six cormorants and a lone black-backed gull stood on a single rock, half awash, while in the adjacent swell twenty-four ducks swam, riding high—ex-

19

actly a dozen couples, or so it seemed, reinforcing my doubts about the natural rightness of the metric system. I also saw four plump but graceful downy gray birds, which later consultation with Roger Tory Peterson's guidebook led me to think were dowitchers or knots; a flock of sanderlings skittering along the water's edge; and, in a pond on the inland side of the road, a heron, standing so still I wondered if it was a statue of a heron, heron-still. Beach rose, beach plum, morning glory, bayberry, and goldenrod grew in niches and patches between the rocks. The sidewalk turned into a genuine boardwalk, on which I headed toward Rye Beach. Six-inch-wide planks, twelve to fifteen feet long, were laid four abreast on the summit of a man-made stone-and-shingle embankment protecting the road from the sea. The planks, clattering a little as I walked along them, made a pleasant change from sand and asphalt. Moreover, the contact with what's there, through the soles of one's feet, that one gets while walking produces a marvelous equanimity. Down below on the road, a yellow Corvette went snorting by, driven by a bare-chested youth who had one arm on the wheel, the other round the shoulders of his girl passenger. He shouted something up at me—words I didn't get, but the tone was arrogant and abusive. I threw him a cheerful, dismissive wave. (If I had been in a car he was overtaking, hearing him shout the same thing, I would have been furious.) On the narrow boardwalk I encountered only a ten-speed Peugeot, pedaled rapidly toward me by a boy in a bright-red T-shirt. I stepped aside onto the stones to let him pass and got a wave of thanks.

I kept up a good pace through Rye Beach—though tempted by a pizzeria, and sudden desire for a *quattro stagioni* of the kind I used to order at Luigino's on West Forty-eighth Street. (The pleasure of eating pizza at Luigino's was finally undermined by continued dynamite blasting as the great office-building boom engulfed Sixth Avenue; and Luigino's in the end went, too.) But this pizzeria was closed. Rye Beach has a short strip of stores, houses on both sides of 1A, and an unfancy beach of gray sand. On the section of it called Jenness Beach, three girls—undeterred by state law—were keeping their eyes on a half-gallon bottle of red Paisano cooling in the foamy edge of the sea.

One doesn't get a great sense of the past along much of this coast—perhaps because of the impact of the summery present, perhaps because the early settlers tended to make their first settlements farther inland (Rye preceded Rye Beach; Hampton, Hampton Beach, etc.)—but Straw's Point, which I was approaching, has not only a history but a prehistory. The section of 1A running up to it is called Cable Road, because in 1874 the first Atlantic telegraph cable came ashore at Straw's Point, from Ireland. The mansard-roofed, clapboard-sided cable station on Old Beach Road is now part of a motel, with bright-red doors and window trim. Before it was Straw's Point, it was Locke's Neck. One of the first settlers, John Locke, came on the canoes of an Indian raiding party here, cut holes in them, and caused the warriors to walk home. One day in 1694, they returned for revenge. They

21

found Locke reaping grain and shot him with his own gun, which he'd left on a nearby rock. But before he died, Locke swung his sickle and cut off the nose of one of his enemies. A state historical marker on 1A near here draws attention to the fact that off the point are the remains of a sunken forest, remnants of the last Ice Age. Large gnarled stumps, with the original Atlantic cable weaving through them, are said to be visible at low tide. It was scarcely forty minutes after high water and I didn't see them. Deprived of pizza and blueberry muffins, and with hope of sustenance a mile away at Rye Harbor, I pushed on.

At 12:05 p.m., after more than eleven miles, I entered the first eating establishment I came to: the Rye Harbor Restaurant, which, for the purpose of taking in northbound travelers, was strategically situated a quarter of a mile south of Rye Harbor itself. Instead of the harbor, a nutrient-looking marsh abuzz with birds and dragonflies could be viewed through the screened restaurant windows. The décor within was seashore driftwood, with fishing nets and lobster-pot markers draped over cheap plywood paneling of the sort that looks like greasy brown linoleum, which was further enlivened with dreadful "original paintings" of schooners, draggers, yachts, and waves breaking on picturesque headlands. The paintings were for sale. However, I was the first lunch customer, and the young waitress—white dress, white shoes—was friendly. I had clam chowder, fried Maine shrimp, a bottle of Heineken's, and blueberry pie with vanilla ice cream—a dish which, in restaurants at least, is invariably better in the relish of anticipation than it turns out to be in the syrupy staleness of fact. (One of life's little lessons which I don't seem to learn.) When I paid the bill, the girl said, "Thank you very much, sir. Have a nice day."

The nice day I was having might have been even nicer if the road had not felt quite so hot through my sneakers. A little roadside marker informed me that 1A is called the Yankee Trail here, and I stepped along the edge of the trail, where tarmac thinned into gravel and sand that was interwoven with lonely blades of coarse grass, hardy weeds, shreds of old beach towels and fiberglass insulation, fragments of brown beer bottles, and flattened Schlitz cans. The early Yankees dredged out the cove here for their fishing boats, and more recent improvers have enlarged it for yachts and lobster boats. A square bite out of the coast, partly closed by a stone breakwater, and with a few necessary sheds and buildings: that's Rye Harbor. I was glad to get onto the beach once more—first on the sands south of Concord Point, on Rye North Beach, and then, after another mile of roadwork, on the beach of Wallis Sands. Each of the New Hampshire beaches seem to lie between similar rocky points and to have a crescent of summer cottages, changing rooms, lifeguard chairs, flags flying above a club or pavilion, and kites flying. But Wallis Sands had a somewhat more intimate family scale than the others. Small children were kneeling, digging deep holes toward China, or sitting with their knees up, patting the sand into the shapes of forts or fishes—one was making a complacent-looking shark. It's nice to see people lying on beaches, face and stomach up, accepting the blessings of the sun, or face down, dozing in the warmth of it. One small child lay bottom up alongside his mother, an arm stretched across her back so that his fingers lay flat in total contact with her skin. A young couple—he in swimsuit, she in halter-neck top and denim shorts—lay face to face, kissing lightly, as if not to get each other sticky or sandy. In the sand nearby, someone had carefully written, in large capitals, DRACULA LIVES FOREVER.

At Wallis Sands, I perched myself on a flat stone, took off my sneakers, and stuck my feet in the sea. Lovely feeling! From my chart, it appeared that the rest of the coastline was rocky; it was going to be edge-of-the-road work for me from here on. Off Portsmouth, the tanker was still there, closer now, but looking as if she were lower in the water. One remarkable thing about this coastline is the lack of oil or tar on it, compared with any British or European beach, where small black globules of the sticky stuff are liable to get on your clothes or skin, and take a lot of getting off. How long this state of Eden will last, who knows? The *Union Leader* that day had a story about five of the six New England governors (free-living New Hampshire for some reason didn't participate) asking for a delay before they responded to a government request for their nominations of areas off their coast that should be preserved from oil drilling. (The governors were waiting for results of studies on fish population and ocean-bottom conditions.) Here the Isles of Shoals were at their closest. Sunlit yellow sand and green hillsides were visible on Appledore, the largest of the islands. Several white-sailed yachts leaned from the afternoon breeze. Small waves splashed over my feet against the rocks.

Undoubtedly, it is the sight and sound of natural movement, the perceptible evidence of time passing, that makes anyone sitting by the sea brood, or, as the poets used to put it, "muse." A century ago, John Greenleaf Whittier was the prime example of this activity in these parts, and wrote a number of now scarcely readable poems (mélanges of earnest newspaper editorials and women's magazine stories in strict meter) with such titles as "Hampton Beach" and "Amy Wentworth." Matthew Arnold's "Dover Beach" is the inimitable star of the genre, rendering, as it does so precisely, the way in which "the tremulous cadence" of the sea, with its "melancholy, long, withdrawing roar," gives one a powerful sense of transience and justifies his cry: "Ah, love, let us be true/To one another!" Perhaps one should react this way only on shingle, on steeply shelving beaches like Dover, but I found myself on Wallis Sands thinking about my Massachusetts friends, whom I had known since the early days of their marriage. They had weathered twenty years of ups and downs, much giving and taking, but now seemed to be giving in to the seductive idea that they could by splitting up reach "a land of dreams,/So various, so beautiful, so new." And perhaps it wasn't just thought of them that made me sad; it was also self-interest, as another marker in my life, a marriage, was swept away on the ebb.

"Enough of this. Got to be moving on," I said

aloud. At this stage in a long walk, one often starts talking to oneself. I'd done about sixteen miles; it was just past two-thirty. I not only spoke encouraging remarks to myself but whistled snatches of "It's a Long Way to Tipperary" and sang the chorus of "The Caisson Song" ("When the caissons go rolling along"). Marching songs, well designed to keep one foot swinging past the other. This was on a rural stretch of road, a little way in from the shore, that bent out around Odiorne's Point, another headland with some history. Among the first voyagers to the spot were Captain Martin Pring, who arrived in his ship *Speedwell* in 1603, looking for sassafras, a laurel with bark and roots then valued for their medicinal properties; the French explorer Samuel de Champlain, who came by in 1605; and Captain John Smith, who visited and admired it in 1614. (He gave the Isles of Shoals the name Smith's Isles.) The first proper settler on Odiorne's Point was a Scotsman, David Thompson, who picked it in 1623 as a "fitt place to build their houses for habitacons" because "it was high, it had good harbor and a fine spring, and the great salt marsh to the west made it easily defensible against savages." The road wound beside the wooded crest of Odiorne's, on the right, and the wide salt marshes, pale green with the afternoon sun on them, stretching away to the left. Along here, I had to make a decision I had been putting off; this involved answering the question: Where does the New Hampshire coast actually stop? In many ways, Odiorne's Point had a good claim to be its termination—and I could have walked out along a little road that ran through a state park to the point, the end of the continuous mainland coast. But my chart showed that New Castle Island, to the north, had a small peninsula sticking out a smidgen to the east of the most easterly point of Odiorne's. It seemed that if I had stood out on the tip of Odiorne's and leaned well forward, I—or my nose—would have been as far east as that New Castle peninsula. There was also the fact that the geological-survey map, showing state borders, made it clear that New Castle Island lay cheek by jowl with the Maine border, running down the Piscataqua River; whereas Odiorne's Point was three-quarters of a mile from this frontier as it ran out to the Isles of Shoals. And there was an even more serious aspect of the situation. Although I sat pondering the problem some two miles as the crow flies from the Ultima Thule of New Castle, the route I would have to take to get there, around various bays and inlets and across bridges, looked to be at least five miles. I and my leg muscles had a little tussle with my conscience then. No one would dispute that—having reached Odiorne's—I had conquered the New Hampshire coastline, would he? *Would* he?

It was the inner glow of glory, therefore (and the fear that I might be denying myself a just helping of it), that kept my feet going. I trudged past Odiorne's Point and westward past Frost Point, and over the bridge that spans an inlet from Little Harbor, which takes a considerable chunk out of the marshes and had to be rounded. I was no longer quite so observant of roadside detail. I failed to proceed farther than I had to off my route in order to see the house, on Little Harbor Road, the WPA guide informed me had been the summer residence of Francis Parkman, the great nineteenth-century historian, and before that had been the home of Benning Wentworth. Benning was one of three Wentworths who were Royal Governors of New Hampshire—in his case, from 1741 to 1767. He held court here (the guide informs us) "in high-spirited style, keeping up the aristocratic tradition of bees-wing port and high play at cards . . . At the close of a banquet celebrating his sixtieth birthday and attended by the cream of New England's aristocracy, he called in Martha Hilton, his housekeeper, and bade the Reverend Arthur Brown, rector of St. John's Church in Portsmouth, read the [marriage] ceremony then and there, which the astonished prelate did." Thomas Bailey Aldrich, the Portsmouth writer (*An Old Town by the Sea*, 1893), called the house "an architectural freak" and "a cluster of whimsical extensions." He went on, "It originally contained fifty-two rooms . . . The chambers were connected in the oddest manner, by unexpected steps leading up or down, and capricious little passages that seem to have been the unhappy afterthoughts of the architect. But it is a mansion on a grand scale, and with a grand air. The cellar was arranged for the stabling of a troop of thirty horse in times of danger."

Route 1A went on into Portsmouth, and a mile or so before reaching that city, I turned off on 1B. This ran past an occasional elderly private house and Mike's Marina, with a motley collection of old boats no longer in their element. Other boats were moored in the creek beside the bridge on which I

crossed to New Castle Island. And there, overlooking the harbor and a golf course, was a sight!
Why it isn't listed among the seven wonders of the
world—or, at least, of New England—I don't
know. But I nominate the Hotel Wentworth. It
must be one of the largest clapboard buildings
extant. Built in the 1870s, four stories high, with
towers at both ends and a Swiss-chalet roof, it
stretches—like the Empire State Building lying on
its side—about a quarter of a mile along the road,
which has the feeling here of being part of the golf
club, with golfers and caddies strolling along it. At
the Wentworth in 1905 stayed the delegates of
the peace conference that brought to an end the
Russo–Japanese War. Walking by it, I felt a bit
dizzy, perhaps from the scale of the building, the
light on the white clapboards, the weird vocabu-
lary of golf that came to me in snatches, and the
fact that I was moving on fast-running-down reserves of energy. I felt overwhelmed by surreal
images of sunlit clarity, as in a Magritte—one such
vision being of the battleship *Potemkin* planked in
clapboards and manned by Lilliputian golfers.

Fortunately, it was only another mile or so,
through a wooded area of prosperous, tucked-away
exurban homes, into New Castle. Once a busy
fishing community and military post, it is now a
rather somnolent, fixed-up place, with narrow,
winding streets that feel like mere paths widened
by use. Old saltbox houses sat on grassy banks.
But there wasn't much to suggest that New Castle
was formerly the seat of the Royal Governor and
his court, a town with crowded docks, taverns,
and prisons; or that in 1682 the place was enliv-

ened by the antics of a stone-throwing devil, who (according to Richard Chamberlain, Secretary of the Province at the time) "threw about, by an Invisible hand"—and particularly at one George Walton and his family—"Stones, Bricks, and Brick-bats of all sizes, with several other things, as Hammers, Mauls, Iron-Crows, Spits, and other domestick Utensils." The only thing flying in New Castle as I hobbled through it was Old Glory, the only noise the ping of halyards against the aluminum flagpole at the Coast Guard station. Here, overlooking the pretty, half-mile-wide Piscataqua toward Kittery, Maine, with Portsmouth and the navy shipyard just out of sight behind numerous small islands, a mile upstream, and to the southeast the mouth of the river and the Isles of Shoals, stood the military buildings and fortifications of several epochs. There were concrete bunkers of a battery put up during the Spanish–American War; a modern, glass-windowed control tower standing near a helicopter pad; the stone walls, with empty window embrasures, of an uncompleted Civil War fort; and, from before the Revolutionary War, the brick-and-masonry walls and bastions of Fort Constitution. I entered the last through a gateway with a wooden portcullis, recently replaced by the New Hampshire Daughters of the American Revolution—an anniversary present celebrating events in December of 1774, when, stirred by an early Paul Revere ride to Portsmouth to say that the British weren't going to allow any more military stores to be shipped to the colonies, four hundred local "patriots" overpowered the five-man British garrison of the fort, then called William and Mary, and carried off, among other things, a hundred barrels of gunpowder, put to use later on at Bunker Hill. This enterprise, says a handy sign, was one of the first overt acts of the American Revolution.

The fort is nicely bare, with crabgrass growing in the open space between the low battlements. I walked through the fort and the adjoining Civil War fortifications and out along a little gray-and-white painted wooded catwalk to a small lighthouse. This was it—the end of the coast. Five o'clock. Gulls and lobster boats made their rackety, preoccupied pronouncements; the big tanker, closer and even lower in the water, either sinking without making a big thing of it or taking on fuel through an unseen pipeline; vivid blues and greens and bright white-gray of sun on rocks. I took a long, sweeping look to stick it all firmly in my mind, and then started back through New Castle, putting to use the good old thumb.

Gettysburg, PA

PHILIP HAMBURGER

Born in Wheeling, West Virginia in 1914, Philip Hamburger has been a staff writer for The New Yorker *since 1939. One of his books,* Our Man Stanley, *was a collection of pieces he wrote for the "Talk of the Town" pages of that magazine. Here, he dramatizes how a brief visit to Gettysburg enlivened the Civil War for even an "ordinary fellow."*

Alt., 520. Pop., 7,960. No more egregious error can be committed by the visitor to Gettysburg than to assume that the Battle of Gettysburg (July 1-3, 1863) is over. In fact, there is reason to believe that hostilities are only just beginning. Skirmishes take place all over town, and the most obscure details of the huge, sprawling battle are made available to strangers, in one form or another, every hour of the day. "I tell you, I was just an ordinary fellow, with an ordinary fellow's interest in the Civil War, until I spent two days at Gettysburg," an ordinary fellow who gave the impression of having been through a protracted siege said not long ago. "Now I think I could lecture at the War College. It all began when I took a room in a motel on the edge of the battlefield. This particular motel lay almost directly in the line of

Pickett's Charge—athwart it, you might say. Pickett's Charge, of course, was the unsuccessful offensive mounted by the Confederate troops on the afternoon of July 3rd, when Pickett and his men marched out from the Confederate left flank on Seminary Ridge and crossed an open field to meet the Union troops head on on Cemetery Ridge. I would place the start of the charge at approximately 3 P.M., Eastern Standard Time. I won't go so far as to say that Pickett's men would have come right *through* my bedroom, but they might well have bruised themselves on the television set against my southern wall. Actually, I feel certain that Pettigrew's men—he was stationed to the left of Pickett—and the men of Archer, Davis, Scales, and Lane would have come right across my bed, knocking over the telephone and the bed lamp. They ran into Meade's men—Hays, Webb, Gibbon, and the rest—and at the Angle it was bloody beyond description, and the Confederates were turned back at the Copse of Trees, at what is known as the High Water Mark of the Confederacy. The Rebels were said to be incapable of ever again mounting an offensive. Pickett's Charge was all over by ten minutes to four, but I kept going in Gettysburg pretty much around the clock, taking bus rides with build-in sound effects describing every last inch of the battle, watching an electric map with hundreds of little lights blinking and winking to show the position of the troops, looking at a cyclorama of the battle, walking over the battlefield, taking a guided tour in my own car, with a hired guide, and buying toy cannons, old bullets, flags, literature of all sorts, and tons of picture postcards. Now, if I had been Pickett . . ."

A man can visit Gettysburg, not even stop at a motel, and garner a rich historical background—merely by buying postcards. Postcards abound. They outnumber the people in the town by approximately twenty to one. They have a tendency to jump off the racks and hop into one's pockets. There are pictures of everything and everybody—Devil's Den, General Warren on Little Round Top, Big Round Top, the Valley of Death, Spangler's Spring, General Lee, General Lee's horse, Culp's Hill, the Wheatfield, the Virginia State Monument, the North Carolina State Monument, the Peach Orchard, McPherson Ridge, Barlow Knoll, Oak Hill, the Copse of Trees, the Angle, General Meade, General Meade's horse, General Meade's headquarters, the Jennie Wade House, and so on. The sense of history that pervades the city often produces an anesthetic effect that can take days to shake off. This happens most often to people who hire an official guide to accompany them as they drive around the thirty-odd square miles that constitute the battlefield. Groups of these guides —elderly men, for the most part—sit and sun themselves in front of small stone houses that are scattered about the edge of the field. Many of the guides would make interesting picture postcards. They leave the impression that they are veterans of the battle. They are staggering repositories of information, much of it in the general area of blood and gore. They feel that, seated beside a person who has hired their services for an hour or an hour and a half while he drives along the quiet tree-lined and gun-lined roads, they have a duty to dwell upon the horrors of war. Actually, bodies no longer lie out on the gently rolling, alternately brown and green fields, but the guides are corpse-conscious just the same, and they cannot pass a gully, an open stretch, or a battery of guns without making vivid references to the toll of human life that was taken at Gettysburg. They savor casualty figures, and roll them over and over on their tongues, with special attention to the number of hours or days that "the dead lay out there in the hot sun." Nor is their arithmetical ardor confined to casualty figures. The cost of various monuments titillates them to a frenzy of statistics, and they cite to the penny the amount expended on every monument they pass. "When I got through with one of those guides," a visitor to Gettysburg remarked recently, "I had the feeling that I had been driving around with a man from Price Waterhouse who had come to the field, eagle-eyed, to examine the books." Most of the guides are brigadiers *manqué*, or at least colonels *manqué*, possessed of a mysterious, superior untapped skill in commanding vast armies of men over broad areas under optimum conditions of strategy and tactics. They find it difficult to concede that the generals who fought the battle knew what they were doing, and they make it clear that if *they* had been consulted, little of what did take place would have taken place. For the most part, they would have everywhere attacked sooner, or later, in a different spot, with different equipment and radically different formations. "By the time I was through with my guided tour, I had no possible way of knowing which side, if any, won the battle," a man who had visited the battlefield said not long ago. "I decided to go home and read a book about it. The book said the North won."

Gettysburg strongly feels the presence of two former Presidents of the United States—one dead, one living. Lincoln is everywhere: in the National Cemetery, where he delivered the Gettysburg Address; in the tiny maroon-and-gray railroad station (now a tourist center) where he got off the train from Washington the afternoon before he delivered the address; in the Old Wills House, where he spent the night before he delivered the address; and on the old streets down which he rode on horseback on his way to the cemetery and the delivering of the address. The casual visitor poking through the souvenir shops is likely to feel that he is almost entirely surrounded by Lincoln— Lincoln staring at him from picture postcards, miniature busts of Lincoln in imitation bronze and silver, and copies of the address on postcards, silk scrolls, and wooden plaques. Gettysburg's living President is Dwight Eisenhower. Pictures of Eisenhower, and of his farm and his wife, are not in short supply, either. The people of Gettysburg may not catch sight of Eisenhower for weeks at a time—he drives from his farm to his office, on Carlisle Street, swiftly and with military precision and efficiency—but they derive comfort from the fact that he is around. "You can go into a lot of towns that call themselves historical—they are more like historical markers than towns, really—and they leave you with a sense of ancient matters settled long ago," a Gettysburg resident remarked the other day. "It's different here. We don't have much in the way of industry—just a shoe factory—and wages are generally low, and the tourists pour through, but we do have this indefinable sense of living history. These two strikingly different men, Lincoln and Eisenhower, have much to do with it. They elevate us and make us feel as though we were actors in some strange pageant that keeps unfolding and is something larger than ourselves."

A recent visitor to Gettysburg, having walked slowly down the main street, past the brooding photographs of Lincoln staring at him from shopwindows along the way, paid a call on General Eisenhower in his office, which occupies a modest three-story red brick building on the campus of Gettysburg College; formerly, the house was occupied by the president of Gettysburg College. The Venetian blinds were always drawn. Visitors encounter an elaborate but unobtrusive security system at the front door—an intercom mechanism through which the visitor announces himself. If he is expected, he is told in metallic tones to enter. Visitors may also be admitted through the back of the house. Several secretaries work there, in an enclosed porchlike extension, amid tall rows of metal filing cabinets with heavy locks. Inside, the house had a comfortable, easygoing air—warm draperies, many oil paintings, rooms lined with bookcases containing bound volumes of government reports. In a large room on the ground floor, the visitor found Colonel John Eisenhower, the President's son. Colonel Eisenhower has left the Army and is now working for a publishing house, helping his father put together his memoirs of the White House years; his desk was covered with galley proofs of the President's work. "He's deep in Volume Two," said Colonel Eisenhower. "Working like fury on it, too, writing all up and down and along the margins of yellow foolscap. He has many of the tools to aid his memory right here, on the back porch, in those files you just passed, and I am cleared to go through them when he needs a fact to refresh his recollection. There are other files out in Abilene, but not of the same importance. And there is a great mass of stuff down at the Library of Congress, in Washington, where my father's assistant on this project, Dr. William Ewald, has stationed himself. When father sits down with pen and paper and relaxes and lets his thoughts spontaneously flow forth, we get some pretty vivid, colorful recollections. These are then typed up and checked over, and then he goes at them again, rearranging and polishing. He's very fussy about his work." The Colonel, who is a tall, slim, engaging-looking man with a casual air, then said, "I have a single-engine Comanche that I keep out at the airport here, and every chance I get, I go up in her, and fly around the countryside, over the battlefield—everywhere. I just wheel around and get out of myself and get off the ground. I feel so free when I am in the air. I am out of myself. I love it."

The President works in a corner room on the second floor. He feels that if he worked downstairs, people would be trying to peer through the windows. Across the hall from his workroom, a retired brigadier general acting as an aide handles the large flow of correspondence and other matters that press into the life of an ex-President. Five stars, forming a circle, are etched in glass on the door leading to the President's workroom. He sits at a wide desk that is almost totally uncluttered, being embellished only by a few gadgets and a tiny silver bust of Lincoln. Behind him are the United States flag and the Presidential flag. The visitor found him relaxed and cheerful, possessed of a strangely old-fashioned and yet military courtesy, his voice soft but somewhat clipped, his words often tumbling out but giving the impression that at his own command they would instantly cease and he would turn his thoughts to other concerns. His cheeks had a healthy tint, and his eyes were clear blue and quietly scrutinizing. "I sit here and admire the watercolor by Andrew Wyeth," he said suddenly, pointing to a framed picture on the wall across from his desk. "I suppose I admire his work above all others. I have no idea how he does it. Just look at those sycamores! Wyeth did that watercolor on my farm, did it in about twenty minutes—faster than I can conceive of a man turning out such a superior piece of work. I hope you noticed my oil by Churchill on the way up the stairs—a favorite scene of mine, a wadi in North Africa. I love the mountain scenes—the Rockies, the Atlas Mountains. I can look at them for hours. I have most of what I need here to work with. It's great fun to test my memory, see what I can remember from the crowded years."

The President took off his glasses and toyed with them. "Twenty-twenty hindsight is so easy, but I find myself trying to track down the minutiae, the considerations that lay behind a decision," he said. "When the war was over, I wanted time to reflect, to think back, but then SHAPE came along, and the Presidency, and all the years. I had wanted to declare myself a one-term President, and then take a long look, have a breathing spell." The President shifted slightly in his chair. "Now, when I look back, I realize that I was never one for bombast, you know. Persuasion was more in my line. And a great many people still look upon me as a rather unwelcome entry." The President smiled, and put on his glasses. He leaned forward intently. "The Gettysburg roots go deep," he said. "That picture over there on that wall, that's my West Point class of 1915, taken right here in Gettysburg on May 3, 1915. We visited here for three days, pored over every inch of the battlefield. There wasn't much about Gettysburg that we didn't study at the Point, and then we came down here to the field itself and studied some more. During the First War, I was stationed here at Camp Colt. Tanks. I went from captain to lieutenant colonel, and I trained my men in discipline and all aspects of this new type of warfare, including machine guns, telegraphy, and the mechanics of tanks. The battlefield fascinated me. I suppose I must have read thirty, forty books on the subject—everything from the Comte de Paris to Haskell. I still read everything I can lay my hands on about the battle. In the old days, during the First War, I would climb into my old Dodge and tour the battlefield and explore every corner of the field and relive the battle. I am still impelled to do it, and from time to time, at dusk, I pack up and look around. Sometimes, I climb one-third of the way up one of those metal lookout towers that are scattered about the field. Don't go all the way up any more. I had a heart attack, you know."

The President pulled a fresh sheet of paper toward him and swiftly, in a few pen strokes, drew the battle lines of Gettysburg, with the fishhook of the Union lines unmistakable. His eyes were brighter than ever now, and he seemed absorbed in the rapid sketch he had made. "Everybody will argue this battle—*everybody*," he said. "I think one would be safe in saying that Gettysburg was the high-water mark of the Confederacy, all right, even though you mustn't forget that Grant took Vicksburg the day after the battle ended here. Meade, of course, had his armies lined up and prepared to fall back to Pipe Creek, near Taneytown. Lee didn't have much here, really, and Meade had a great deal. Certainly Lee might have attacked Washington and Baltimore, thrown panic into the North, and appealed to much Northern sentiment to end the war. Let me tell you, the sense of history is here. With you all the time. Oh, you just get me started on the Battle of Gettysburg and there's no telling where we'll end up!"

The President pulled another sheet of paper toward him and began to jot down some notes. "Back to work," he said.

The Old Wills House, where Lincoln spent the night before the dedication of the National Cemetery, lies two blocks down from Eisenhower's office and across from the Hotel Gettysburg, on the town's main traffic circle. It is now a museum of sorts, open to the public for a small fee. A room on the second floor is papered in bluish gray with a rose design, and contains a huge fourposter bed and heavy red draperies. A stovepipe hat lies on the bed, an old morning coat beside it. On a wooden table near one window are a white china pitcher and a towel rack, on which a few starched towels hang. In a chair by the bed, with a table before it, is a six-foot-four, life-size wax image of Lincoln. He is a startling figure, seated at the table in his shirtsleeves, wearing glasses with thin metal frames, and holding a piece of paper. Visitors to the museum are asked to forget themselves for the moment, let reality slip away, and try to believe that the paper he holds is a rough draft of the Gettysburg Address. The six-foot-four image and the small, stuffy room produce a strange effect. When the lights dim, the men, women, and children huddled on chairs around the room fall into an uncomfortable silence. Recorded music is heard from somewhere, with the old strains of "The Battle Hymn of the Republic" becoming louder and louder. (Sane men keep telling themselves, "Hokum, hokum," but it is a losing fight, with the battlefield and the cemetery a scant half mile away in one direction and a living ex-President a scant two blocks away in another.) Suddenly a voice is heard. It is an actor, recorded, impersonating Wills. "There are fresh towels here, Mr. President, and paper on the desk," says a voice. "May the night bring you a pleasant sleep." Then the voice of an actor impersonating Lincoln is heard saying, in measured tones, "Thank you,

Wills, thank you. You are most kind." The silence becomes almost unbearable, but then one can hear the scratching of a pen on paper and, once again, the voice of Lincoln, quietly reading the words of the Gettysburg Address. When the lights go up, the wax Lincoln is still there at the table, the paper in his hand, and the people file out with odd looks on their faces.

The lady in charge of the Wills House, who has collected fifty cents from every adult and twenty-five cents from every child to visit there, refers to the wax figure as "Mr. Lincoln." There appears to be no doubt in her mind that Mr. Lincoln lives in the house. She says she believes that on certain days one can see his shirt front rise and fall as he breathes. Many visitors, she says, swear that Mr. Lincoln stands up several times during the queer séance to move around the room, and that when they reach out to touch him, they feel flesh.

Fred King on the Allagash

EDWARD HOAGLAND

Born in New York City in 1932, Edward Hoagland was called "the Thoreau of our time" by the Washington Post. *His books and articles deal with wilderness areas of North America and Africa. In this extract from* Walking the Dead Diamond River, *which was nominated for the National Book Award, Hoagland describes the activity and the characters he encounters along Northern Maine's Allagash River.*

One of the arguments used by the logging industry in opposing proposals that a few wilderness areas be set aside is that there is no real wilderness left in the Northeast, anyway, or east of the Mississippi, or in any mountain range in the West that may be discussed—no tract of forest that hasn't already been logged, no river drainage that hasn't been dammed. It's all gone now, say the lumbermen complacently. But it's all that we have, the conservationists insist, and so the battle is joined.

On the Allagash watershed in northern Maine, woods that have been logged over three or four times, a compromise was struck. The lumbermen gave up very little of their land, and yet the first of the nation's officially "wild" rivers was brought under state control—conveyed, in effect, to the canoeists. Because of where it is and because the acreage involved is small (24,000 acres in government hands, versus 1.1 million, for example, in the Boundary Water Canoe Area of Minnesota), the Allagash Wilderness Waterway has quickly come under recreational pressure, perhaps representing the managerial dilemmas other areas will soon face. I wanted to see what it was like, and—most unfashionably in this democratic age—hired a guide so that I could use my paddle as a writing table part of the time and, being a novice, not bother with questions of navigation.

Fred King was talking about bush pilots in the motel at Shin Pond, where we met. He said there were old pilots and bold pilots, but he knew of one who was both old and bold. This man would fly out a sick fisherman at night in a little plane with no instruments, by moonlight alone. Fred King keeps track of these things. He's fifty-eight, looks forty-five, has short hair which is bluish gray, round glasses, a boyish doggy grin, a face deeply cut by grinning and a mouth big enough to grin with. It's a pleasing face; his body is straight and quick like a chipmunk's and he has an immediate laugh, provocatively loud, and likes to stop still when on the move and sound off on the matter at hand, then impulsively move forward again, seeming never to walk if he can run. At home in Augusta he keeps a jug of Allagash water to mix with his drinks, and doesn't much like December because of the short days; "I'd sell December awfully cheap." Until he became too controversial for the local talk show, he would go on TV in December, in his red guide's shirt, and kill the long evenings that way.

It's only been in the past ten years that Fred has canoed. His father died when he was young, and though he had started in college with the idea of graduating as an engineer, he quit and went off for two years to the woods, wintering in a cabin he built for himself six days distant by team and wagon from the community of Ashland, Maine. He was trying to trap—this was in the middle of the Depression—but went about it wrong. The right-headed way to learn how to trap would have been to pair up with an older fellow and learn from him, he says. Instead he had a full-time job just surviving, and during the first winter had to reinforce his roof with material hauled on a toboggan from an abandoned shanty several miles away.

He still likes to be by himself. His ideas sound as if they had been worked out in isolation in the woods and perhaps spoken first in a loud voice all alone. He has a tight shipshape cabin on Chemquassabamticook Lake where he goes in midwinter and works on improvements, hauling now with a snowmobile. He's got to break trail for the snowmobile on snowshoes—it's not like the ads—but he loves the rigor of the winter woods, cooks for himself and sleeps fitfully, listening to the radio and waiting for his mouse trap to snap. The mice he feeds to the gorbies—Canada jays—outside.

Fred worked on highway crews and during World War II was a shipyard pipe-fitter in Portland, but has been self-employed ever since. He would buy a piece of land and build a house on it, doing all the work, then "find somebody fool enough to buy." By fifty he tired of that, not so much because it was strenuous as because he wanted to go back to his original vision of himself. Though not an exceptional woodsman, he's taken the trouble to learn some of the historical lore, and particularly to latch onto a few of the vanishing old rivermen and listen and learn from them, trying modestly to carry on some of the traditions in their name. He also has a kind of guffawing admiration of wealth: more successful men who have blasted a steadier ascent in the world he calls "roosters." "Quite a rooster," he'll say of a fellow who wears nifty clothes nowadays, and will boisterously recite a ditty he learned in school:

> "Dear Lord, in the battle that goes on
>   through life,
> I ask but a field that is fair . . .
> A chance that is equal to all in the strife,
> And the courage to do and to dare.
> And if I should win, let it be by the code,
> With my faith and my honor held high,
> And if I should lose, let me stand by the
>   road and cheer as the winner goes by."

Another old chestnut of his is, "So late we get smart, so soon we get old."

The Allagash flows north for ninety-some miles. Its headwaters connect several lakes, and were tampered with in the 1840's by loggers who were competing to float the logs south to the Penobscot and down to Bangor instead of north on the Allagash to Canada by way of the St. John River.

The tampering has since been set straight, and now a parking lot has been laid out beside the Great Northern Paper Company's bridge at Chamberlain Lake, a two and a half-hour drive from the nearest town. Fifty-four hundred people were waterborne on the Allagash in 1970, a number that's rising 15 percent a year and is concentrated in the two warmest months, so that the state authorities know that soon they will have to institute a system of advance reservations. The campgrounds, however, are tactfully dispersed, and though logging is going on within four hundred feet of the water, a screen of trees, deceptive but pristine-looking, has been left, like the false fronting of a movie-set street.

We put in at Chamberlain on July 17th in a brisk splashing wind, our old-fashioned cedar canoes contrasting with the light aluminum canoes more modernist types were using—the Sierra Club fellows with their families and dogs who fill up this stage set and offend Fred King's sense of what's wild. The vacationers who employ King like his big tents and good steaks on ice and the canned provisions and sauces he brings, though they're not sure they're roughing it properly. The chic way to travel requires carrying thin packets of freeze-dried food, and not much of it, and feather-light sleeping equipment such as backpacking mountaineers have more reason to want—a line that Fred doesn't swallow at all. In the first place, the men he admires, "Moosetowners" who are now in their eighties, used to earn their living poling thirty-foot bateaux up the Allagash loaded with tons of supplies. The measure of manhood was not roughing it on dehydrated foods but hefting a great big load on a portage and living well. Also, the Maine woodsman usually respected the rich as people who had won their spurs in another world, and did not expect them to prove themselves in the woods with feats of do-it-yourself, but were perfectly willing to cater to the "sports" a bit for good pay. Fred says the Sierra Club characters (most of them "lefties"), with their "tin," "bang-bang" canoes, look like internees as they stand in a row waiting for reconstituted soup to be ladled into the tin bowls they hold. Instead of enjoying a meal, they study their maps as if they were eating them.

We sports in his party probably weren't up to the role. Sports lately are "pilgrims," he says laughingly, "groping for something." They believe, as he does too, that even in its protected status the Allagash River is being altered irrevocably, and so they have rushed to experience it before the herds finish it off. But his customers admire the conservationists and disdain the lumbermen who controlled the region until now, while he admires the lumbermen and has little use for the Johnny-come-lately conservationists. They think that a rainy day on a canoe trip is a disaster and therefore to be wet and uncomfortable on a rainy day is natural, whereas he thinks that rain is natural and that to be wet and uncomfortable on a rainy day is unnecessary and unnatural.

We had sun, the trees thrashed in the wind and the surface rippled in shark's-teeth patterns as we went up the lake, until we turned close to the western shore. There were mud beaches every quarter-mile. Chamberlain is an expansive lake, with salmon and togue, and is potentially dangerous when the wind rises. As we crossed toward Lock Dam the waves ruffled up to the gunwhale. King said that a canoeman's basic instrument was his pole, not his paddle (referring again to the old-timers), so that this deep-water stuff was an uneasy business for them. We were using an outboard motor, however. I was a passenger in the bow, his other customers, a Long Island couple, being towed in the second canoe.

The lock tender himself was a summer visitor, a white-haired salesman with an ulcer whose wife wrote children's books. He gave us a couple of minutes of lively water to get us started down the two miles of river that flows into Eagle Lake. Its pitch for a moment looked steep, brimming around us, and we could see varicolored streaks, as lurid as tropical fish, on the rocks underneath us where canoes had scraped. King gave a lesson in snubbing downstream with a pole, the bow being loaded heavily and the steering done by holding the canoe's stern in position, letting the current work on the bow. We saw a muskrat, a loon, and beaver-work in the winding channels, and then emerged on a wide, even prettier lake, the shoreline more indented than Chamberlain's, with moosier swards by the water and a hillier setting, with plenty of leafy hardwoods high up and behind. Terns, ducks, two loons, and an osprey flew over, and we had a fresh breeze at our tail. The loons whinnied in clarinet tones. At Pillsbury Island a boy's camp was in possession, with a great many canoes. We were using the motor all the way, intending to put twenty miles behind us, because in these public playgrounds one must travel out of phase with the particular contingent of enthusiasts who happened to start down the chute the same day, yet not catch up with the parties who set out previously.

We ran into waves tipped with whitecaps, the wind shifting into a headwind, and a heavy-blue curtain lowered in front of us. The murky curtain turned purple, the water turned black and the wind hard and strong—the waves coming in gusts, the canoe shipping water—as we met the storm. It was a smothering front, and passing beyond it, we were soaked by a pellety rain, but found some protection in the lee of Farm Island, then in a narrows, where we tied up at Priest's Camp. In the drumbeating rain as, laughing, we threw up our tents, Fred pretended we'd almost drowned to make it more dramatic for us. He said that when he first began guiding he'd been scared he might do something wrong and had gone to an old-timer for advice: "Just take lots of eggs and jam, Fred."

We were sharing the site with a middle-aged Boston couple, the man equipped with mutton-chops and a mustache like an English eccentric, and two local Maine fishermen who, trusting in the fact that it was mid-July, had neglected to bring a tent. Fred probably would have lent the Boston people some scraps of canvas, but he left the Maine men to sleep in discomfort under their canoe because they ought to have known better. My own companions were from Oyster Bay, the husband, Jim, once a Marine first lieutenant, now a market-research chieftain, well-heeled, revisiting his memories of sleeping on the ground in the Pacific theater thirty years ago, which he'd promised himself that he never would do again. He had four kids at home, a narrow head, a large jaw and a pouchy face that looked as if he had laughed at his boss's jokes about five thousand times too often, a face that looked as if maybe he had been served up one of his kids at a business lunch once and had gone ahead and eaten it anyway. But he was smoothly bright and intelligent, what is called an omnivorous reader, slept lightly, and was skillful and pleasant and easy with people. His wife, Audrey, whom I liked better, wore a tously blond wig over long black hair that she thought was "too oily," had a touching squint, a good heart and dental trouble. She was soft-natured, vaguely appealing, more loving than loved, a hard struggler; she loyally tramped after her husband in all his nerve-testing undertakings—climbing to fire towers, and so on—and was never allowed to be tired or scared. On Long Island, she said, she ran with him around the high-school track every morning at six o'clock, although she hated it. After twenty-eight years of marriage the word "dear" sounded sad when he said it, but they'd brought along nine days' worth of mixed martinis in plastic bottles, as well as a dose of the anti-Semitism which is sometimes an ingredient of stories around the camp fire. Fred partook too.

Next morning we went to look at a relict tramway which had hauled saw logs in the first years of this century, and a railroad spur used for pulpwood later on, both constructed in order to get the logs from this lake into a different drainage that would carry them south. During the 1920's as many as five thousand men worked here. Beans were cooked all night in holes in the ground; the hogs that went on the table along with the beans were kept on Hog Island. Farm Island was for pasturing the oxen, but half of it was never cleared and is still black spruce. Black spruce and white, and sedges and cattails, cover this industrial blur where "Dynamite" Murphy, the dynamiter, and other famous figures once worked. Now a mother duck was running on the water with flapping wings, teaching her babies to fly. I'm such a child of the times that although half of my ancestors were lumbermen in the West, when talking to a proud lumberman of today I all but blush for him as he recounts his exploits, so King and I didn't always see eye to eye at the railroad site.

We circled the lake, slipping into each estuary and up Soper Brook, then up Snare Brook. Dozens of ducks; fish nests down through the water, scooped in the gravel. A great blue heron flew up. A dragonfly chased by a kingbird got away by dodging close to our bow. The brooks were silty but the wetland grasses were a tender light-green. After a half-mile or so the alder growth would close in and beaver cuttings would block the brook, and where we had to stop we'd see moose tracks. When we walked, Fred was quick, and with his small intelligent face looked like a professor afield, though his right arm was beginning to go bad on him—too much holding a chain saw. In the black-fly season he sometimes sews his socks to his pants to protect his ankles, and leaves them on for four or five days, he said.

53

We admired clusters of magnificent white pine left by the spruce and fir loggers of recent times. The original booty up here was pine. Some trees were a hundred and fifty feet high, seven feet thick at the butt, and wanted for naval masts. Before chopping such a whopper, the loggers would throw a nearby spruce against it, climb to the top of the spruce and so reach the climbable branches of the pine, from which they could see for ten miles across a great spread of spruce forest to other "veins" of pine.

We stayed at Priest's Camp a second evening, enjoying a rainbow. A boys' outing party arrived, and there was a special avidity in the way King and Jim and Audrey watched them set up their camp: *these* boys weren't smoking pot. Rain fell hard most of the night, until a clearing shower came just at dawn. Then trilling loons and King's cry, "Wake up, wake up, up with the butter-cups!" I imagined him as the "cookee" around a logging camp in the old days whose light weight kept him from competing in physical feats with some of the men but who bubbled with jokes whenever they broke off work for a meal. He said, though, that he hadn't developed much interest in people until his late forties, having been concerned before then with excavations, machinery and phys-ics.

We always started earlier than anyone else, just as we seized the best campgrounds and pushed past the trippers at every point, but the advantage of this for observing game was lost, either because of the outboard motor or else King's loud anec-dotes echoing on the water. At such times, before the sun rose, when for an hour we had the Allagash to ourselves, he exasperated me and I was sorry I'd come with a guide, but of course from his standpoint this silence-on-the-waters was more Sierra Club nonsense. The old-timers moved through frontier America hollering as loud as could be, unless they were hunting—cutting the silence with hoots, dispelling some of the loneliness of the woods and warning the panthers and bears away. To this day, in parts of Alaska where there are grizzlies a prospector will put a stone in a tin can inside his pack, so that he walks with a constant *click-click*.

In the passage from Eagle to Churchill lakes we saw mergansers, scaups, herons, gulls, and an osprey again. Baby ducks fled in front of us like fish flipping along the surface to dodge a deep shark, the mother among them flittering strongly to set the example. A logging bridge crossed above us; we saw an otter underneath. The shores displayed "cat spruce" (white spruce), sleek and bristly, beaver houses, cedars and drowned-looking alder-covered beaches leading to a fir point where the Indians used to camp to escape the flies. On Churchill, with the sun a silvery band on the water, we caught up with a swimming cow moose midway across. Her body was invisible; her head was like a blunt boat, the ears the housing, and her hairy neck hump nearly underwater. It was a groping blind-looking head, sightless as a whale's, a feeling and suffering-looking head, the nose so huge and vulnerable that other undiscovered senses might have been contained inside. Two terns were diving on her with creaky cries. Her ears lay back as her big pumping legs hurled her ashore, and she swerved to look at us, first over one shoulder, then over the other.

Churchill is a rangy lake, the shore opening and narrowing, with a mountain skyline. Heron Lake, formerly a holding pen for the logs, leads on to Churchill Depot dam. The ranger there, whose name is Clyde Speed, talked about the moose that he sees, and we toured the outdoor museum of log sleds, water sleds, old bateaux, Lombard tractors, Watson wagons, and looked into the boarding house, and engine and blacksmith shops, all defunct. Lombard steam log-haulers preceded the internal-combustion engine in the woods for a decade or two around World War I. Each of them could do the work of sixty horses, a blue flame issuing like a blowtorch from the exhaust pipe on a cold night. They were precursors of the tank and farm tractor because they ran on a caterpillar tread. In 1938 Fred King had walked to this spot to explore; he loved its tall tamaracks and big pines and gave us a chance to poke about. In places like this he always announced that he was only a "fake woodsman," and that although occasionally he spoke for some of the old fellows who couldn't go on TV themselves and spout off, if we wanted to meet the real thing we'd have to go farther afield.

The Chase Rips, the only risky spot in ninety-two miles, began here. Fred had been casual in speaking of it, once suggesting that Jim perhaps might want to practice a bit with his pole in Soper Brook, but now as we lugged our craft down below the dam (paying Clyde Speed to truck the duffels around) he began to hum nervously. We watched other voyagers as their canoes first entered the current like the little cars at a carnival being gripped by the cogs of a loop-the-loop.

I had an easy time in Fred's bow. Often he takes old people through these rapids who can give him no help, who are getting their final look at the outdoors. But Jim and Audrey, suddenly realizing they hadn't practiced enough in Soper Brook, were on their own, Jim cautiously trying to get the feel of the pole, hanging himself up against the bank several times. King, who had drifted ahead almost too far to shout, yelled at him to stand up and move more toward the middle of the canoe. "Stand up! You don't fight Joe Louis sitting down. Get on your hind legs!" He'd stripped to the waist. A moosefly bite him, and he laughed and said, "They'll bite a chunk out of you and fly up on a branch and sit there right in front of you eating the chunk."

The river before us fell off, abrupt as the end of a table; all of a sudden it didn't appear to be there. Then, curling up like a hairdo, it fluffed around us, high at the prow, as we slid down into the rapids themselves. The noisy water was popping in points, peaks and tufts, blotting out all other sights and sounds. We could have been surrounded by other canoes and not noticed them. This was the first pitch, full of rocks, several hundred yards long. The second was shorter but "downhilly," the many rips sticking up as if to chum with us, as the water curled and crabbed around. Riffles, bumps, a wild backdrop of trees. Jim was way back in the first pitch still but beginning to grab hold of the river's hand now. "Good boy!" King shouted to him, a regular educator, jittery on his behalf. "We'll make you an honorary Moose-towner. I ain't got the authority, but I can recommend you." Everywhere on the river there was midmorning light and a hiss as of thousands of snakes, the water backing up recalcitrantly into cowls. Jim's canoe came stumbling, angling along like a cub, edging to the bank, but he jumped out at every juncture to wade and push, as a canoeman should. We all took a breather together against some shore rocks to eat raisins and talk.

The third pitch was energetic with knobby rocks sticking up like bad luck itself, every one striped with canoe-belly paint. King had broken canoes here—a rock square-on at 45 degrees will do it, plunging through the bottom. A friend of his tried out a plexiglass design here but gave his bowman heart failure, the rocks skinning by just an inch or two under his feet. A canoe should go where water goes. "Where's the water?" a canoeman asks himself in the rapids when perplexed. Then, camping alone at supper, all the company he has is the bugs in his cup.

Poling is like snowshoeing and paddling like skiing, and we were able to paddle for a little while. We passed several parties who were "frogging" (walking) their way down the channel, leading their canoes, having become discouraged from tipping over so much. The river was gala with rocks, a hustling hubbub. King's craft snuggled in like an invited guest—but, no, a big jar. We skidded and sidled by the tough spots. Fred said not to try to signal to Jim or he'd misunderstand, and it would distract him. Soon he did tip and swamp, the canoe underwater. "Not too bad being in the river, just lots of water and rocks," Fred said, jumping in too to help hold and right their canoe and recover their gear that was floating downriver. Now that their string of conquests had broken, the two of them fell out again twice in quick succession, but learned to leap when they felt themselves going so that at least the canoe didn't sink. "Once they get wet they'll get wet again." Watching, Fred sang with tension.

After having covered a mile and a half (it seemed much more), we stopped at a place called Big Eddy to dry out and have lunch underneath an old cedar, the water purling like Hiawatha's. When other people passed, we'd hear their piping shouts for a moment, but both the river and the dramatic forest—blue firs and black spruces—made them mirages.

We pushed on, the Allagash partying along, popping with rocks but forty yards wide, leaving plenty of current, till it tipped down steeply again and we slid at the edge of whole thievish mobs of rocks that nattered away, feeling their tug, zipping by Harrow Brook. There were scraps of canoes that had wrecked and washed down, becoming wedged in the rocks; some had been drawn up on the bank where they covered small piles of firewood, because a great many people had crawled ashore and spent time recuperating here. Jim and Audrey fell overboard twice more, though the river wasn't as severe. First he lost his balance; the next time she did. He was strong and uncomplaining but heavy and had lost his confidence, and Fred gradually formed the opinion that he was awkward and that over-education had spoiled him. Fred stopped really rooting for him, though continuing to mutter encouragement—whether or not Jim and his wife were able to hear. Being as safe as a sack of peas in Fred's bow, I felt guilty for having it all so easy and knew that I would have looked worse.

We enjoyed peaceful minutes of drifting too, with the bottom brown mud, just a few round white rocks dotted about, and the banks grassy, cedars leaning over the water, and white-collared birds darting close to our heads. Then for three hundred yards the river would turn feisty, roaring, tergiversating, as busy as rush hour, each rock having its say. We twisted through new rips and rapids, eluding sweepers, seeing the trout jump, and dragonflies in a mating clinch; jays called in the trees. The clouds were lovely, if we took time to glance upward. There were still-water sloughs, and gulls on the mud-banks, and parakeet cries from the bear-jungle. Then a swift chute, dark choppy water, on into a wide, luxurious pool. Buzzing birds in the woods, occasional pines, more shaggy cedar, big pairs of spruce, a heron flying high with folded neck, a gangly flying loon, some green grassy islands. A winter wren sang. Then again the water crawled with ripples, with stream birds flying up, the water slanting alive with bubbles over a gravel bar.

After these last corrugations a wide boggy low-slung valley interrupted the forest, and there were red-winged blackbirds, bitterns, and other signs of slower water. We saw a speck of a bird diving on an eagle or osprey, harassing it for several minutes; hummingbirds and robins do this. The Allagash is thought to be visited by three or four eagles.

The bogs gave way to Umsaskis Lake, which after the rapids seemed placid and big, with bumpy timbered hills all around. We rested our backs, using the outboard. Fred said that in the years following the invention of outboards the Moose-towners kept trying them out and discovering that they could pole upstream faster than a motor could go, so the older men never did bother adopting them.

We'd covered twenty miles, and camped on July 20th in the Thoroughfare leading from Umsaskis into Long Lake. The Oyster Bay couple were telling about their trip down the Colorado River and I was talking about other rivers I'd seen, when I realized that we were making poor Fred jealous; he wanted our attention fixed on the Allagash. They talked about their vacation in Japan too, where Jim wouldn't take his shoes off. "We beat the sons of bitches, so there's no reason why we should take our shoes off."

It was warm and the frogs on the Thoroughfare started croaking at 8 P.M. As I stood listening, the local ranger, making a last swing past, stopped to find out if everything was all right. He said that people in trouble generally just stand on the bank looking out, don't wave or shout. Sometimes he wonders how long they'd stand there if he didn't come over—two days, three days?—before they began to wave and yell.

Fred keeps a jeep at Umsaskis. The next day he drove us forty miles across International Paper

Company roads to Chemquassabamticook Lake, where we boated to his cabin. The spot is close to Canada, and during Prohibition a good deal of booze was hauled to Fred's lake, where the canoemen took over and carried it via the waterways to Moosehead Lake and other resorts farther south. We passed some cabins of the era with double-split roofs: cedar shakes overlying a layer of earth, covering an inner roof composed of spruce poles.

Fred's maternal grandfather went to California for the Gold Rush, sold mining timbers there and brought back fifty thousand dollars in gold. Gone now, Fred laughs, with a backward jerk of his head as if he were swinging an ax. His cabin is at what sixty years ago was One Eye Michaud's logging camp; and he's found the "greenhouse" (root cellar), the old beanhole, lined with rocks, with charcoal at the bottom, the outline of the bunkhouse, and that of a trapping cabin which must have predated Michaud. In his own cabin, built of peeled logs that he rolled up on skids to the height of the eaves, he has a hundred-year-old pair of caribou-hide snowshoes, and other antiques; even a scrap from a cedar tree where he cut some life-saving kindling one snowy night when he was caught on the lake by a bitter headwind and had to sit out the storm on the shore. He got under a spruce with the biggest fire he could scrape together and thought of all the things he'd done wrong in his life. Later he came back and cut that particular spruce for his new ridgepole, dragging it home on a sled made from two fenders.

His curtain rods are old setting poles; his

clothesline is tied between saplings skinned by the beavers. He had a potato garden to tend, and we went out to see the stump of a virgin pine with the marks of the broad-ax that cut it still visible and a forty-year-old birch tree growing on top. We saw two barred owls calling each other, and a woodpecker drinking down ants on a stump, and moose and deer prints on the sandy beach, among the debris of mussel shells the gulls had dropped. In the winter it's so cold that the wings of the ravens flying overhead seem to squeak like an ungreased hinge. One Eye Michaud is said to have wanted to maintain his reputation as a hard man, and so, out here in winter weather, a four-day walk from the nearest town, he might fire somebody and then, leaning into the kitchen, announce, "Don't give this man any food!" It kept up appearances, and the fellow's knapsack was immediately filled.

Fred used to sneak up here years ago, even building himself a squatter's shack on a ridge of rock maple and yellow birch, since logged. The logging roads now extend everywhere, if one looks down from the air, like tributaries that join the main arteries leading to Canada and the pulp mills. We visited a fire warden named Leslie Caron with a round wrinkled face such as befits a man born in the puckerbrush, who as a boy had carried the mail by dogsled. He said the weather forecasters "must have read last year's almanac," and that he would retire and "be a free nigger" next year. Fred told about catching a six-pound lake trout and taking it up to the watchman in the fire tower on Ross Mountain as a present, assuming he'd catch another on the following day. He didn't, and as soon as the fellow climbed back to his tower, his dog got hold of the fish and ate it. Now the spotting is done by airplanes. Caron in a jeep chases out to where they are circling and tells them where he is in relation to them, because they can't see him through the cover of trees. Then they tell him where the fire is in relation to him.

In the morning the sunrise was golden through the thick trees. A soupy mist covered the lake, which smoked like a hot spring. Two connubial loons floated side by side, then dived together. The water was as dark as blueberry jelly. We drove back to the Allagash and got under way toward Long Lake again. There we encountered some Explorer Scouts, the vanguard of a program which will scatter ten thousand boys every summer through northern Maine; also a private boys' camp, forty-four kids in twenty canoes.

Fred said there are three kinds of bears in Maine: black bears, maybe a few brown bears, and *Jalberts*. Sam Jalbert was born on a rock in the Allagash, and when he was three days old he fell off and has been in the river ever since. He poled upriver so much he grew arms as thick as his neck, and hands as wide as a shovel. He raised a family of ten kids and had to kill a lot of deer out of season to do it. Used to take sports down the Chase Rapids too. Once he stood on his hands in the stern and steered by tipping and balancing his body. The Jalberts helped dig the channels and build the dams, and this twenty miles we were doing today was Jalbert country, where they logged and had their landings. The logs couldn't simply be set on the river ice or they would be lost in the frenzy of spring break-up; they were kept at strategic points along the bank, then rolled in when the river began to relent but before it lowered.

Chemquassabamticook Stream came in from the west through a moosey flat—Fred has poled up there to his lake from the Allagash, taking all day. We saw a swimming beaver and three otter, two of which ran up on the bank like muddy rascals. Here at Harvey Pond is an old farm clearing, once a freight depot during the towboat era, before that a place where people stopped for vegetables as far back as 1820, along the so-called California Road, a wilderness path which headed west. The original Harvey was a squaw man with a long white beard and twelve kids who married and settled here, liking the warmth and bustle after a lonely life.

An osprey and some splendid ducks flew overhead. There was a last dam, with lilies and water weeds and fish jumping. A channel was maintained by the towboaters for the rest of the way to the St. John, and we sought this out where there were rapids. A couple of horses would drag upstream a boat sixty feet long and ten feet wide (One Eye tried one seventy-two feet long). Barrels of pork and beef weighing three hundred pounds were placed in the bow, barrels of flour behind them, and buckets of lard and blueberries alongside the tiny cabin in the stern. Coasting back, the horses got a free ride.

We passed bits of islands covered with driftpiles, saw a doe and a fawn, a sheldrake with seven ducklings, a squirrel swimming the river, its tail like a rudder. A heron flew up and stood for a minute atop a fir tree. The river curved gently in a stretch sweet as honey, softening its watery sounds so that we could hear the white-throated sparrows. After tilting again with a few rocks we entered a dead water which lasted for an hour's paddling, birds warbling all around, the water smooth, black and waxed. Tying the canoes together, we drifted as a raft, eating Fig Newtons, and hearing chain saws. Sweeney Brook, Whittaker Brook and Jalbert Brook joined the current. Fred told the story of a guide on the St. John who used to drift along with a gallon of booze at his side. When he and his sports approached a series of rapids and they shouted across to him from their canoe over the roar of the water to ask how to deal with it, he would raise his tin cup and tell them, "I'll drink to that."

While Fred's "brain was in neutral" we hit some rocks, then met more brief rustling rips, rollicking through the Long Soo Rapids for a mile or so, through lovely still country. Only the water popped, a confabulation of rocks, with sandbars and other complexities and many dead elms and ashes that the ice had girdled in the crush of the spring. Fred sometimes picks fiddlehead ferns for his supper here. Entering Round Pond, we paddled to his favorite campground, and baked some bread, cut up chub for trout bait, and watched the ravens harassing the squirrels. Jim fished a springhole while I went to see Willard Jalbert, the Old Guide, as he likes to call himself, having become a bit of an institution. His description of fighting rearing bears with a double-bitt ax sounded as if he'd been looking at *Field and Stream* covers, but last fall at eighty-three he had shot a deer, and still could wend his way through the rapids with an outboard full-throttle, or hold his canoe where he wanted it with his pole while casting with his free hand. He once rode a log over the fourteen-foot drop of the Long Lake Dam, and used to play tricks on the ospreys, throwing out chub for them—a fish that is the butt of many river jokes—attached by a line to a log. "Everybody for himself and God for us all," he would call, going into the rips. But it has all somehow ossified now that the wilderness is gone.

At dusk we went for a joyride on the windy water. A thin-lipped bright sunset, a loon's giddy titter like a police whistle with water in it. Rain with thunder during the night.

From before sunrise, hard logging was going on at Round Pond, all by Canadian labor, the logs being trucked to St. Pamphile. The truth is the Yankee big-timber-logger has been a myth for several decades, and old-timers like the Jalberts disguise their dismay at the fall-off in gumption among young Americans by grumbling that the hunting is tailing off because these Canadian woodsmen must be shooting the deer, tucking their carcasses among the logs and smuggling them out of the country.

We got started at 6 A.M., a sailing hawk peering down at us. A mist almost the color of snow lay between the lines of trees, so that although the weather was warm it was a wintry scene. In the Round Pond Rips a couple of ducks babbled in the thick of the fun, the water reverberating around them. Next, the Musquacook Rips and islands. King's echoing voice in the quietness irritated me exceedingly because this was not *my* sixtieth trip, but as he spoke of his "walking stick," which was his pole, and his "rain shirt," his poncho, exclaiming resoundingly, "Bubbles mean troubles," I had to remember that this was real history he was reliving, that he was a link with the boisterous rivermen whose intent was to knock down the forests and let the light in.

A buckskin-colored deer exploded with springy bounds. We saw a merganser family, a ridge scalped by a tornado. In a dead water we looked down and saw grasses growing on the bottom, while a whole populance of insects bounced in the air. The sun streamed through the morning vapors in warm yellow combinations on the west bank, but on the east the view was still snowy-looking. The black-growth forest humped into low hills. We floated past grassy islands, then sibilant stretches, the water combing through the rocks, turning the big ones yellow with reflected light and leaving a platter of calm downstream of each. There's a disastrous-sounding crunch when a canoe hits a rock and the floor lifts under one's feet, but the sound is worse than the results. We passed an old shack with a sod roof, now burgeoning with raspberries, and saw Savage Brook debouch through its delta, and Five Finger Brook. The water itself looked like running gravel, and we passed several old cabins that used to belong to characters like Sporty Jack (so called because of a birthmark he sported), and the Cunliffe Depot, the abandoned headquarters of a logging boss who rivaled Michaud. Michaud's hay farm was two miles below, now devoid of buildings but spacious after so many miles of woods. Then beaches and finally a slough called Finlay Bogan, where we saw kingfishers, fish jumping, islands foliaged with willows and silver maples, ice-scarred. It became a still, rainy day with some occasional neighborly thunder. We ran by a few gentle rapids and shoals, seeing huge waterlogged stumps that were shaped like moose. The river here was a dream—rustling, windy, wild-looking and lush—chipper with birds, overhung with sweepers, dense with slow channels forking between the islands. It was beautiful and remote. The pioneers chose inter-vale land such as this whenever they could because the river had already partially cleared it for them and laid down topsoil in which the natural wild grasses had seeded, so that their stock could browse.

At the approach to Allagash Falls the water grew deep, the bottom rocky and the forest black. Fred began to hum as we entered the rips that led to the lip, and we squeezed over to the east bank and camped in the crook of land where the portage begins. The water is churned butter-yellow as it goes over, and it spouts off the rocks below like the wake of a ship. I swam in the bombast below the falls, in deep potholes where the water was warm. It's a fat, plentiful falls, not notably high; once some daredevils went over in a bateau and survived. Looking down from above at the charade of destruction, suddenly I missed my wife. It was so lonely watching the water go over and smash that the mosquitoes began to seem friends. Fred, who was turning ornery now that the responsibilities of the trip were nearing an end, shouted from the supper fire, "Beavertail sandwiches" (Spam).

In scratchy places the channel generally stuck close to the outside bank. We'd try to go where the water went but not where it was making a fuss. Below the falls the Allagash achieved its maturity. It was plump, and the birds were dashes of white overhead, singing from every side. In a dead water, a large tributary, Big Brook, flowed in. Then McGargle Rocks, two short rapids with a pool between. We saw various map-eater parties in bang-bang canoes. Between McGargle and Twin Brooks is a nondescript stand of fifth-growth white birch and knobby pulpwood, not showing the logging industry at its best. As usual, Fred's voice scared off the moose in front of us; once we saw a stream of fresh pee on the gravel where one had fled.

The Twin Brooks enter the Allagash directly opposite each other in the midst of a rapids. There was a roar, and the channel was first on the left and then crossed over while we hopped about in the swells. " 'I'm lost!' the Cap'n shouted," Fred yelled in the fastest turbulence amid the rocks, before we slid into a pool where a seagull sat. We'd covered eight miles in two hours.

The water got moving again. The government-owned wild area ends at Twin Brooks, and soon we saw log trucks alongside the bank, and a ramshackle structure, the Allagash Inn, at Eliza Hole. The Allagash Inn was One Eye Michaud's jumping-off point on the river, where he kept his successive wives. Two of the four were mail-order floozies who decamped with his assets, but when he was old and pitifully sick and poor, the first of them came back and nursed him.

One expects to arrive at some signs of civilization at the mouth of a river. Ahead we could see the ridge carved by the St. John. The Allagash makes an S-turn to delay joining it, through Casey Rapids. We saw two last deer, smelled a skunk, an animal that prefers a civilized habitat, and heard new bird calls—field and song sparrows, bobolinks, meadowlarks. Crows had replaced the wilderness ravens.

Then the jukebox of the Allagash Pool Hall. Allagash proper is a sad shantytown, a sleeping shell of the Moosetowners' settlement, with everyone drawing food stamps now, but there are canoes on the lawns. It's ragged, not even quite right for potato country, backed smack up against New Brunswick. The old-timers, lame with arthritis after so many years of exposure to rain and cold, when often they slept in the snow next to a small fire, have become supersensitive to the cold. They find it torturing, tack up insulation everywhere, or pray for the money to winter in Florida.

I had a butterscotch sundae and a strawberry milkshake. Fred King departed like a boy let out of school: no more entertaining or catering to us, no more wincing at the bumps delivered to his canoes. He would drive south until he got tired and sleep by the side of the road. Our vehicles had been brought around from Chamberlain Lake, but Jim and Audrey's new Chrysler had not weathered the trip well. The two of us left them changing a tire, putting gas into the empty tank from a one-gallon can and reminding each other that no minor mishap should spoil such a fine trip.

From *Travels with Charley: In Search of America*

JOHN STEINBECK

In his novels and stories, John Steinbeck (1902–68), defended migratory farm workers and other disinherited working people. He won the Nobel Prize for Literature in 1962, the same year he wrote Travels with Charley, *his only travel book. In this trip from Aroostook County, Maine, through Vermont and New York State to Erie, Pennsylvania, Steinbeck takes a wide ranging view of the Northeast as he shares the road with his favorite ambassador.*

Maine seemed to stretch on endlessly. I felt as Peary must have when he approached what he thought was the North Pole. But I wanted to see Aroostook County, the big northern county of Maine. There are three great potato-raising sections—Idaho, Suffolk County on Long Island, and Aroostook, Maine. Lots of people had talked of Aroostook County, but I had never met anyone who had actually been there. I had been told that the crop is harvested by Canucks from Canada who flood over the border at harvest time. My way went endlessly through forest country and past many lakes, not yet frozen. As often as I could I chose the small wood roads, and they are not conducive to speed. The temperature lifted and it rained endlessly and the forests wept. Charley never got dry, and smelled as though he were mildewed. The sky was the color of wet gray aluminum and there was no indication on the translucent shield where the sun might be, so I couldn't tell direction. On a curving road I might have been traveling east or south or west instead of the north I wanted. That old fake about the moss growing on the north sides of trees lied to me when I was a Boy Scout. Moss grows on the shady side, and that may be any side. I determined to buy a compass in the next town, but there wasn't any next town on the road I was traveling. The darkness crept down and the rain drummed on the steel roof of the cab and the windshield wipers sobbed their arcs. Tall dark trees lined the road, crowding the gravel. It seemed hours since I had passed a car or a house or a store, for this was the country gone back to forest. A desolate loneliness settled on me—almost a frightening loneliness. Charley, wet and shivering, curled up in his corner of the seat and offered no companionship. I pulled in behind the approach to a concrete bridge, but couldn't find a level place on the sloping roadside.

Even the cabin was dismal and damp. I turned the gas mantle high, lit the kerosene lamp, and lighted two burners of my stove to drive the loneliness away. The rain drummed on the metal roof. Nothing in my stock of foods looked edible. The darkness fell and the trees moved closer. Over the rain drums I seemed to hear voices, as though a crowd of people muttered and mumbled offstage. Charley was restless. He didn't bark an alarm, but he growled and whined uneasily, which is very unlike him, and he didn't eat his supper and he left his water dish untouched—and that by a dog who drinks his weight in water every day and needs to because of the outgo. I succumbed utterly to my desolation, made two peanut-butter sandwiches, and went to bed and wrote letters home, passing my loneliness around. Then the rain stopped falling and the trees dripped and I helped to spawn a school of secret dangers. Oh, we can populate the dark with horrors, even we who think ourselves informed and sure, believing nothing we cannot measure or weigh. I knew beyond all doubt that the dark things crowding in on me either did not exist or were not dangerous to me, and still I was afraid. I thought how terrible the nights must have been in a time when men knew the things were there and were deadly. But no, that's wrong. If I knew they were there, I would have weapons against them, charms, prayers, some kind of alliance with forces equally strong but on my side. Knowing they were not there made me defenseless against them and perhaps more afraid.

Long ago I owned a little ranch in the Santa Cruz mountains in California. In one place a forest of giant madrone trees joined their tops over a true tarn, a black, spring-fed lake. If there is such a thing as a haunted place, that one was haunted, made so by dim light strained through the leaves and various tricks of perspective. I had working for me a Filipino man, a hill man, short and dark and silent, of the Maori people perhaps. Once, thinking he must have come from a tribal system which recognizes the unseen as a part of reality, I asked this man if he was not afraid of the haunted place, particularly at night. He said he was not afraid because years before a witch doctor gave him a charm against evil spirits.

"Let me see that charm," I asked.

"It's words," he said. "It's a word charm."

"Can you say them to me?"

"Sure," he said and he droned, *"In nomine Patris et Fillii et Spiritus Sancti."*

"What does it mean?" I asked.

He raised his shoulders. "I don't know," he said. "It's a charm against evil spirits so I am not afraid of them."

I've dredged this conversation out of a strange-sounding Spanish but there is no doubt of his charm, and it worked for him.

Lying in my bed under the weeping night I did my best to read to take my mind out of misery, but while my eyes moved on the lines I listened to the night. On the edge of sleep a new sound jerked me awake, the sound of footsteps, I thought, moving stealthily on gravel. On the bed beside me I had a flashlight two feet long, made for coon hunters. It throws a powerful beam at least a mile. I got up from bed and lifted my 30/30 carbine from the wall and listened again near the door of Rocinante—and I heard the steps come closer. Then Charley roared his warning and I opened the door and sprayed the road with light. It was a man in boots and a yellow oilskin. The light pinned him still.

"What do you want?" I called.

He must have been startled. It took him a moment to answer. "I want to go home. I live up the road."

And now I felt the whole silly thing, the ridiculous pattern that had piled up layer on layer. "Would you like a cup of coffee, or a drink?"

"No, it's late. If you'll take that light out of my face I'll get along."

I snapped off the light and he disappeared but his voice in passing said, "Come to think of it, what are you doing here?"

"Camping," I said, "just camped for the night." And I went to sleep the moment I hit the bed.

The sun was up when I awakened and the world was remade and shining. There are as many worlds as there are kinds of days, and as an opal changes its colors and its fire to match the nature of a day, so do I. The night fears and loneliness were so far gone that I could hardly remember them.

Even Rocinante, dirty and pine-needle-covered as she was, seemed to leap over the road with joy. Now there were open fields among the lakes and forests, fields with the crumbly friable soil potatoes love. Trucks with flat beds loaded with empty potato barrels moved on the roads, and the mechanical potato digger turned up long windrows of pale-skinned tubers.

In Spanish there is a word for which I can't find a counterword in English. It is the verb *vacilar*, present participle *vacilando*. It does not mean vacillating at all. If one is vacilando, he is going somewhere but doesn't greatly care whether or not he gets there, although he has direction. My friend

Jack Wagner has often, in Mexico, assumed this state of being. Let us say we wanted to walk in the streets of Mexico City but not at random. We would choose some article almost certain not to exist there and then diligently try to find it.

I wanted to go to the rooftree of Maine to start my trip before turning west. It seemed to give the journey a design, and everything in the world must have design or the human mind rejects it. But in addition it must have purpose or the human conscience shies away from it. Maine was my design, potatoes my purpose. If I had not seen a single potato my status as *vacilador* would not have been affected. As it turned out I saw almost more potatoes than I needed to see. I saw mountains of potatoes—oceans—more potatoes than you would think the world's population could consume in a hundred years.

I've seen many migrant crop-picking people about the country: Hindus, Filipinos, Mexicans, Okies away from their states. Here in Maine a great many were French Canadians who came over the border for the harvest season. It occurs to me that, just as the Carthaginians hired mercenaries to do their fighting for them, we Americans bring in mercenaries to do our hard and humble work. I hope we may not be overwhelmed one day by peoples not too proud or too lazy or too soft to bend to the earth and pick up the things we eat.

These Canucks were a hardy people. They traveled and camped by families and groups of families, perhaps even clans: men, women, boys, girls, and small children too. Only the nurslings did not work at picking up the potatoes and placing them in the barrels. Americans drove the trucks and used a windlass and a kind of davit to pull the filled barrels aboard. Then they drove away to deposit the crop in the potato barns with earth heaped high about their sides to prevent freezing.

My knowledge of Canuck French derives from motion pictures usually with Nelson Eddy and Jeanette MacDonald, and it consists largely of "By gar." It's odd, but I didn't hear a single one of the potato pickers say "By gar," and they must have seen the pictures and known what is right. The women and girls wore pants usually of corduroy and thick sweaters, and they covered their heads with bright-colored scarves to protect their hair from the dust that rises from the fields with the smallest wind. Most of these people traveled in big trucks covered with dark canvas tarpaulins, but there were some trailers and a few camper tops like Rocinante. At night some slept in the trucks and trailers, but also there were tents pitched in pleasant places, and the smells that came from their cooking fires indicated that they had not lost their French genius for making soup.

Fortunately the tents and trucks and two trailers were settled on the edge of a clear and lovely lake. I parked Rocinante about ninety-five yards away but also on the lake's edge. Then I put on coffee to boil and brought out my garbage-bucket laundry, which had been jouncing for two days, and rinsed the detergent out at the edge of the lake. Attitudes toward strangers crop up mysteriously. I was downwind from the camp and the odor of their soup drifted to me. Those people might have been murderers, sadists, brutes, ugly apish subhumans for all I knew, but I found myself thinking, "What charming people, what flair, how beautiful they are. How I wish I knew them." And all based on the delicious smell of soup.

In establishing contact with strange people, Charley is my ambassador. I release him, and he drifts toward the objective, or rather to whatever the objective may be preparing for dinner. I retrieve him so that he will not be a nuisance to my neighbors—*et voilà!* A child can do the same thing, but a dog is better.

The incident came off as smoothly as one might expect of a tested and well-rehearsed script. I sent out my ambassador and drank a cup of coffee while I gave him time to operate. Then I strolled to the camp to relieve my neighbors of the inconvenience of my miserable cur. They were nice-looking people, a dozen of them, not counting children, three of the girls pretty and given to giggling, two of the wives buxom and a third even buxomer with child, a patriarch, two brothers-in-law, and a couple of young men who were working toward being brothers-in-law. But the operating chieftain, with deference of course to the patriarch, was a fine-looking man of about thirty-five, broad-shouldered and lithe, with the cream-and-berries complexion of a girl and crisp black curling hair.

The dog had caused no trouble, he said. The truth was that they had remarked that he was a handsome dog. I of course found myself prejudiced in spite of his deficiencies, being his owner, but the dog had one advantage over most dogs. He was born and raised in France.

The group closed ranks. The three pretty girls giggled and were instantly smothered by the navy-blue eye of the chieftain, backed by a hiss from the patriarch.

Was that the truth? Where in France?

In Bercy, on the outskirts of Paris, did they know it?

No, unfortunately they had never been to the fatherland.

I hoped they might remedy that.

They should have known Charley for a French national by his manners. They had observed my *roulotte* with admiration.

It was simple but comfortable. If they found it convenient, I should be pleased to show it to them.

I was very kind. It would give them pleasure.

If the elevated tone indicates to you that it was carried on in French, you are wrong. The chieftain spoke a very pure and careful English. The one French word used was *roulotte*. The asides among themselves were in Canuck. My French is ridiculous, anyway. No, the elevated tone was a part and parcel of the pageantry of establishing a rapport. I gathered Charley to me. Might I expect them after supper, which I smelled on the fire?

They would be honored.

I set my cabin in order, heated and ate a can of chili con carne, made sure the beer was cold, and even picked a bouquet of autumn leaves and put them in a milk bottle on the table. The roll of paper cups laid in for just such an occasion had got squashed flat by a flying dictionary my first day out, but I made coasters from folded paper towels. It's amazing what trouble you will go to for a party. Then Charley barked them in and I was host in my own house. Six people can squeeze in behind my table, and they did. Two others beside me stood up, and the back door was wreathed with children's faces. They were very nice people but quite formal. I opened beer for the big ones and pop for the outsiders.

In due course these people told me quite a bit about themselves. They came over the border every year for the potato harvest. With everyone working, it made a nice little pool against the winter. Did they have any trouble with immigration people at the border? Well, no. The rules seemed to relax during the harvest season, and besides, the way was smoothed by a contractor to whom they paid a small percentage of their pay. But they didn't really pay him. He collected directly from the farmers. I've know quite a few migrant people over the years—Okies and Mexican wetbacks, and the Negroes who move into New Jersey and Long Island. And wherever I've seen them there has always been a contractor in the background to smooth the way for them for a consideration. Years ago the farmers tried to draw more labor than they needed so that they could lower wages. This seems to be no longer true, for government agencies channel only as many laborers as are needed, and some kind of minimum wage is maintained. In other cases the migrants have been driven to movement and seasonal work by poverty and terrible need.

Surely my guests for the evening were neither mistreated nor driven. This clan, having put their own small farm to bed for the winter in the Province of Quebec, came over the line to make a small nest egg. They even carried a little feeling of holiday with them almost like the hops- and strawberry-pickers from London and the Midland cities of England. These were a hardy and self-sufficient people, quite capable of taking care of themselves.

I opened more beer. After the night of desolate loneliness I felt very good to be surrounded by warm and friendly but cautious people. I tapped an artesian well of good feeling and made a small speech in my pidgin type of French. It began: "Messy dam. *Je vous porte un cher souvenir de la belle France—en particular du Departement de Charente.*"

They looked startled but interested. Then John the chieftain slowly translated my speech into high-school English and put it back into Canadian French. "Charente?" he asked. "Why Charente?" I leaned down and opened a compartment under my sink and lifted out a bottle of very old and reverend brandy brought along for weddings, frost bite, and heart attacks. John studied the label with the devout attention a good Christian might give to the holy sacrament. And his words were reverent: "Jesus Christ," he said. "I forgot. Charente— that's where Cognac is." Then he read the purported year of the bottle's nativity and softly repeated his first words.

He passed the bottle to the patriarch in his corner, and the old man smiled so sweetly that for the first time I could see he lacked front teeth. The brother-in-law growled in his throat like a happy tomcat and the pregnant ladies twittered like *alouettes* singing to the sun. I handed John a corkscrew while I laid out the crystal—three plastic coffee cups, a jelly glass, a shaving mug, and several wide-mouthed pill bottles. I emptied their capsules into a saucepan and rinsed out the odor of wheat germ with water from the tap. The cognac was very, very good, and from the first muttered *"Santé"* and the first clicking sip you could feel the Brotherhood of Man growing until it filled Rocinante full—and the sisterhood also.

They refused seconds and I insisted. And the division of thirds was put on the basis that there wasn't enough to save. And with the few divided drops of that third there came into Rocinante a triumphant human magic that can bless a house, or a truck for that matter—nine people gathered in complete silence and the nine parts making a whole as surely as my arms and legs are part of me, separate and inseparable. Rocinante took on a glow it never quite lost.

Such a fabric cannot be prolonged and should not be. The patriarch gave some kind of signal. My guests squirmed out of their squeezed-up seats behind the table and the adieux, as they should be, were short and formal. Then they went into the night, their way home lighted by the chieftain John carrying a tin kerosene lantern. They walked in silence among sleepy stumbling children and I never saw them again. But I like them.

I didn't make down my bed because I wanted to start very early. I curled up behind the table and slept a little while until in the dim false dawn Charley looked into my face and said "Ftt." While

I heated my coffee, I made a little sign on cardboard and stuck it in the neck of the empty brandy bottle, then passing the sleeping camp I stopped and stood the bottle where they would see it. The sign read: *"Enfant de France, Mort pour la Patrie."* And I drove as quietly as I could, for on this day I intended to drive a little west and then take the long road south down the long reach of Maine. There are times that one treasures for all one's life, and such times are burned clearly and sharply on the material of total recall. I felt very fortunate that morning.

On such a trip as mine, so much there is to see and to think about that event and thought set down as they occurred would roil and stir like a slow-cooking *minestrone*. There are map people whose joy is to lavish more attention on the sheets of colored paper than on the colored land rolling by. I have listened to accounts by such travelers in which every road number was remembered, every mileage recalled, and every little countryside discovered. Another kind of traveler requires to know in terms of maps exactly where he is pin-pointed at every moment, as though there were some kind of safety in black and red lines, in dotted indications and squirming blue of lakes and the shadings that indicate mountains. It is not so with me. I was born lost and take no pleasure in being found, nor much identification from shapes which symbolize continents and states. Besides, roads change, increase, are widened or abandoned so often in our country that one must buy road maps like daily newspapers. But since I know the passions of the mapifiers I can report that I moved north in

Maine roughly or parallel to U.S. Highway 1 through Houlton, Mars Hill, Presque Isle, Caribou, Van Buren, turned westward, still on U.S. 1, past Madawaska, Upper Frenchville, and Fort Kent, then went due south on State Highway 11 past Eagle Lake, Winterville, Portage, Squa Pan, Masardis, Knowles Corner, Patten, Sherman, Grindstone, and so to Millinocket.

I can report this because I have a map before me, but what I remember has no reference to the numbers and colored lines and squiggles. I have thrown this routing in as a sop and shall not make a habit of it. What I remember are the long avenues in the frost, the farms and houses braced against the winter, the flat, laconic Maine speech in crossroad stores where I stopped to buy supplies. The many deer that crossed the road on nimbling hooves and leaped like bounding rubber away from the passing Rocinante. The roaring lumber trucks. And always I remember that this huge area had once been much more settled and was now abandoned to the creeping forest, the animals, the lumber camps and the cold. The big towns are getting bigger and the villages smaller. The hamlet store, whether grocery, general, hardware, clothing, cannot compete with the supermarket and the chain organization. Our treasured and nostalgic picture of the village general store, the cracker-barrel store where an informed yeomanry gather to express opinions and formulate the national character, is very rapidly disappearing. People who once held family fortresses against wind and weather, against scourges of frost and drought and insect enemies, now cluster against the busy breast of the big town.

The new American finds his challenge and his love in traffic-choked streets, skies nested in smog, choking with the acids of industry, the screech of rubber and houses leashed in against one another while the townlets wither a time and die. And this, as I found, is as true in Texas as in Maine. Clarendon yields to Amarillo just as surely as Stacyville, Maine, bleeds its substance into Millinocket, where the logs are ground up, the air smells of chemicals, the rivers are choked and poisoned, and the streets swarm with this happy, hurrying breed. This is not offered in criticism but only as observation. And I am sure that, as all pendulums reverse their swing, so eventually will the swollen cities rupture like dehiscent wombs and disperse their children back to the countryside. This prophecy is underwritten by the tendency of the rich to do this already. Where the rich lead, the poor will follow, or try to.

Some years ago at Abercrombie and Fitch I bought a cattle caller, an automobile horn manipulated by a lever with which nearly all cow emotions can be imitated, from the sweet lowing of a romantic heifer to the growling roar of a bull in the prime and lust of his bullhood. I had this contraption on Rocinante, and it was most effective. When its call goes out, every bovine within hearing distance raises its head from grazing and moves toward the sound.

In the silver chill of the Maine afternoon, as I bucketed and lumbered over the pitted surface of a wood road, I saw four lady mooses moving with stately heaviness across my bow. As I came near they broke into a heavy-cushioned trot. On an impulse I pressed down the lever of the cattle caller and a bellow came out like that of a Miura bull as he poises before firing himself at the butterfly sweep of his first veronica. The ladies, who were on the point of disappearing into the forest, heard the sound, stopped, turned, and then came for me with gathering speed and with what looked to me like romance in their eyes—but four romances, each weighing well over a thousand pounds! And much as I favor love in all its aspects, I trod my accelerator and got the hell out of there fast. And I remembered a story of the great Fred Allen. His character was a Maine man telling of a moose hunt. "I sat on a log and blew my moose call and waited. Then suddenly I felt something like a warm bath mat on my neck and head. Well sir, it was a moosess licking me and there was a light of passion in her eyes."

"Did you shoot her?" he was asked.

"No, sir. I went away from there fast, but I have often thought that somewhere in Maine there's a moose with a broken heart."

Maine is just as long coming down as it is going up, maybe longer. I could and should have gone to Baxter State Park, but I didn't. I had dawdled too long and it was getting cold and I had visions of Napoleon at Moscow and the Germans at Stalingrad. So I retreated smartly—Brownville Junction, Milo, Dover-Foxcroft, Guilford, Bingham, Skowhegan, Mexico, Rumford, where I joined a road I had already traveled through the White Mountains. Perhaps this was weak of me, but I wanted to get on with it. The rivers were full of logs, bank to bank for miles, waiting their turn at the abbatoir to give their woody hearts so that the bulwarks of our civilization such as *Time* magazine and the *Daily News* can survive, to defend us against ignorance. The mill towns, with all respect, are knots of worms. You come out of serene country and suddenly you are tossed and battered by a howling hurricane of traffic. For a time you fight your way blindly in the mad crush of hurtling metal and then suddenly it dies away and you are in serene and quiet countryside again. And there is no margin or overlap. It is a mystery but a happy one.

In the short time since I had passed, the foliage of the White Mountains had changed and tattered. The leaves were falling, rolling in dusky clouds, and the conifers on the slopes were crusted with snow. I drove long and furiously, to Charley's great disgust. Any number of times he said "Ftt" to me and I ignored him, and barreled on across the upraised thumb of New Hampshire. I wanted a bath and a new bed and a drink and a little human commerce, and I thought to find it on the Connecticut River. It is very strange that when you set a goal for yourself, it is hard not to hold toward it even if it is inconvenient and not even desirable. The way was longer than I had thought and I was very tired. My years spoke for my attention with aching shoulders but I was aimed at the Connecticut River and I ignored the weariness, and this was utter nonsense. It was nearly dark when I found the place I wanted, not far from Lancaster, New Hampshire. The river was wide and pleasant, bordered with trees and edged with a pleasant meadow. And near the bank there stood what I was lusting for—a row of neat little white houses on the green meadow by the river, and a small, compactly housed office and lunch room with a sign in the roadside that bore the welcome words "Open" and "Vacancy." I swung Rocinante off the road and opened the cab door to let Charley out.

The afternoon light made mirrors of the windows of the office and lunch room. My whole body ached from the road as I opened the door and went in. Not a soul was there. The register was on the desk, stools at the lunch counter, pies and cakes under plastic covers; the refrigerator hummed; a few dirty dishes soaked in soapy water in the stainless-steel sink, and a faucet dripped slowly into it.

I banged the little bell on the desk, then called out, "Anybody here?" No answer, nothing. I sat down on a stool to await the return of the management. The numbered keys to the little white houses hung on a board. The daylight slipped away and the place darkened. I went outside to collect Charley and to verify my impression that the sign said "Open" and "Vacancy." By now it was getting dark. I brought out a flashlight and looked through the office for a note saying "Back in ten minutes," but there was none. I felt strangely like a Peeping Tom; I didn't belong there. Then I went outside and moved Rocinante out of the driveway, fed Charley, made some coffee, and waited.

It would have been simple to take a key, leave a

note on the desk saying that I had done so, and open one of the little houses. It wasn't right. I couldn't do it. On the highway a few cars went by and crossed the bridge over the river, but none turned in. The windows of the office and grill flashed under approaching headlights and then blacked out again. I had planned to eat a light supper and then to fall dog-weary into bed. I made my bed, found I wasn't hungry after all, and lay down. But sleep would not come to me. I listened for the return of the management. At last I lighted my gas mantle and tried to read, but with listening I could not follow the words. As last I dozed, awakened in the dark, looked out—nothing. My little sleep was troubled and uneasy.

At dawn I arose and created a long, slow, time-wasting breakfast. The sun came up, searching out the windows. I walked down to the river to keep Charley company, returned, even shaved and took a sponge bath in a bucket. The sun was well up by now. I went to the office and entered. The refrigerator hummed, the faucet dripped into the cold soapy water of the sink. A new-born, heavy-winged fat fly crawled fretfully over a plastic pie cover. At nine-thirty I drove away and no one had come, nothing had moved. The sign still read "Open" and "Vacancy." I drove across the iron bridge, rattling the steel-tread plates. The empty place disturbed me deeply, and, come to think of it, it still does.

On the long journey doubts were often my companions. I've always admired those reporters who can descend on an area, talk to key people, ask key questions, take samplings of opinions, and then set down an orderly report very like a road map. I envy this technique and at the same time do not trust it as a mirror of reality. I feel that there are too many realities. What I set down here is true until someone else passes that way and rearranges the world in his own style. In literary criticism the critic has no choice but to make over the victim of his attention into something the size and shape of himself.

And in this report I do not fool myself into thinking I am dealing with constants. A long time ago I was in the ancient city of Prague and at the same time Joseph Alsop, the justly famous critic of places and events, was there. He talked to informed people, officials, ambassadors; he read reports, even the fine print and figures, while I in my slipshod manner roved about with actors, gypsies, vagabonds. Joe and I flew home to America in the same plane, and on the way he told me about Prague, and his Prague had no relation to the city I had seen and heard. It just wasn't the same place, and yet each of us was honest, neither one a liar, both pretty good observers by any standard, and we brought home two cities, two truths. For this reason I cannot commend this account as an America that you will find. So much there is to see, but our morning eyes describe a different world than do our afternoon eyes, and surely our wearied evening eyes can report only a weary evening world.

Sunday morning, in a Vermont town, my last day in New England, I shaved, dressed in a suit, polished my shoes, whited my sepulcher, and looked for a church to attend. Several I eliminated for reasons I do not now remember, but on seeing a John Knox church I drove into a side street and parked Rocinante out of sight, gave Charley his instructions about watching the truck, and took my way with dignity to a church of blindingly white ship lap. I took my seat in the rear of the spotless, polished place of worship. The prayers were to the point, directing the attention of the Almighty to certain weaknesses and undivine tendencies I know to be mine and could only suppose were shared by others gathered there.

The service did my heart and I hope my soul some good. It had been long since I had heard such an approach. It is our practice now, at least in the large cities, to find from our psychiatric priesthood that our sins aren't really sins at all but accidents that are set in motion by forces beyond our control. There was no such nonsense in this church. The minister, a man of iron with tool-steel eyes and a delivery like a pneumatic drill, opened up with prayer and reassured us that we were a pretty sorry lot. And he was right. We didn't amount to much to start with, and due to our own tawdry efforts we had been slipping ever since. Then, having softened us up, he went into a glorious sermon, a fire-and-brimstone sermon. Having proved that we, or perhaps only I, were no damn good, he painted with cool certainty what was likely to happen to us if we didn't make some basic reorganizations for which he didn't hold out much hope. He spoke of hell as an expert, not the mush-mush hell of these soft days, but a well-stoked, white-hot hell served by technicians of the first order. This reverend brought it to a point where we could understand it, a good hard coal fire, plenty of draft, and a squad of open-hearth devils who put their hearts into their work, and their work was me. I began to feel good all over. For some years now God had been a pal to us, practicing togetherness, and that causes the same emptiness a father does playing softball with his son. But this Vermont God cared enough about me to go to a lot of trouble kicking the hell out of me. He put my sins in a new perspective. Whereas they had been small and mean and nasty and best forgotten, this minister gave them some size and bloom and dignity. I hadn't been thinking very well of myself for some years, but if my sins had this dimension there was some pride left. I wasn't a naughty child but a first rate sinner, and I was going to catch it.

I felt so revived in spirit that I put five dollars in the plate, and afterward, in front of the church, shook hands warmly with the minister and as many of the congregation as I could. It gave me a lovely sense of evil-doing that lasted clear through till Tuesday. I even considered beating Charley to give him some satisfaction too, because Charley is only a little less sinful than I am. All across the country I went to church on Sundays, a different denomination every week, but nowhere did I find the quality of that Vermont preacher. He forged a religion designed to last, not predigested obsolescence.

I crossed into New York State at Rouses Point and stayed as near to Lake Ontario as I could because it was my intention to look at Niagara Falls, which I had never seen, and then to slip into Canada, from Hamilton to Windsor, keeping Lake Erie on the south, and to emerge at Detroit—a kind of end run, a small triumph over geography. We know, of course, that each of our states is an individual and proud of it. Not content with their names, they take descriptive titles also— the Empire State, the Garden State, the Granite State—titles proudly borne and little given to understatement. But now for the first time I became aware that each state had also its individual prose style, made sharply evident in its highway signs. Crossing state lines one is aware of this change of language. The New England states use a terse form of instruction, a tight-lipped, laconic style sheet, wasting no words and few letters. New York State shouts at you the whole time. Do this. Do that. Squeeze left. Squeeze right. Every few feet an imperious command. In Ohio the signs are more benign. They offer friendly advice, and are more like suggestions. Some states use a turgid style which can get you lost with the greatest ease. There are states which tell you what you may expect to find in the way of road conditions ahead, while others let you find out for yourself. Nearly all have abandoned the adverb for the adjective. Drive Slow. Drive Safe.

I am an avid reader of all signs, and I find that in the historical markers the prose of statehood reaches it glorious best, and most lyric. I have further established, at least to my own satisfaction, that those states with the shortest histories and the least world-shaking events have the most historical markers. Some Western states even find glory in half-forgotten murders and bank robberies. The towns not to be left behind proudly announce their celebrated sons, so the traveler is informed by signs and banners—Birthplace of Elvis Presley, of Cole Porter, of Alan P. Huggins. This is no new thing, of course. I seem to remember that small cities in ancient Greece quarreled bitterly over which was the birthplace of Homer. Within my memory an outraged home-town citizenry wanted Red Lewis back for tarring and feathering after he wrote *Main Street*. And today Sauk Centre celebrates itself for having produced him. We, as a nation, are as hungry for history as was England when Geoffrey of Monmouth concocted his History of British Kings, many of whom he manufactured to meet a growing demand. And as in states and communities, so in individual Americans this hunger for decent association with the past. Genealogists are worked to death winnowing the debris of ancestry for grains of greatness. Not long ago it was proved that Dwight D. Eisenhower was descended from the royal line of Britain, a proof if one were needed that everyone is descended from everyone. The then little town where I was born, which within my grandfather's memory was a blacksmith shop in a swamp, recalls with yearly pageantry a glowing past of Spanish dons and rose-eating senoritas who have in public memory wiped out the small, desolate tribe of grub- and grasshopper-eating Indians who were our true first settlers.

I find this interesting, but it does make for suspicion of history as a record of reality. I thought of these things as I read the historical markers across the country, thought how the myth wipes out the fact. On a very low level the following is the process of a myth. Visiting the town where I was born, I talked with a very old man who had known me as a child. He remembered vividly seeing me, a peaked, shivering child walking past his house one freezing morning, my inadequate overcoat fastened across my little chest with horse-blanket pins. This in its small way is the very stuff of myths—the poor and suffering child who rises to glory, on a limited scale of course. Even though I didn't remember the episode, I knew it could not be true. My mother was a passionate sewer-on of buttons. A button off was more than sloppiness; it was a sin. If I had pinned my coat, my mother would have whaled me. The story could not be true, but this old gentleman so loved it that I could never convince him of its falsity, so I didn't try. If my home town wants me in horse-blanket pins, nothing I can do is likely to change it, particularly the truth.

It rained in New York State, the Empire State, rained cold and pitiless, as the highway-sign writers would put it. Indeed the dismal downpour made my intended visit to Niagara Falls seem redundant. I was then hopelessly lost in the streets of a small but endless town in the neighborhood of Medina, I think. I pulled to the side of the street and got out my book of road maps. But to find where you are going, you must know where you are, and I didn't. The windows of the cab were tightly closed and opaque with streaming rain. My car radio played softly. Suddenly there was a knock on the window, the door was wrenched open, and a man slipped into the seat beside me. The man

96

was quite red of face, quite whisky of breath. His trousers were held up by red braces over the long gray underwear that covered his chest.

"Turn that damn thing off," he said, and then turned off the radio himself. "My daughter saw you out the window," he continued. "Thought you was in trouble." He looked at my maps. "Throw those things away. Now where is it you want to go?"

I don't know why it is a man can't answer such a question with the truth. The truth was that I had turned off the big highway 104 and into the smaller roads because the traffic was heavy and passing vehicles threw sheets of water on my windshield. I wanted to go to Niagara Falls. Why couldn't I have admitted it? I looked down at my map and said, "I'm trying to get to Erie, Pennsylvania."

"Good," he said. "Now, throw those maps away. Now you turn around, go two traffic lights, that'll bring you to Egg Street. Turn left there and about two hundred yards on Egg turn right at an angle. That's a twisty kind of street and you'll come to an overpass, but don't take it. You turn left there and it will curve around like this—see? Like this." His hand made a curving motion. "Now, when the curve straightens out you'll come to three branching roads. There's a big red house on the left-hand branch so you don't take that, you take the right-hand branch. Now, have you got that so far?"

"Sure," I said. "That's easy."

"Well repeat it back so I'll know you're going right."

I had stopped listening at the curving road. I said, "Maybe you better tell me again."

"I thought so. Turn around and go two traffic lights to Egg Street, turn left for two hundred yards and turn right at an angle to a twisty street till you come to an overpass but don't take it."

"That clears it up for me," I said quickly. "I sure do thank you for helping me out."

"Hell," he said, "I ain't even got you out of town yet."

Well, he got me out of town by a route which, if I could have remembered it, let alone followed it, would have made the path into the Labyrinth at Knossos seem like a throughway. When he was finally satisfied and thanked, he got out and slammed the door, but such is my social cowardice that I actually did turn around, knowing he would be watching out the window. I drove around two blocks and blundered my way back to 104, traffic or not.

Against the Sea

PAUL THEROUX

Novelist and travel writer Paul Theroux was born in Medford, Massachusetts, in 1941. He served in the Peace Corps and later taught in such distant lands as Malawi, Uganda, Singapore, and Italy. His travel accounts include his rail journeys, The Great Railway Bazaar *and* The Old Patagonian Express, *and* Kingdom by the Sea *in which he described a walk around the coast of England. In one of the few pieces he has written about his native Massachusetts, world traveler Theroux paddles from his summer home on Cape Cod to Plymouth, Mass., in search of adventure and concludes that for him "travel is mostly in the mind."*

Travel is an attitude. It is not a matter of place, though some places, more than others, appear to be convincing backdrops for adventure. But I have come to believe that travel is mostly in the mind.

A person goes to Bangkok and returns with a pile of lurid snapshots and a few yards of raw silk and believes that to be travel. Travel is supposed to be swimming pools and sunshine and the whole supine experience of feeling very rich because everyone else is very poor. I don't condemn it as a vice, though I think it is helpful to recognize that there is an implied snobbery in this sort of vacationing. At its best it is harmless, but it is also thoroughly predictable.

The adventure of travel is something else, something personal and enigmatic, and I usually associate it with high-risk, high-gain activity. This might mean an assault on the north face of the Eiger, but it could also mean a rainy afternoon in Red Hook, or the choppy seas off Scusset Beach, in Massachusetts.

Adventure may be deliberate. There is a travel company in California that organizes eight-day trips to the North Pole for $7,000. But adventure is more likely to be accidental. Classically, it is the picnic that turns into an ordeal ("George! George! Drop the keys!" of the Charles Addams cartoon), the hunting expedition that becomes a nightmare (the "Moby-Dick" experience that is more vulgarly served up in efforts like "Deliverance"), or the jolly, away-from-it-all sea voyage that is interrupted by killer whales and is later retold in a book like "Survive the Savage Sea."

I like the idea of travel as a solitary enterprise, something that involves maps and planning, forethought, consultation, even secrecy. In spite of the planning, the unexpected usually occurs. True travel is launching oneself into the unknown—a sort of confrontation. There is no excuse for it except the excuse that one offers oneself—simply that you want to do it. And to me the most compelling trip holds the prospect of the unknown near home.

November had dripped into my soul, and my remedy for that gloom lay in battling through the surf from my house in East Sandwich across the bay and around the corner to Plymouth. The season would make it dangerous and difficult, and therefore rewarding. Half the thrill of it was that I had never done it before—and so it would all be enlightening.

Circumstances are everything. In the summer, tiny tots bob about, sitting in inner tubes on the sunny sea off Sagamore; but in winter no one goes very close to the water for fear the waves will rise up and overwhelm him and snatch him away. The prevailing wind is northwesterly, cold and hard. I have a passion for small boats, but sailing is impossible in such seas; rowing is out of the question, and even the large yachts are in dry dock for the winter. Next year, people say, and stuff their hands deeper into their pockets, and they go on surveying the wild sea from the safety of shore—the breakers and dumpers, and hurrying whitecaps and the clash of clapotis, the flying spray and the claw-shaped overhanging wave crests that look like something by Hokusai.

Yet paddling a kayak off the New England coast, even in winter, is not very strange. Sea-kayaking, which has been carried on for centuries by the icebound peoples of Alaska and West Greenland and Patagonia, has caught on as a sport and recreation in recent years. It has allowed people to travel to places that are unreachable in any other sort of boat. A kayak can go almost anywhere in practically any weather. In the right hands it is probably the most adaptable and seaworthy vessel afloat. Kayaks have been paddled across the Atlantic and through the Caribbean and up the

Alaskan coast and down the Nile and the Amazon. In 1979, Charles Porter of Maine rowed his Klepper kayak around Cape Horn—incidentally making him the first man to go around the Horn backward. Last year, in the Patagonian winter, two Germans paddled around the horn in two Klepper folding kayaks.

There have been paddlers in kayaks at the Horn for hundreds of years. When Darwin first saw them he was scornful. He saw in the kayak a mark of the Fuegan Indians' savagery. These Indians were no better than animals, he said, because they had not improved their kayaks. "The canoe," he wrote in 1837, "their most ingenious work, poor as it is, has remained the same as we know from Drake, for the last two hundred and fifty years." Darwin was mistaken in his conclusion. Four hundred years later the kayak is still unchanged in its basic design, because for its size it is as near as possible to being a perfect boat. In one sense it is not even a boat, but rather something that you wear that keeps you afloat.

This trip had not been a casual decision. A month before, I had spent some time in Southeast Asia. *That* had been a casual decision. But kayaking alone in a November sea off Massachusetts had required quite a lot of forward planning. I needed equipment and practice; I had to study the weather, and I had to overcome certain fears. I felt weak and ignorant, and I was afraid of tipping over in a cold sea and having to make what kayakers call a "wet exit."

My fear of falling in was so great that the first chance I had I decided to throw myself in—to break the suspense. I was wearing a wet suit, but even so, the shock of the cold seawater gave me a lasting headache. I was also worried by high waves. To prove to myself that I could maintain my balance in them, I went out one day and paddled in a sea that was producing four- and five-foot waves near shore. I had also been fearful of the cold, but I quickly discovered that in a well-found kayak one is almost impervious to cold—in fact, perspiring and overheating are much greater problems.

I estimated that with detours it would be just about 30 miles from my home inlet to Plymouth. I was especially eager to get close to a blurred gray bluff on the off-Cape coast that I could see on clear days from my kitchen window. That was about 10 miles away; but I had never been there. I liked the idea of visiting my view. After a month or more of practice and nerving myself for the trip, I set off, passing a man fishing at the inlet. A man fishing is not easy to distract, but when this wading one saw me he lowered his tackle and called out, "This I've got to see!" The surf was up. I was heading out into three-foot dumpers.

I was grateful to the fisherman for a remark that seemed to signify my departure. And I was pleased that he had noticed me, because in a vainglorious way I was proud of setting out on such a cold morning. I was also a little apprehensive: the turbulent aftereffects of a hurricane were still in the air and on the sea. But it was also strange to be witnessed doing this. Because writers are mainly sedentary people we have a tendency to over-dramatize physical effort; the non-writers I know who are travelers take things pretty much in their stride and seldom make a meal of their adventures. The fisherman's attention made me self-conscious, and I took a formal sort of care in negotiating the waves, going up and over them and punching with the paddle. Then I was beyond them, in relative safety.

The sea was scattered with whitecaps. Apart from the fisherman, there was no one on the beach, and except for a distant ship, there was nothing on the sea. I was alone and rather excited at the prospect of this unusual outing. It was like answering a dare. I was certainly trying to prove something to myself, and I was enjoying the pleasure of having ignored dire warnings. Most people are only too happy to discourage you from doing anything that looks risky, and I found that whenever I mentioned that I was going to spend part of November kayaking on the New England coast, people tried to put me off. Too cold, too windy, they said; too dangerous alone, and what about the sharks? I suppose people say those things because they don't want to be held responsible for another person's foolishness, and because they cannot imagine anyone doing something they would not do themselves.

But the dire warnings filled me with resolve; they were the very stuff of adventure and they were as good as a salutation, and so are bad weather and dim prospects and risk. There was a 15-knot head wind. "If the human race has one common denominator, it is hatred of head winds," as John McPhee has written.

The first day I paddled to Cape Cod Canal,

which is a wonderful cut from Cape Cod Bay to Buzzards Bay—it was proposed by early settlers in the 17th century and finally opened in 1914. When I crossed the eastern entrance a strong current was running out of it, because the tide was rising (the Canal current floods east and ebbs west). With both the wind and the tide against me I was pushed a distance offshore and had to thrash hard to get back near land. I had lunch farther on at Sagamore, under a cliff. There, a dog walker told me he had seen a shark that morning.

"Its dorsal fin was about this size," he said, measuring two feet with his mittens. "And it wasn't flopped over, so I know it wasn't a sunfish. Must have been 10-12 foot long."

Soon after that, night fell. It came quickly, like a shade being yanked at 4 o'clock, and then there was nothing I could do but put in.

I did not see any sharks the next day, but I saw hundreds of eider ducks, and grebes, and golden-eyes and canvasbacks. And cormorants gathered on rocks, looking as though they were posing for medallions as they held their wings out to dry. The beach had an empty, scoured look, and it was bleak and curiously inanimate—in great contrast to the waves just offshore and the foamy corrugations on the horizon. At times I could not see over the tops of the waves when I paddled into the troughs between them.

Eventually I was close to the cliffs that I had seen from my kitchen window—the long, eroded headland near Center Hill Point. The waves broke over my deck, and occasionally over my head, and streamed over my sprayskirt. I did not tip over and I stopped worrying about it. It was heavy going in such a strong wind, but I was in no particular hurry. I knew that my destination was merely an excuse to take the trip.

If I needed any justification, I had it on the third day. Paddling in a shallow rocky bay near a place the chart said was Churchill's Landing, I saw half a dozen bobbing boat moorings—or were they lobster markers? They began to disappear. Then some returned; there were 10. Soon I saw that these shmoo heads were unmistakably seals. They came closer and surrounded me, and I counted 17 of them. They were funny, friendly and nimble, their whiskers dripping, their bald heads gleaming, like enchanted beach toys. Their odd upthrust and swiveling heads made me laugh, and I was delighted when they followed me toward Manomet Point.

Seeing those seals and creeping up on them and being followed by them was worth my month of preparation. The whole point of travel is discovery, and few experiences can match the satisfaction of such an extraordinary discovery near home. The way seals play can make you believe in the possibility of a peaceable kingdom, and that vision stayed with me and gave me zest for the next leg into Plymouth.

It was no distance, of course, but the trouble was that as soon as I rounded the point I received the full unimpeded blast of the northwest wind. I was off White Horse Beach and was struggling through the surf. But I reminded myself that I was not in a hurry. I had chosen an unusual means of getting to a familiar place; when I was younger I headed for unusual places by conventional means. This time I was lured by what was visible, and the prospect of the unknown, and on the way had seen marvels.

To avoid the breakers smashing on Rocky Point, I detoured into Plymouth Bay and headed for the breakwater at the harbor. There I was sheltered by the high ground of the mainland, and with the wind deflected I paddled into Plymouth. If I had come in a car I probably would have driven through without stopping. But because I had come in a kayak I was grateful for this safe arrival and this pleasant landfall.

I went into the post office to send a postcard. I was wearing sunglasses and a wet suit and rubber booties. I had mitts called "pogies" on my hands. I was windblown and on my suit were rimey stripes of sea salt. In a secret, self-dramatizing way I felt like Ishmael.

The women at the counter said, "Where have you been?"

I told her—out there, kayaking.

"What are you doing that for—a coffee commercial?"

From *Travels in America 100 Years Ago*

THOMAS TWINING

Thomas Twining (1776–1861), served in the India service for England and visited the United States in 1795 on a trip home. In this lively account, he travels by stagecoach and horseback through Maryland and Pennsylvania and visits with General and Mrs. Washington as the president contemplates his retirement.

10th May.—At 6 A.M. I set out for Philadelphia. Among the passengers who almost filled the wagon was Mr. Hancock, son of Mr. Hancock of Massachusetts, the countryman and colleague of Mr. Adams, the Vice-President. A trifling circumstance showed the general feeling of respect towards General Washington. Mr. Hancock having learned that I was bearer of the picture of the General, communicated this incident to the rest of the company, upon whom it seemed to make an extraordinary impression, procuring me their congratulations on being honored with such a charge, and particular marks of their attention during the remainder of the journey.

Breakfasted at Harford. Stopped a few minutes at Charlestown, from the neighborhood of which is a fine view of the Chesapeak. Dined at Havre de Grace. The dinner, though not remarkable for its excellence, afforded by its singularity much amusement. The first dish being pork, to which one of the passengers, a Frenchman, had a great dislike, he waited for the second, but this being pork also his national irritability was much excited, and broke through all bounds when he found that the remaining dishes were only varieties of the same hated food. The Frenchman, who had perhaps calculated on a fine trout from the Susquehannah, expressed his dissatisfaction in very warm terms; and when finally a rather high bill was placed before us, he positively refused his share of the contribution. The American *in*sisted, the Frenchman *re*sisted, and seconded his declaration by twice raising his knife and striking the handle of it with great violence against the table. It would have been fortunate if his resentment had ended here, for lifting up his knife a third time, while he looked angrily at the master of the inn, he brought the end of it down, not upon the table, but on his plate and broke it to pieces. The landlord was far from disposed to soothe the increased vexation of his offended guest, but said with an air of triumph, "Monsieur will now pay for the dinner and the plate too"; and in fact, instead of reducing his bill or the Frenchman's portion, he charged as liberally for his porcelain as for his pork; leaving the Frenchman no other satisfaction than that of complaining during the rest of the journey that he had paid dear for a dinner he had not eaten, and for more plates than he had broken. For myself I not only made a good dinner, the pork being excellent, but learned a circumstance which itself was worth my share of the reckoning. I was informed that great numbers of pigs were turned loose into the woods of the Susquehannah, where they run wild, living and growing fat upon the acorns and nuts of various sorts which abound there. Before winter the poor animals are hunted, and such as are caught—for many probably escape—are killed for home consumption and exportation. I was told that a similar plan was adopted in other parts of Maryland, and it most likely extended to other states.

I had heard on board the *India,* and indeed Sir Robert Abercromby had before mentioned the circumstance to me, that in some parts of America the pigs were fed on peaches. I now found that this was the fact, and not so extraordinary a one as it had at first seemed to be. I had observed to-day, as I had in other parts of Maryland, that almost every farm-house and cottage had a peach orchard attached to it, as an apple orchard would be in England. The peaches were distilled into brandy, but the pigs fed upon the refuse, as well as upon such fruit as fell from the trees.

As we crossed the Susquehannah, I cast a farewell look upon the wild beauties of that river. It was dark before we reached the "Head of Elk." Here things were much changed since I passed before. There was indeed the same number of beds in the room, but the landlord was no longer surly, but extremely civil, and gave us a supper that made the best possible amends to the Frenchman for the loss of his dinner.

11th May.—Leave the "Head of Elk" at five

o'clock. Breakfast at Newark, and at three in the afternoon reach Philadelphia. Finding dinner prepared at the inn, I dined there and afterwards proceeded to Fourth Street, where Mr. and Mrs. Francis, and the good-tempered negress, and all my friends, were glad to see me. My notes say, "Glad to get to a good mattress again." In the evening I went to the play, the "Moghol Tale."

The excursion which I had made had quite succeeded. The country, towns, villages, state of society, were full of interest in their present condition, while their futurity presented a picture the most pleasing—the forests I had passed through converted into fertile plains, and the solitary banks of the Potomac, the Susquehannah, the Elk, and the Patapsco, covered with a free and intelligent population. One of the many improvements already spoken of is the junction of the Chesapeake and Delaware by cutting through the isthmus which now separates them. There will then be an inland water communication between Philadelphia, Annapolis, Alexandria, and Washington.

12th May.—Hearing that the American ship *Atlantic* would sail in a few days for England, I walked down to the Delaware, and liking the appearance of the vessel, I took my passage in her, engaging one of the state-rooms, a name rather absurdly bestowed upon a very small berth by the side of the great cabin or public-room, and feebly lighted from it by a glass in the door. The ship appeared to be about 300 tons, or nearly the size of the *India*. Called afterwards at Mr. Bingham's, where I found my Cabul sheep grazing in good

111

health on the garden lawn. Visited Dr. Ross and other friends.

13th May.—At one o'clock to-day I called at General Washington's with the picture and letter I had for him. He lived in a small red brick house on the left side of High Street, not much higher up than Fourth Street. There was nothing in the exterior of the house that denoted the rank of its possessor. Next door was a hair-dresser. Having stated my object to a servant who came to the door, I was conducted up a neat but rather narrow staircase, carpeted in the middle, and was shown into a middling-sized, well-furnished drawing-room on the left of the passage. Nearly opposite the door was the fireplace, with a wood-fire in it. The floor was carpeted. On the left of the fireplace was a sofa, which sloped across the room. There were no pictures on the walls, no ornaments on the chimney-piece. Two windows on the right of the entrance looked into the street. There was nobody in the room, but in a minute Mrs. Washington came in, when I repeated the object of my calling, and put into her hands the letter for General Washington, and his miniature. She said she would deliver them to the President, and, inviting me to sit down, retired for that purpose. She soon returned, and said the President would come presently. Mrs. Washington was a middle-sized lady, rather stout; her manner extremely kind and unaffected. She sat down on the sofa, and invited me to sit by her. I spoke of the pleasant days I had passed at Washington, and of the attentions I had received from her granddaughter, Mrs. Law.

While engaged in this conversation, but with

my thoughts turned to the expected arrival of the General, the door opened, and Mrs. Washington and myself rising, she said, "The President," and introduced me to him. Never did I feel more interest than at this moment, when I saw the tall, upright, venerable figure of this great man advancing towards me to take me by the hand. There was a seriousness in his manner which seemed to contribute to the impressive dignity of his person, without diminishing the confidence and ease which the benevolence of his countenance and the kindness of his address inspired. There are persons in whose appearance one looks in vain for the qualities they are known to possess, but the appearance of General Washington harmonized in a singular manner with the dignity and modesty of his public life. So completely did be *look* the great and good man he really was, that I felt rather respect than awe in his presence, and experienced neither the surprise nor disappointment with which a personal introduction to distinguished individuals is often accompanied.

The General having thanked me for the picture, requested me to sit down next the fire, Mrs. Washington being on the sofa on the other side, and himself taking a chair in the middle. He now inquired about my arrival in America, my voyage, my late journey, and his granddaughters, Mrs. Law and her sister, who had accompanied me to Alexandria. He asked me my opinion of that town, and seemed pleased with the account I gave of the extraordinary activity I had observed there. In the course of the conversation I mentioned the particular regard and respect with which Lord Cornwallis always spoke of him. He received this communication in the most courteous manner, inquired about his lordship, and expressed for him much esteem. Speaking about the intercourse between India and America, I said that I thought the United States had gained a great point by the right of trading conceded by the thirteenth article of Mr. Jay's treaty, and I mentioned at the same time the facilities of which this commerce was susceptible, to the equal advantage of America and India, now that it rested upon a legal basis.

I stated these opinions because the treaty in question, which had been approved by the existing Government, had caused some unreasonable animadversion amongst the opposers of the administration at this period. I observed that the measure was one to which the East India Company might object, as interfering with their chartered privileges, although in a manner favorable to the commercial population of India; but that it was in every respect advantageous to the United States, enlarging a communication that before was confined, and legalizing what was arbitrary and subject to prohibition.

The General asked me some questions about Calcutta, the natives of India, the Ganges, and the interior of the country. Upon my inquiring if coal had yet been found in the States of the Union, he said that it had been discovered in various parts, and that mines would doubtless be opened and worked when the diminished abundance of wood should direct the public attention to this subject.

After sitting about three quarters of an hour, I rose to take leave, when the General invited me to drink tea with him that evening. I regret to say that I declined this honor on account of some other engagement—a wrong and injudicious decision, for which I have since reproached myself. No engagement should have prevented my accepting such an invitation. If forwardness on such occasions be displeasing, an excess of delicacy and reserve is scarcely less to be avoided. However, this private intercourse with one of the most unblemished characters that any country had produced had entirely satisfied me, and greatly exceeded my private expectations, which had been limited to the usual transient introduction at a public levee. This, then, forms one of my most memorable days. The moment when the great Washington entered the room, and Mrs. Washington said, "The President," made an impression on my mind which no subsequent years can efface.

SOUTHERN
UNITED STATES

Notions and Theology: Peddler in the South

HARRY GOLDEN

Harry Golden (1902–1981), born in New York City, became nationally famous as editor of the Carolina Israelite, *a paper he wrote entirely himself for a quarter century, favoring such subjects as civil rights, socialism, and Zionism. It was once called the "most quoted newspaper in America." In the following first-hand account of a peddler's travels, Golden narrates as Morris Witcowsky, who was born in Russia in 1862, and died in Philadelphia in 1948.*

My name is Morris H. Witcowsky. I was eighty-four years old last April and for the last eleven years since 1935 I've been living in the Jewish Home for the Aged in Philadelphia.

I was a peddler in the South for over thirty years. I peddled all over North Carolina, South Carolina, and Virginia, and finally bought a store in Newport News which I ran for sixteen years until my retirement.

It's funny what stories you remember, usually events which, at the time, you thought were least important.

First let me tell you about my name. This is important.

You and I have been corresponding and talking together and you know me as Morris H. Witcowsky, but that's only since I entered the Home for the Aged here in Philadelphia. I mention it now because my name has a lot to do with my peddling.

In Yanceyville my uncle fitted me out with goods and my first trip was a short one. I was to peddle into Virginia and go as far as the town of Danville. He gave me all the instructions to make my trip safe. Actually he gave me a route made up of customers he himself had been calling on for three or four years. He told me where I should watch out for a bad dog, a big problem with peddlers, and he told me of the places where I could barter for food. He also marked down the homes where the people did not like peddlers, and the homes where I would be welcome.

The first thing I discovered was that to tell a customer my name was Morris H. Witcowsky was out of the question. They looked at me as if I didn't know who I was or what I was trying to do or say, so I just said, "My name is Morris." It was natural. Years later when I had peddled all through South Carolina, North Carolina, and Virginia, every customer called me Morris and some of the ladies called me Mr. Morris, so I left it that way. I've forgotten whether I ever did this legally or not but my son who died after World War I was Samuel Morris all of his short life. For myself, I just put the middle initial which stood for Hyman in front of my name and so all my life as a peddler on the road and as a merchant in Newport News I was H. Morris. That's how I signed my checks and that's how I signed my receipts and that's what I was always called.

For the first four years I peddled with a pack on my back. This pack when full of merchandise weighed about a hundred and twenty pounds, eighty pounds strapped to the back and a forty-pound "balancer" in front. It is not as serious as it sounds. You get used to it. Anyway it gives you tremendous shoulders and arm and leg muscles. Leather suspenders and a wide leather girdle helped a peddler support the pack. It relieved the peddler of all the pressure on one area. You learned early how to remove the pack, lay it neatly on the ground, open it, and choose exactly the merchandise ordered or what you wanted to show. Another great joy was taking those straps off at night. You slept like a baby. During those years when I peddled with a pack I sold mostly soft goods and notions: ribbons, thread, needles, piece goods, garters, men's socks, and women's stockings. I also carried buttons, bone and pewter buttons, and combs. The combs and the buttons, and even what we call today costume jewelry such as earrings, were a side line. But they sold well. Little boxes of loose dressmaker's pins, and shoelaces, too, were always in my pack.

When I began to peddle with horse and wagon in 1891, I added to my stock and was able to carry heavy merchandise including tinware and a whole line of shoes, and every once in a while the wholesaler would have a special on clocks or books, especially New Testaments and songbooks, and I sold quite a few copies of *The New England Primer*. With the horse and wagon I was able to add considerably to the most profitable item, piece goods. It gave me great pleasure to sell piece goods because for years afterward, when I called on these people, I would still see them wearing the dresses and the coats they had made from piece goods I had sold them.

In my time, I also carried ax handles and pots and pans. There was an occasional special on knives which went very well, and quite a few luxury items. I remember selling a great number of little china dogs. The child would grab the china dog and the mother looked a little sad that day as if to say, "Why didn't you hide that or why did you have to show that?" But she wasn't mad about it for too long.

Now I have to explain how I came to this little town, Yanceyville, North Carolina, and how my uncle, also from Vilizh in the province of Vitebsk, got to this little town of North Carolina in the South. It is not a mystery. The people who did the big business with the peddlers in the South were suppliers, or as we called them, "wholesalers," most of whom were up in New York, Philadelphia, and Baltimore—such firms as Finer & Sons and H. B. Claflin, in New York, and the Baltimore Bargain House. A peddler with small capital couldn't go to New York or to Baltimore to get his supplies, as he needed them every week or so. There were various subcontactors, or jobbers, who handled merchandise which they bought from the big suppliers in New York, Philadelphia, and Baltimore. There were jobbers in Norfolk, Virginia, and in North Carolina one was in Yanceyville and another in Mount Gilead.

But there's more to this story of Yanceyville than the fact that a wholesaler had a little warehouse. Originally, this warehouse was owned by a man named Fels who had been a jobber for a Philadelphia wholesaler maybe thirty or forty years before, even before the Civil War. During his years of peddling and then selling to other peddlers, Mr. Fels recognized the great possibilities in the marketing of a low-priced household soap, which he made himself. Eventually this became the Fels-Naptha Soap Company. (The money this family accumulated has gone since for education to such places as Antioch College in Ohio and the observatory and planetarium in Philadelphia, and one of the sons of the original Fels, Joseph Fels, contributed several million dollars to advance the economic philosophy of Henry George of the Single-Tax movement.) The Fels family was gone from Yanceyville when my uncle got there. The warehouse was still operated for the use of ten or twelve peddlers working in Virginia and North Carolina, and my uncle replaced the agent the Baltimore Bargain House had originally sent there. It was at my uncle's suggestion that Philip, my companion and later my brother-in-law, should go to Knoxville, Tennessee. There was a peddler's route open there that had given a good living to a man who had suddenly decided to give it up and go into business in New York.

A welcome for the peddler was by no means unanimous. There were quite a few people who would have nothing to do with us. Perhaps they were prejudiced against the first peddler they saw and they just never bothered to test others. At any rate, you learned who these people were and avoided them, and you made certain that you were not stranded before nightfall near a home where you were not welcome. These homes, however, were few and far between. Even those customers who shook their heads and said, "Nothing today," were nice to us. You would be surprised how often they refused to take anything for a night's lodging. But, when this happened you immediately opened your packs and put some little things on the table for each of the children and the presents were always accepted with thanks.

Your story about the Indians calling us peddlers "egg-eaters" interests me. In the thirty years I peddled in Virginia and the Carolinas I did not meet Indians. But they were right. I ate eggs and no meat while I was out peddling. I got the eggs from the farmers on my route. In the early days I bartered eggs for some of my merchandise wherever I went and immediately boiled them. After a few years my customers knew me, and the housewife put six or eight hard-boiled eggs in my pack without negotiations.

Quite frankly, I was not very religious. But I observed the Sabbath and the High Holy Days. Later in life I made it my business to observe the "Yarzeit," that is, the anniversary of the death of each of my parents. I believe that not eating pork or ham or shrimp or lobster was more a matter of habit with me than religious observance. I couldn't possibly observe the dietary laws to the letter and I am sure I didn't. But I never touched any meat that wasn't kosher.

I got home every Friday afternoon. In Richmond the Jewish people had a "shohet", a ritual slaughterer and my wife bought the meat there. But on the road I ate eggs, vegetables, and fruits. Later on, when I had a horse and wagon I even carried my own dishes. When I started out late Sunday afternoon my wife gave me jars of everything I would need. I also took with me two loaves of bread. But I can well understand that the Indians would call us "egg-eaters" because no matter how much I was able to bring along from home in my wagon I was constantly looking for eggs. Eggs are what you would call the staple diet of the Jewish peddler in America.

You wanted to know about my customers during all those years in North Carolina, South Carolina, and Virginia? First of all, I only made about one trip a year in South Carolina and that was with specials the suppliers gave us, like clocks or a whole stock of knives. My work in South Carolina was, of course, when I was already peddling with the horse and wagon. In North Carolina I worked from Yanceyville to Statesville, down to Charlotte, then to Winston-Salem and Greensboro, and three times a year I would go across the State toward such rural communities as Monroe, Rockingham, Troy, and Mount Gilead. In Mount Gilead there was another jobber with a small warehouse. I do not want you to get the impression that these people did a big business and made lots of money. Usually this jobber was a peddler himself, but he had accumulated enough capital to have stock which he could supply to other peddlers. This was the extent of his extra operation. In other words, he not only earned a living through his peddling but there may have been eight or nine peddlers from whom he earned a commission for selling them goods on the spot.

My route northward took me through Reidsville, North Carolina, up into Danville, Virginia, and through the towns of South Boston, Alta Vista, Buena Vista, and Appomattox which, of course, was famous for the last battle between the North and the South. I made friends on all these routes. I remember a family in Rustburg, Virginia, who always insisted that I stay overnight and discuss the Bible with them.

I found this happened over and over in these three States. I thought about it all these years and long ago came to the conclusion that Jewish peddlers, who couldn't even speak the language well, had a special status with the Protestant Christians of the South. For the first few years all I could say in English were words to identify the merchandise, call out the prices, and say "good morning," "good evening," and "may you and your children be inscribed in the book of life."

I was reminded of this feeling for the Hebrew religion wherever I went. I read such names as Pisgah, Cedars of Lebanon, Mount Olive, Mount Gilead, Mount Hebron, Nebo, Ararat; and in Virginia and North and South Carolina I saw road signs for Christian churches called Bethel Chapel, sometimes Beth El, usually Baptist. This familiarity with the Torah was good for both the Jewish peddlers and the people to whom we sold, particularly the Negro people.

Many times a customer on my route, Negro or white, would ask me questions about the Bible. I would come to a farmhouse and see the farmer walk across the field to meet me and the wife come out of the house. As I went toward the farmer, he would say to me, "We had a big argument at the prayer meeting. . . ." The farmer would tell me the argument was something about Daniel in the lions' den, or maybe it was about Jonah, and he would ask me to settle the argument, because I was a Jew and they all looked upon me as an authority. I have told my friends here at the Home all about this and they don't half believe me. It is interesting that many of these Christians in North Carolina, South Carolina, and Virginia with whom I became so intimate, looked upon me as a Christian, some sort of a Jewish Christian. This came as a surprise, and when I began to explain what a Jew was they looked at me as though I were talking nonsense. I remember well being asked time and time again, "Are you a Baptist Jew or a Methodist Jew?"

Along about 1911 I began to sell on credit. The peddlers had experienced a serious depression. The storekeepers were multiplying and they were selling on credit. It is true that we still had our Negro trade. It was not big enough or important enough for the white storekeeper to go after so he left it to us.

But the white trade almost disappeared for us because the storekeeper in town extended credit. Selling on credit presented a problem, and the problem was the matter of financing as well as collecting. You need capital to sell on credit. But by this time I had accumulated a couple of thousand dollars and I thought that I would try extending credit. I am glad I did. I took the advice of two brothers who had just come from Russia, at least twenty years younger than I, Moses and Harry Richter. They were peddling in central and eastern North Carolina and I met them at our jobber's house in Mount Gilead. I understand that they have done very well and are among the leading citizens of North Carolina.

Selling on credit to the Negro was called "having a book on the schwartzes," which meant carrying a ledger sheet for a Negro customer. Do not misunderstand me. "Schwartzes," which means "the blacks," was not a sign of disrespect. As a matter of fact, I look back on it and realize that we performed a great service for the Negroes of the South between the years of 1900 and 1920. We were probably the first white people in the South who paid the Negro people any respect at all, who regarded them as equals. A customer is an equal, and when you sell a person merchandise on credit, you respect him. Some of the white merchants sold to Negro tenant farmers on credit but this was an entirely different thing. They sold him seed and a mule and whatever else he may have needed for his crop, but they sold to him on credit only on the same ledger sheet with the name of the farmer from whom the Negro was renting or for whom he was sharecropping. The "boss man," as the Negro called the white farmer, had to go surety on the credit sheet for the Negro's supplies.

But with our "book on the schwartzes," we put the Negro's family name in the book and we let them try on the merchandise and once I learned the names, I did not say, "Uncle" or "Auntie," but "Mr." or "Mrs." whatever their name was.

The first man with the "book on the schwartzes" was a peddler who was working with the Richter boys out of Mount Gilead, North Carolina. He carried household goods and sold entirely to Negroes. Since this peddler was doing well I decided that when I started to sell on credit I would also include some household items. Until I quit peddling and bought the store in Newport News, I made my rounds with these items, but as the years went on I cut down to just a few. I handled mattresses which I sold to the Negro housewife for ten dollars to be paid off at the rate of twenty-five cents a week.

While all my white customers called me "Mr. Morris," now my Negro customers were beginning to call me "the matritz man." Collections were good. The women always had the money for me and I learned that even when on rare occasions they moved away, they caught up with me somewhere to pay me. In those days the Negro women did not buy any frills or luxuries of any kind, except a gold-filled brooch. I sold many hundreds of these. The women wore them on Sundays when they went to church. The fleur-de-lis design was the most popular. I sold gold wedding bands to many Negro women. These cost ten dollars, paid at the rate of twenty-five cents a week. Clocks were popular. They bought one or two models, the "half-hour strike," or the "banjo type." The price was eight dollars, and the installments were also twenty-five cents a week.

I began to sell to many of the Negro people after I got the horse and wagon. My white customers bought the notions, and sometimes the luxury items for the children, also the ribbon and more particularly the goods by the yard, but the Negro women bought mostly ready-to-wear things. For the Negro women I had aprons for forty cents and housedresses at eighty cents, and late in the fall I put on the wagon two dozen winter coats at seven dollars each, which I sold on credit, and always got rid of my stock.

We learned a trick after a while that made us most welcome in the home of the Negro tenant farmer as well as in the shacks of the "city" Negro living at the edge of town. The Negroes were beginning to come to the towns in 1905. They worked in the tobacco warehouse pulling the vein out of the tobacco leaf. I understand that in recent years this job is done by machinery. What we learned then was to permit the Negroes to try on the hat or the housedress or the coat, and we let their children try on shoes. In those days, the white merchants did not permit the Negroes to try on any ready-to-wear merchandise. The Negro could buy goods only by pointing to what he wanted or asking for it, and both he and the merchant did the best they could in fitting him in this way. But it was understood that if a Negro tried on any of the merchandise, the merchant would lose his white trade. We peddlers were more or less itinerants and we knew this was the only way we could do business. We took no chances. We did not even offer any of this ready-to-wear apparel to our white customers, so they could never say a Negro had tried it on. We made sure that there was never the slightest suspicion of this. I never encountered any trouble along this line. As a matter of fact, on many occasions I sold the white farmer and his wife and children and the Negro tenant farmers and their families at the same time, all standing around my wagon smiling and feeling good. There might be two Negro women behind my wagon trying on housedresses over the clothes they were wearing, while the white farmer and his wife looked through my tinware and their children handled the ribbon and the few toys I carried.

Beginning in 1919, till the time I stopped peddling, I was home every Friday night, and sometimes I'd be home during the week, too. I would take short trips for maybe two days. If I took a long trip I made sure that I started on the way home Thursday so I'd be home for the Sabbath. My son was growing up and doing well in school, and I was beginning to think of a store. I told all my friends to keep their eyes open for a good proposition in Richmond, or Norfolk, or any other city in Virginia.

Soon enough the store came along in Newport News and I bought it. It was a five-ten-and-twenty-five-cent store stocking toys, school supplies, notions, and some soft goods such as underwear and hosiery. When I sold out, I received four thousand dollars in cash and promissory notes for seven thousand dollars payable at semi-annual intervals over a period of three years. I had no close relatives left. My father and mother had died in 1906 and 1909 respectively, and of the rest of our family only a sister was left. She was then a grandmother, and I last heard from her in 1929. So I turned over this four thousand dollars and the promissory notes to the Jewish Home for the Aged, as a gift, and the reason I mention it is because I want to point out that this was the sum total of my estate which I began to build in Yanceyville, North Carolina, in the year 1885. But do not shed any tears for me. We never wanted for anything and my wife and I had a good life. Much hard work and lots of sadness about our only child, but it was a good life. We lived well, we had good clothes, and I kept up my insurance. I do not ever remember borrowing anything from anybody or ever being in debt beyond the current transaction with the wholesaler.

I had credit with all the suppliers, but I paid my bills as quickly as possible. I am not one of these peddlers who became a merchant prince, but do not misunderstand me, I am not making fun of that. Some peddlers did indeed become merchant princes, and in the case of the Fels family it happened right in front of our eyes, so to speak. They were gone when I got to Yanceyville but when we peddlers met anywhere in those days we spoke of the Fels family and Fels-Naptha soap. I knew maybe twenty peddlers in my territory, and none of us ever became rich. We all worked hard and I think those I knew would say the same thing; maybe some of them built up bigger estates than I, but we all knew that the dollar was hard to come by and we learned to respect it.

When you peddle for an entire week with a pack on your back and have $8.40 for your share at the end of the week, it is a lesson in respect for work and its rewards, no matter how small. And so for the rest of my life $8.40 was identified with walking through a countryside in a strange land for an entire week—this you do not forget so easily. I had great respect for that eleven thousand dollars I turned over to the Home. I can say like a big shot, "I turned over my estate and my insurance to the Home." This was a big thing for me. It was a mountain of an estate considering the work that went into it. I'm now in my eighty-fourth year and my health is good and my memory is good, as you can see. I think I was in a valuable profession. I do not know how many others, in different trades and professions, can say, "With each customer I left not only the joy of a new possession but perhaps a bit of information, some news maybe or even an interpretation of a Biblical text." Whether I knew what I was talking about or not when it came to theology did not really matter, did it?

Morris H. Witcowsky
Born: Vilizh, Russia; April 9, 1862
Died: Philadelphia, Pennsylvania; February 4, 1948

Needles in the Dark

PETER AND BARBARA JENKINS

Peter and Barbara Jenkins recorded their cross-country hike after Peter had trekked alone with his dog from upstate New York to Louisiana. That adventure was recorded in an earlier book entitled A Walk across America. *He met Barbara Pennell in New Orleans; they married and "set out to discover America together." In this disturbing encounter in Louisiana they discover an America few would wish to experience but, undaunted, they manage to strap on their backpacks and greet a new day.*

Our squints returned as we walked west. We weren't a quarter mile away when I realized I didn't know the name of the place where I'd bitten down on that rough pearl. I looked back and could see nothing. The reflections from the oil-black road and white shells hazed everything into wavy oblivion. It was too hot to go back. I still had the pearl.

I was walking quite a ways in front of Barbara. After all those oysters, frog's legs, boiled shrimp, and iceberg Cokes I surged with power. The winds of freedom blew through me again and made me feel I could discover everything there was to know in an hour, made me shiver with overflowing en-

134

ergy. I felt I could walk across America this afternoon. It wasn't the sugar from the Cokes either. It was having everything I needed to live on my back. It was never rounding the same corner, never seeing the same face. It was a feeling as strong as a Gulf Coast lightning bolt. It was so good to be on the road again.

I had been soaring inside myself for what seemed like a moment; it may have been an hour. When I looked back for Barbara, she was way back. I stood still. There were no trees except the cypress and willows that grew out of swamps; I wasn't about to float under them for what little shade they might give. When she got closer, I could see that she was favoring her feet, walking like the road was a café's grill heated extra-hot for the lunch rush. She got closer; she was limping.

"B.J., what's wrong? You step on something?"

She could have cried, but she wouldn't. "My feet, they, they hurt so bad. Are they always going to hurt like this on the walk?" Her mouth was strung tense. I knew that although she'd get used to it, there would always be some pain. I couldn't tell her that, though.

"You know it's possible that your feet are not strong enough to wear Adidas running shoes. When we get to Morgan City, we'll get you a pair of boots. I'm sure that will make a lot of difference, honey. That sound OK with you?"

"OK," she said, her voice trailing off into the pizza-soft road. "Will you please tell me how long it's going to take us to get to Morgan City?" she asked.

I swung my pack down to my feet and got out

my 1976 Louisiana state map. Like most maps, the water was blue, the land white, the roads black and the interstates red. The parish boundary lines were yellow. But that map transmitted false information. Most of the "land" was underwater, and the people lived on their own islands. They had built them in the swamp with imported dirt and sharp-edged white shells. Walking a few hours on the shells was like walking on the dull edges of a million razor blades.

Their islands were surrounded by huge expanses of the greenest greens I'd ever seen. Lily pads reflected the sun like round green mirrors and they served as these Cajun people's grass. When the hyacinths flowered, they turned hundreds of acres of bayous into a delicate purple field. There were trees, undergrowth, vines, and weeds that choked out the light.

When we camped by these swamp thickets, I expected to wake up with vines growing around our necks. A rabbit would have had trouble going more than ten feet. There was a lot of life in there; almost all of it slithered in the dark.

Three days later we stumbled into Morgan City. Barbara had to settle for a pair of boots that were black and looked like Israeli combat boots. I tried to explain that they needed to be broken in. She couldn't wait any longer. Her feet had to have some support walking on the slanted sides of the road on the unstable shells. She said we'd have to pray for the best.

We crossed a high bridge into a little town. We'd

been on the road now together for almost two intense weeks. Some of the places on the Louisiana map sounded menacing. Bayou Goula, Montegut and Grosse Tete were good places to detour.

On our left only a couple of hundred yards off the bridge was a building set maybe seventy-five feet back. There was a shell parking lot that looked like a bomb zone, it was littered with so many potholes. They were filled with hot, muddy water and probably filled with jiggling mosquito larvae. It was before midday and there was only one car parked under a sliver of shade.

A man, his face draped with saggy flesh, came out of the raised building. His skin was the color of a coffee milk shake; his hair, bleached rust red by the sun and thick as wool. I was looking at a bumper sticker that said something about Cajuns but was covered with oily dust. I asked him if I could wipe it off. His eyes were lily-pad green. It said, "Cajuns Live Longer . . .They'll Eat Anything."

"This place have anything to eat?" I asked.

"It depens," the man said. In some places in this country they would call this man a Creole, in others, a Cajun. Some would call him a mulatto, some a tan. Some could call him black. Others would call him nigger and there'd be fighting. In a few places he'd pass for white, especially if he stayed out of the sun. He had calf-high white rubber boots on, and that meant he worked fishing, shrimping, oystering or frogging.

"What does it depend on?" I asked.

"It ain' got notin' to do wit' your color. Da peoples dat run it dey black. Bu' da ol' lady in dere she jus' don' like certain peoples. If she don't, you betta leave, yu hear?" The heat of these southern Louisiana summers melted words together.

"Why does she not like certain people?" I wondered.

"I can't tell youse dat. Jus pay my words mind . . . pleez." He sounded serious. He backed out carefully, avoiding all the potholes.

"Peter," Barbara said, having overheard us, "let's go further into town and find someplace else. That guy made me nervous. Why did he say what he did about some old lady?"

"Let's try this place since we're here. We can always leave," I said.

The weathered building had no sign to announce its intentions, only a plastic Coca-Cola sign in one of the dusty windows. There were stains of purple, pink and yellow that had once coated the bare wood. The dominant color now was wind- and rain-pelted gray.

There were two steps and a screen door for ventilation. There was no air conditioning and almost no light to see by. A big fan sat on the center table and went back and forth, back and forth. It had an old cord that looked frayed and was right next to the table we sat at.

There was no old woman in the place, only three black men. They weren't Creole; they were blacker than the dark room. As we sat down, one turned on a light. They could see us better, and we could see what else was in here. There were a few windows up high, making me think that this may have been an old country store before. This was sugarcane plantation area and maybe this had been one of the old plantation stores for the slaves. The high windows were covered thick with spider webs. The light filtered through the webs, covered with dust and moths, in opaque slivers. The floor gave when people walked.

The men sat with their strong backs to us. Behind the bar, surrounded by many half-emptied bottles of liquor, was a statue of Jesus. There were some candles. They were purple or black, standing in plates on both sides of the statue. There was a bowl of something that looked like white sugar. In the plates were all kinds of Mardi Gras beads and piles of other things I could not see from our table. There was a cheap metal peace sign hanging over the saint and a cutout picture of Jimi Hendrix with his face and puffy Afro covered by red and green lights. There was no jukebox, but in one far corner was a table with an old mono-record player. It rested next to a pile of frayed album covers. On the back wall, taped with yellow Scotch tape, were many pictures of other saints. I could only recognize the Virgin Mary.

The more I saw, the less I wanted to stick around. But I was desperately thirsty and sitting down felt so good.

I kept smelling the stale air that had lingering odors of smoke, grease, some type of strange incense, chickens, body odor, fresh country air and food. Where is the person who runs this place? We'd been sitting here for about ten minutes. The men hadn't moved. Then from the back, where I guessed there might be a kitchen, came a loud noise. Something had been thrown into some very hot grease. Maybe they were a wire box of french fries or some delicious seafood, maybe shrimp. Never had I heard anything fry and pop and crackle so loud. What could possibly be frying so loudly?

From underneath the building came a scream. A shrill noise of something getting killed, bitten. Something jumped up from the earth underneath the building and hit the floor. There was a thump, then another squawking shriek. Then everything broke loose. "That dawg mus' not been fed again."

Now a woman's voice was screaming, her voice directed underneath the building to the dog that must have been killing all the chickens there. The back door opened and slammed again. It was one of those worn-out doors that begged not to be slammed. Maybe the spider webs held it together, too.

On another wall I saw a picture, all in vivid reds, flesh tones and purples, of a heart. If I remembered right, it was the Sacred Heart of Jesus. What strange things to have in a seafood place.

Maybe it was one of those chickens that was in the deep fryer. It still crackled loudly. Out of the kitchen I heard steps coming, soft, but firm and padded. Neither of us had said anything. We were frozen in our seats. Swaying through the door was a wide-faced, blue-tongue Chow, one of the most ferocious dogs anywhere. It was red, like an Irish setter, except for a bald patch under its neck. Maybe it had been in a bad fight. These kinds of dogs were known to be very mean. Cooper had fought a few of these dogs and won every fight but one. I'll never forget the first time one attacked him. He was only ten months old and that Chow tried to kill Cooper. We had been having a Halloween party at college in a graveyard. We were huddled around a fire when the Chow walked quietly up to baby Cooper and wagged its tail. Then it went right for his throat. I had no choice but to reach into that swirling pile of dog muscle and hair and teeth to save Cooper. One of them bit through my hand, but I kicked the Chow in the head and held Cooper. He couldn't stop shaking from fright all that night from the attack. I'd never liked Chows since. This one acted as if it owned the building.

He smelled me first, stopped, looked in my eyes and then went to Barbara. She was normally kind of nervous around strange dogs, but this one she just stared at. It stared back like no dog I'd ever seen. I'd seen dogs that thought they were humans and looked at you that way, but this dog thought it was something more. What, I didn't want to know. After checking us out, it went back through the kitchen, stayed there a minute or so, and then the back door slammed shut once more. I wondered when that door was going to fall apart.

I turned to Barbara and was about to tell her that we'd better leave when someone started moving through the kitchen. The loud frying sounds had stopped. A black woman came through the door. She was silhouetted against the light so I could not see her face. She had a lithe body and she looked somewhere in her thirties.

"What do you people want here?" she asked with a slight French twang. Her diction was clear and her delivery dramatic.

141

"Could we see a menu?" I asked. She moved around so that she was facing the bar.

"We don't have a menu. In fact, we don't serve food here anymore." Her face was long with continually moving white eyebrows that arched high against her cocoa-colored skin. There were few wrinkles except for deep ones at the sides of her mouth. She couldn't be in her thirties, I knew, now that I could see her face and hands. Her hair was the whitest thing in this place except for her teeth and the teeth of her Chow. The dog was now back inside, lying against the front door. Anyone that came in or out would have to walk over it and brave its teeth.

"Do you have anything cold to drink?" I asked her. One of the men called her Miss Sweet when she first walked in. But there was nothing about her that seemed sweet. Her eyes pierced like a bayonet. Her voice was both whispery and grating. She didn't like us, and I didn't think it had anything to do with the fact that we were white.

"That depends what you drink," she answered, shifting her eyes from me to Barbara. Barbara had been very quiet since we'd come in. She looked my way, and I could tell this lady made her very uneasy. She wasn't about to go over that dog, though.

"We were hoping that you had some cold Cokes or maybe some orange juice. You see we've been out traveling in the heat all day."

"Yes, I know. We only have beer and I think," she was saying as she walked over to the bar, "we have a couple of Seven-Ups. You want one, sir?"

"Thank you, I'll take one and also one for my wife." She gazed at Barbara.

"I only have three left. I'm not going to give one to her. I have to save two for others that might come here tonight." She lit one of the purple candles next to the strange statue. This just didn't seem like a place that would have a statue of Jesus. I'd never felt such strange feelings swirling around. They seemed to be generated by the woman and the dog. She brought the 7-Up over and gave it to me.

"That'll be a dollar fifty," she whispered.

I would never argue with someone like her. I pulled two dollars out of my pack. She didn't return the change; she just sat down in a chair at an empty corner table. She crossed her legs, the way only thin people can do, and stared. Mostly she wouldn't take her eyes off Barbara. I'd seen Barbara handle all kinds of weird people and I knew that sweet as she looked, she was afraid of no one. Barbara moved her eyes back and forth, first looking at me to make sure I was still there and then a quick glance to see if the strange woman was still staring at her. She always was. The three black men at the bar did not say a word.

Then there was a noise, footsteps, as someone came up the back steps again. The woman, the skin pulled very tight across her narrow face, still sat in the corner and bobbed her leg up and down slowly. She had hold of her hands and was taking each finger and squeezing it from the base to the tip. Her hands were oddly much darker-colored than any other visible part of her body.

When the back door closed, this time it didn't slam, and no one came through into this main room. Miss Sweet got up from her chair, keeping her eyes on us like a cowboy getting up about to draw his gun.

I heard her speak to someone. She sounded mad.

"Wha' you boys doin' here?" she yelled as her way of talking changed. "You suppos' to be in schoo'. You knows you mama don't allow you here. Get out!"

"But, Maw Maw, we both gots a paddling at schoo' and we rans from dere. We wanna be wit' you and watch you doin'—"

She interrupted and it sounded as though she'd put her hand over the mouth of the boy that was talking. "Shut up and get *out* there and sit down."

"Yes, Maw Maw," the boys answered. Many kids in the South called their grandmothers Maw Maw.

The boys were about fourteen. They were both thin as sugarcane stalks and their presence added some degree of normality to this eerie place. By now we'd finished the 7-Up and I was wanting to leave. The more aggressive boy walked over to the old record player, like the kind we used to use as kids and play Walt Disney records on. He took an album from the top of the stack and put it on. The woman had gone over and lit another candle, this time the black one. As soon as the record dropped down and the first notes came out of the speaker, she stood up abruptly and rushed over to it. The record sounded like some kind of chanting or moaning. It was hard to really tell because we didn't hear enough. She pulled one of the boys into the back and I heard a loud slap. Sounded like he'd been stunned to the face with her powerful hands. When he came back out, there were no tears, just a dazed look set deep in his eyes, as though this had happened many times before. He walked over to the stack of records and looked through them. When he found what he had been looking for, he put it on. It was a scratchy old James Brown album. His "get down and boogie" music lightened the heavy atmosphere.

Before he went back and sat down by his grandmother, I asked him if he would move the dog for us. He said he'd have to ask *her*.

He walked over to where she sat like some queen. She said something, which took longer than "Yes, move that dog!" The boy, dressed in a striped T-shirt, jeans and orange sneakers, came back and pulled up a chair. He had a stare as vivid as a hex. He seemed to have inherited that from his grandmother. "She say I can move da dog, but firs' she wan' me to tell youse sometin'. She say dat you, mister, better leave. She don' like you eyes. She say dey too open."

With that we both got up very slowly. I had a feeling that there were invisible spirits zooming back and forth over our heads. It was a heavy feeling, almost cold. It made the back of my neck tight as a steel rod. It also made the front of my head pound. I'd heard stories here and there about demons and possession. A few movies had made me shiver, but I always knew they were actors on a screen of light. But if any of it was possible, then there were demons banging on the ceiling and slithering on the floor in here. I wanted to break and run. Barbara's eyes figured out every exit. Since we'd been standing, she kept either her hand or shoulder touching me, as if she were afraid I'd disappear.

The sitting queen, as skinny as a caved-in black Barbie doll, stared, her legs still crossed, her boys guarding her sides, her blue-tongued Chow at her feet. They looked like they should have been in stone in front of some pyramid. I'd never felt any human, man or woman, that gathered a force about her by doing so little. The three men still sat at the bar.

We got to the door. I opened it and fought myself to hold it for Barbara. When she was safely in the potholed shell parking lot, I slammed it. I almost expected to have the building disappear and to wake up in the middle of some jungle thicket, sweating from a bad dream.

Normally, when we left a stopping place, it took a few minutes to get our packs on and every strap adjusted, the hip belt tightened and our shoelaces tightened. This time we both ran with our packs hanging off one shoulder. When we got back onto old Highway 90, I glanced back and saw and heard nothing. The place looked as if screams should have been echoing off the thickets of spider webs.

We were moving again. I told Barbara we were not going to stop anywhere else in this town. We'd gone a couple of hundred yards, and there was the rest of the town. A few harmless-looking gas stations, a small bank, an everything-for-everybody store that had groceries, clothes, bamboo fishing poles, some chicken feed piled up by the front door and rolls of chicken wire. An old black man, his skin shiny, rode by on a green and yellow John Deere tractor. He wasn't going that much faster than we were. Waxy-leafed magnolia trees stood among shacks and trailers in the middle of yards that were scratched bare of grass by chickens and rooting hogs.

We were leaving town and could see again the endless fields of cane. Someone called out from behind us. Sounded like a kid on a bicycle. We always attracted children on bicycles when we walked through towns. Often we gathered a small parade, and sometimes, when we got from one city limit sign to the other, there was an escort of ten bicycles.

"Hey, mister," someone said.

It was Maw Maw's two boys on bikes with high handlebars. One of them had a basketball in his right arm and pedaled with no hands.

When they caught up with us, they asked the usual first questions. "Where you peoples headed?"

I gave the usual answer.

"You tinkin' 'bout movin' here?" They'd never seen anyone on foot with packs like us before, they said.

"No, we're just walkin' through town, headed for Texas." The sun was still midday-blinding and even with my mirrored mountain climber's sunglasses I had to squint some. They were in front of us, their backs to the west and the sun. I couldn't really see much but their outlines. They were both sugarcane thin.

"Whys you gonna go to Texas? Dem peoples

ain't got notin' but desert, ain't dat right?" he said to his silent friend. "You peoples married?" The one talking had a small paper bag in his hand.

"Yep," I said.

"Ain't many strangers come tru dis place."

"Because it was on the road we had to take to walk across southern Louisiana. You ever been to New Orleans?" I asked.

"No, man, dat's way far from here."

Barbara still wanted to get far away from here and she had walked ahead. She stood under a grandmother live oak that sent its octopuslike branches out over the road.

"Do you boys have any more questions?" I said, looking toward Barbara and wanting her close to me in this hostile town.

"We come afta youse wit' sometin' to say. Dat lady back where you bought a Seven-Up, she says dat if youse a-plannin' to move here and tries to take over any of her territory, she says she gonna get youse." I could see that the bag he had was stained with grease or something.

"What do you mean?" I demanded.

"My maw maw, she a powerful lady. Everyone 'roun' here is afraid of her, man. Youse bes' jus' get outta here."

"What kind of power you talking about?" Barbara was standing under the tree still, with her hand on her hip. I knew she was mad at me spending too much time talking to these boys. She was really in a hurry.

"She's got da voodoo powers. She can gets you, mister. Kills you, too." He said all this not vengefully, not boastingly, just stating facts, like he'd

148

seen it happen many times before. "Youse betta not be movin' heres."

"I can guarantee to you we are just traveling through."

"I never seen my maw maw not likes two peoples so fas' as youse. She say dat you woman got the spirits and tryin' to turn dem again' her. Ain't no one crazy 'nough to tries dat, mister." He shifted the bag to his other hand. "She say dat she put a hex on you wife. Youse betta gets outta heres, fas'."

I didn't need to hear any more. As I turned to leave, the boy, still sitting on the long seat of his bike, spoke again. This time there was hostility in his words. "Hey, mister. Where you goin', I ain't finish." His friend was backing up.

"I don't care whether you're finished or not." I turned around and began walking.

He rode up to me, pulled his small bike over and blocked my way. "You peoples don' acts like youse heard wha' I says 'bout my maw maw. She powerful: she say she can make devils go in peoples. She say she know Satan. I know she do."

I stepped around him again and began walking faster. He rode by me and pulled over again. "One las' ting, mister. She told me to giv' youse dis bag. Youse better takes it or sometin' double bad gonna happens." The bag was a regular grocery bag, medium-sized and filled with something. There was a rubber band holding it closed. He reached out to hand it to me and I saw there were red stains coming through the sides by the bottom. I touched the side and it was something kind of soft, something hard. I let it fall to the ground.

The boy rode off. His friend, the silent one, had already gone.

I walked away from that bag as fast as I could. Then I thought, What am I afraid of? I've never run away from anything like this. I was letting that bag scare me and I had no idea what was in it. I turned around and walked back to it. I reached down to pick it up. What could it be? I straightened back up and decided to take my sunglasses off so I could see what was in there. I bent back down and again saw those stains. They were blood red; that was no ketchup leaking through. There was no way I was going to open that paper bag.

I overheard some men talking. I could pick up only a few words and when we opened the door to the small gas station, they switched in mid-sentence from English to Cajun French.

"What do you suspect those people are doing hiking through here this time of year?" one dark-haired farmer said in fast, clearly spoken French. If only I could have had an accent as pure as that when I took French in high school.

"Maybe they are crazy!" They roared, laughing with that French sparkle in their eyes, so typical of Cajuns.

I waited till they stopped laughing. *"Bonjour, comment vas-tu?"* That meant, "Hello, how are you doing?" *"Il est très chaud, oui?"* That meant, "It is very hot, yes?"

"Bonjour." The least shocked farmer smiled. *"Tu parle cajun?"* He had said hello, his tan face turning bronze red. Cajun is their special brand of

French, mixed with some English, and Spanish. It was as blended as the best of their gumbo.

"*Non*," I answered, smiling. "I only speak a little French I learned in high school." I switched back to English.

"You sure caught us good that time." They all walked a bit closer to us.

"Can I ask you something?" I didn't bother making any small talk.

"Sure." When they spoke English, they had the faintest of French intonations.

"Something really strange happened to us back there. It looked like a bar or restaurant." Barbara was leaning against the front of the white painted building. We stood under a tin roof that shaded all of us.

"We stopped in this place and this old black woman, she was thin and had a dog, acted very strange. She wouldn't even sell my wife a soda, give us any water, or sell us food."

They looked at each other as though they knew who I was talking about.

"What's so odd about her not wanting to sell you a soda? Maybe she didn't like you being in there. That's mostly a place where black people go."

"That's only the beginning," I said, feeling those tightening muscles in my neck. "When we were there, she lit these candles that were in odd saucers filled with sugar or something."

"What color were the candles?" one interrupted, his eyebrows furrowed.

"One was black; the other was purple."

"I don't know about the purple one, but I know

that the black candle has something to do with death. That lady is known all over, by black and white alike, as a voodoo queen. That voodoo and hoodoo has been practiced in these parts for over a hundred years."

"What else did she do?" the thinnest farmer asked.

"Nothing except stare at us. That is, until we left. After we were about a half mile down the road from the place, her grandson and his friend rode up and asked us if we were planning to move there. Then he handed me a bag."

"*Oh, mon Dieu!*" one exclaimed. "That must have been bad!"

"Did you look to see what was in the bag?" the other man asked.

"No, I didn't open it. It felt kind of soft, though. Do you men have any idea what it was?"

"It could have been a chicken foot, a rooster's head or other things. She may have been trying to put a hex on you both."

"Have you ever seen any of these hexes work?" I pressed.

The thinnest farmer answered. "I used to laugh at all that when I was a young man. But I seen too much to laugh anymore. I seen people go crazy and then found out one of the voodoos had put them under a hex. I've seen deaths and heard worse. Killing babies, even cutting cattle in horrible places as parts of their rites. I still don't believe it, but I don't mess with them either. One of our neighbors supposedly had a cleaning lady who was one who claimed to have the powers. A lot of bad things happened to that couple when the wife began getting into the voodoo."

The other interrupted. "If I was you people, I'd just keep on going and forget about it." He glanced at his fellow farmers, giving them a silent message to quit talking. I thanked them for their time, wishing in a way that I'd forgotten about it before asking these men all the questions.

"There is no way that I'm going in there," Barbara said. It would be dark in an hour or so and we were about to enter the woods. It looked impenetrable.

"Barbara, we don't have any choice." I had to fight back the dagger-mean words that the clinging heat brought on. "We have got to camp soon, before dark, and this is the only place I can see anywhere." It wasn't like finding a camping spot in most areas. Normally we were surrounded by thousands of acres of farmland, which always had some bordering woods or unplanted dry land. Not in these parts. The sugarcane grew very close together and higher than my head. There was no way to camp in it. This small patch of woods looked like our only chance. I took off my pack and let it rest on B.J.'s leg. If dusk came before we were in our tent, any exposed skin would be dark brown with hundreds of mosquitoes. They'd pierce the skin like a hundred voodoo pins. Except these pins suck blood.

As I attempted to enter, I ripped at vines and tore at briars. They wove around and around each other. I was learning how to weave my body into the growing tropical maze and I was making some

153

progress. I saw a clearing. It was very small, about the size of a large car. Rich yellow rays of sunlight broke into the clearing in beams, the way light can pierce stained glass in a gray-rock church.

It looked good, so I called to Barbara that I'd found something. I liked this, especially after that bloodstained bag, because it was hidden from the road. I didn't want anyone to know where we camped tonight. The clearing was bare of any growth and had a blanket of dried leaves and cypress needles. How strange for a place to be so nude in the center of this orgy of green. It looked high enough and dry, and when my foot hit it, I found out why there was nothing there. My foot sank and so did most of my leg into something indescribable. It was warm partway down, and very smooth.

It was quicksand! I yanked my leg out of there with a frantic pull and half twisted my knee off. I burst through a lot of briars as they ripped my bare legs. When I got to the road, my arms and legs had red rip marks as blood came out of the thorn cuts. Also, I'd mashed against some red-purple berries and they added to the stains. My right leg was covered with black, stinking mud. It was as warm as grits.

"We can't camp in there. That clearing is a bog or a quicksand pit or something. Let's get down the road." We'd been so tense all day that we'd eaten nothing but some vitamins and crackers. Barbara looked as tired as a salmon after spawning. One more ripple in the road and she looked like she'd roll over and die.

With no place to sleep and the swarms of dark-

ness ready to attack us, we were facing a night-
marish ending to an agonizing day.

"B.J., we need to walk fast, please. I can see at
least three-quarters of a mile down the road and
there's nothing but sugarcane." At the outside we
had less than an hour of light left. Knowing we
had so little time to get in our tent gave me a
frantic feeling.

About a half mile away I could see a few trees
that looked as though they had survived since the
earth's beginning. Lightning, hanging ropes, and
sharecroppers had only taken pieces from them.
They were laden with strands of gray moss that
hung to the ground, heavy with humidity and
stillness. In the wind they acted like a horse's tail,
stirring up the bugs.

It was a ring of live oaks. Here in southern
Louisiana, where the ground was wet, a ring of
wise ol' oaks meant that they were protecting either a fine southern mansion, a school, a graveyard or a Catholic church. I saw, in between the
outstretched arms of the oaks, a cluster of stucco
buildings painted a bright salmon pink.

It was a Catholic church set in an old-world
courtyard. There was a graveyard, too, in this
small clearing ringed by the live oaks. The Spanish moss made the oaks mysterious and sort of
scary. I looked back to Barbara, knowing that
we'd have to have a graveyard for our camping
grounds.

The clouds of swamp vampires would be on us
by the thousands in minutes. Already a few early
risers were buzzing in my ears. I'd seen a farmer's

hat that had said, "MOSQUITO, LOUISIANA'S STATE BIRD."

"B.J., we're going to camp in this graveyard," I said. "Let's hurry and get off the road before anyone sees us." I leaped the ditch; a car with its lights on was coming.

"No way! I'm not going to camp in a graveyard. Especially one like this." She stood on the road. Because the land was so swampy, everyone in southern Louisiana was buried aboveground. Not like some of the Indian tribes on wooden platforms but usually in sun-bouncing bone-white tombs. The older ones were built with brick, covered with white plaster.

Sometimes these white tombs were so old that resurrection fern grew from the cracks in the plaster. This stunning green fern dried to an ugly brown when it was dry. When it rained, it resurrected. There was such little space between each tomb. Some just had concrete slabs holding the dead people inside. I heard something that sounded like rock against rock. I wouldn't have lived if someone had come out, resurrected! It was only a baby racoon running over one of the graves.

"Barbara, I am not jiving with you, girl. GET OVER HERE. We must get our tent up!"

"I'm not camping in there." She crossed her arms. I hoped no police car would pass by. It would definitely stop.

"Where, then, do you think we should go?" I asked. I could barely keep myself together, such was the intensity of torture I experienced when attacked by mosquitoes.

"The only place I'll go is in the sugarcane fields.

Look over there. There's some kind of tractor. Maybe they've been harvesting some. There may be a clearing."

We had to walk through the graveyard. There were rows of white crosses in the now-red sky. There were figures of Jesus. There were statues of Mary and many angels flying.

As we walked around the city of death, I saw huge cockroaches scurry across the white and cracking plaster. They were as big as small mice. Barbara was holding on to my pack and I don't think she saw them. I hoped one would not jump on her.

On one of the biggest tombs, which seemed to house a whole family, the brick front was crumbling. Grass, weeds, ferns and vines grew from within, where the bodies were. If I'd had a flashlight, I'd never have looked inside. On a black wrought-iron cross four or five lizards were soaking up the last bit of heat. They were chameleons and they were all vivid green. The biggest one had half its tail missing. Barbara didn't see them either. Fortunately she didn't see too well when the light was dim.

We neared the fence that would hold no snakes back. It would not keep back any lizards, opossums, roaches, rats or armadillos either. The darting blurs of nighthawks and bats replaced the white flocks of egrets that were already roosting. As I lifted my pack to the other side of the rusting fence, there was a neon green thing zipping toward me. It was a long snake, thin as a pen. When my pack hit the weedy ground, it turned back into the sugarcane field. The fence creaked as I climbed over. Everything metal seemed to be rusting down in this special world. Barbara didn't see the snake, thank God.

We found a road-wide section of the field that had been harvested. Maybe they'd taken it early as a test or something. Maybe this would be OK for sleeping. The nights in our tent without air conditioning in mid-July made Devils Island sound like paradise.

A closer look and I saw that the sugarcane was grown on mounds, and when it was cut, there was left a section of the stalk about three inches long. Its point was cut at an angle and became a spear. Sleeping on the mounds and the sugarcane was like being dropped into a pit in Vietnam filled with pungie sticks.

We had maybe five minutes to get into the tent, so I chose the flatter-looking mounds and pulled the tent out. At least we'd be hidden in case the voodoo lady came after us. I tried to center the tent so that we'd each lie in between the rows. The valleys weren't wide, but on our sides maybe . . . Well, I could set it up so that only one of us could have a valley. I let Barbara have it. Today had been extra-stressful on her and it showed in her eyes. There was no sparkle; even her delicate lips, which usually turned up in warmth, turned down. What an introduction to our first weeks of the walk! This section had been the most tormenting so far. I told her that, but she acted as if I were just trying to make excuses. I gave up and just hoped that she'd make it through these swamps, cockroaches and black candles.

Sleeping that night was impossible. It was like

being on a bed of nails. Every time I would turn in another direction, another sugarcane spear would jab me somewhere. If it were just the spears, it would have been semi-bearable. But it never cooled off. It was so hot that if I had been tortured by an enemy, I would have told him anything for air conditioning, a cool shower, a dry sheet.

From the way our bodies were stabbed I knew the tent was being pierced too. I was worried that snakes would crawl in. Mosquitoes, fire ants and worse could attack. I couldn't share my nightmare fears with Barbara. We'd been lying next to each other for hours, both knowing we were awake, yet unable to speak. All I could hear were her lungs straining through the thick, slimy air.

Our night of agony, surrounded by tall sugarcane that blocked even the whispers of breeze, could have ended peacefully if only there had not been that sound outside the tent. At first I was so miserable that I didn't notice it. After I told myself to concentrate on anything but the spears and sweat-soaked tent, I heard it. It wasn't a sound that you would call loud, but one that began like a murmur and grew with concentration and imagination.

The first thing I heard was a kind of low hum. As I listened closer, trying to sort out the usual tree frog songs, it became a drone. The sound was steady and seemed to be moving around outside the tent like a misty ghost. I concentrated. After I had been on the walk for so long and living in the woods, my hearing had improved remarkably. I had become able to discern much in the night's soft sounds. I'd never heard this sound, though.

I turned and kind of leaned up against the tent walls. A second later it felt as if a hundred tiny needles were piercing my skin. Mosquitoes were biting me thought the tent. All they wanted was for us to come out with them. That's why we couldn't escape this insect-droning night hell. The drone was the clouds of mosquitoes. There were so many out there waiting for our blood that we could actually hear them.

The more I tried to shut out their echoing drone, the louder it got. The harder I tried to lie still and sleep, the more conscious I became. The more I thought of waking Barbara and making a run for it, breaking into the church, even a tomb, the louder their noise became in my head.

The wicked clouds of bloodsuckers had eternal patience. They never gave up on our coming out to them. I knew that they had smothered and killed 2,000-pound cattle, swarming so thickly on their faces. I prayed and waited for the light, so that they would go back, like Dracula, when the light appeared. The light took over from the dark so slowly, so leisurely. I wanted to scream at it to rise faster, to burn away the clouds of blood-hungry insects.

There came a time that morning when we could stand being inside the stench of our nylon tent no longer. It was either our sanity or our blood. We talked about it and decided to give them some of our blood. I thought of even leaving the tent right where it stood and just running away. But then what would we do tomorrow night? So I told Barbara to get all her stuff packed up and get dressed in long pants and to spring to the road and wait for me there. If need be, I said, just start walking and I'd catch up.

She got packed up and took off. A gray cloud followed her as she ran with that thirty-five pound pack. The cloud gave up on her halfway to the road and came back for me.

When I was packed, I reached my arm out into their midst. I opened the mosquito netting ever so slightly to unzip it so I could get out, and my arm was covered in seconds. It was like the commercial on TV where the man sticks his arm in a tent filled with mosquitoes and shows how great his repellent works. Mine never worked.

I reached up for the cool metal zipper to open the tent and I felt something slimy on it! I shook my hand in horror. It was a bright green tree frog.

I burst out and ripped at the pegs that held the tent in the ground. Some wouldn't come out, the ground was so hard. I slapped at the whirling insects that blackened my bare legs and my sunburned arms.

The mosquitoes flew in my eyes and I couldn't see. I rubbed at them: then there were dead pieces floating in my tears. They attacked my ears, flew up my nose. The mosquitoes didn't care whether I screamed or not.

I had half the tent down. Another cloud, like a wave of World War II bombers, came in from the dense sugarcane. I could not see Barbara. She must have been running down the road.

With my pack already on my back I slapped with my free hand continuously, my arms and legs were still covered, and the gorged mosquitoes were fat and red with my blood. Some even fell off dead, they drank so freely. I was so mad, trying to kill them, that I left welts and bruises on my skin. At last I made it to the road.

Dragging the tent down the road like an escaped patient from a padded room, I saw Barbara way down the road. The sun was up now, and the mosquitoes seemed to have thinned out.

As I rolled the tent up on the early-morning road, I thought for a moment that maybe we were crazy, subjecting ourselves to the kind of day and night we'd had yesterday. Then I thought of what lay ahead and behind and thought about what I'd be doing if I wasn't on the walk. I strapped the tent on top of my blue backpack and hit the road. It was a new day.

South by Southeast

WILLIAM LEAST HEAT MOON

Born in 1945, William Least Heat Moon is a former college professor who set out, in the spirit of his Sioux ancestors, to follow the backroads and discover for himself the little-known towns and people of America. His resulting travelogue, Blue Highways, *was considered a masterpiece and a joy to read by critic and ordinary reader alike. His trek through the backwoods of Georgia and Louisiana explores the unsung side of America for which he was searching.*

On Georgia 155, I crossed Troublesome Creek, then went through groves of pecan trees aligned one with the next like fenceposts. The pastures grew a green almost blue, and syrupy water the color of a dusty sunset filled the ponds. Around the farmhouses, from wires strung high above the ground, swayed gourds hollowed out for purple martins.

The land rose again on the other side of the Chattahoochee River, and highway 34 went to the ridgetops where long views over the hills opened in all directions. Here was the tail of the Appalachian backbone, its gradual descent to the Gulf. Near the Alabama stateline stood a couple of LAST CHANCE! bars—those desperate places that run at a higher pitch than taverns part of the whole fabric of a town; there's an unnaturalness in them, isolated as they usually are from the ordinary circuits of people. On into Talopoosa County and Alexander City (just north of Our Town), where I found a place for the night by the tennis courts of the community college. That evening was to change the direction of the journey.

The woman was an authority. Whatever there was, she knew it. Her face, pallid like a partly boiled potato, looked as if carved out with a paring knife. She was a matron of note in Alexander City. Two other women, dark in eighteen-hole tans, sat with her on a bench alongside the tennis courts, while their daughters took lessons under the lights. The discussion on the bench was Tupperware. The potato had just said, "For a shower gift, you can't do better than a Pak-N-Stor." Another explained how her eldest had received an upright freezer full of nesting food containers from the Walkers.

"That reminds me," said the third woman, "how is Mildred?"

"How good can you be, taking cobalt?" the authority answered.

A daughter in pearl-mint lipgloss jogged up to a handsome man standing by the courts. On his shirt, a famous little crocodile was laughing at something. Her damp haltertop and tennis shorts clung to her like tattoos. She didn't mind my staring. "Buy me a cola drink, Daddy."

A sunburned man at the end of the bench said, "Doesn't she get her share of attention! Goes to school in the North. Nobody here can touch her."

"North, South," I said, "makes no difference."

He said nothing. The girls returned to their lessons, the father went back to courtside, and the women talked about aboveground swimming pools. The sunburned fellow muttered, "That your green van?" I nodded and told him I was looking around the South. He asked, "You go through Atlanta?"

"Trying to stay out of cities."

"Not seeing the South then. Better go back." He moved down the bench. I smelled booze. "I went to Emory University for five years. Drove a city bus in Atlanta to pay for my schooling." As he rambled, I watched the players chase tennis balls. He said something about a "martyr bus."

"What's a martyr bus?"

"M-A-R-T-A. Metropolitan Atlanta Rapid Transit Authority, otherwise known as Moving Africans Rapidly Through Atlanta."

"I don't get it."

"The blacks—you know, the domestics living in Buttermilk Bottom, the goddamn ghetto—they take buses to the suburbs to clean houses."

"I see."

"No, you don't. You're goggling the coeds in their cute tans. Listen, church in Atlanta, down on West Peachtree, had a signboard. Big letters. WHERE THE FOLKS ARE FRIENDLY. Same church that wouldn't let a black preacher speak at a worldwide Methodist conference."

"Nothing particularly Southern about that."

He wasn't listening. He was convincing me. "I can tell you about a boutique in Underground Atlanta that sold little plastic ax handles signed by a former governor. Even being a Yankee, you might've heard of Lester Maddox taking his stand in front of his Pick-Rick restaurant with a goddamn ax handle in his goddamn hands. I mean, he got elected governor because he got photographed with a goddamn ax handle. I wasn't with MARTA then, but if I'da been, I'da driven my bus right into Lester's fucking cream pies."

The blue crocodile man turned to us. He said, "Easy, Marlin. Ladies about. We've heard all that stuff by now. Times have changed for ideas like that."

"Changed?" He looked at the tall man. "I'll tell you change." He turned to me, his sunburn reddening. "Here's change: a monument to the boll weevil in Enterprise, Alabama, because it broke King Cotton's back so beans and corn could take over. Here's change: Atlanta Klan rally, Klan as in KufuckingKlux, year or two ago. Little ad in the *Constitution* advertising the rally. At the bottom it says, 'Bring your own robe.' Organization changed from furnishing the stinking bedsheets."

Looking at me, the handsome man put his hand on Marlin's shoulder. "You're the one needs changing, Marlin. Next thing, you'll be spouting again about your great-grandaddy up in the quarry at Sylacauga cutting marble for the Supreme Court building. Hear yourself: it's all old talk now."

To me, Marlin said, "I drove a bus, and he drives a real estate office. You figure it out, Yankee." He got up, knocked the man's hand from his shoulder, and put his face close to mine. In a mocking, *Gone-with-the-Wind* accent, he said, "Why don't y'all git youah fuckin' eyes off the darlin' belles' butts and go ovah to Selma? See

166

what Uncle Remus got to say since he done give up the cake walk."

He went off up the hill. That was it.

By midmorning I was following route 22, as I had from the Alabama line, on my way to Selma. The truck license plates said HEART OF DIXIE, and I was going into the middle of the heart. West of the bouldery Coosa River, I saw an old man plowing an old field with an old horse, and once more I wasn't sure whether I was seeing the end or beginning. Then an outbreak of waving happened—first at Maplesville, again in Stanton, again in Planterville; from galleries and sidewalks people waved. Where folks were friendly.

It was late afternoon in Selma, and big trees along Broad Street, a clean and orderly avenue, shaded the way; citizens swept porches and talked over hedges. At the bottom of Broad, the Edmund Pettus Bridge arched high above the Alabama River. The span, named after a Confederate private who mustered out as a brigadier general, was the point where mounted troopers forced a halt to Martin Luther King's first attempt to march to Montgomery. But the afternoon I saw the bridge, it looked silvery and quiet, more ordinary than historic.

Water Avenue intersected Broad Street and ran parallel to the river on the high, north side. West on the avenue was a boarded-up building of Doric columns and an inscription chiseled in stone: HARMONY CLUB. East stood two- and three-story brick buildings with ornamental ironwork supporting galleries that gave the street an aspect of the Vieux

Carré in New Orleans. What little remained of Selma's old commercial architecture—buildings Walker Evans photographed during the Depression—was here.

I looked along Broad Street for a beer to chase the heat and furnish opportunity for conversation; two places appeared to be bars, but signs outside gave no indication. Water Avenue, down where Confederate shipfitters had built ironclads to fight Farragut at Mobile Bay, was quiet but for an old cotton warehouse with a buzzing electric sign: MICKEY'S PLACE. A second sign above showed a champagne glass, a plus symbol, and a human figure either dancing or falling over dead.

Mickey's was, in fact, a tavern and the sign a Bible Belt hieroglyphic to say that. I was the only customer. The barmaid, in her early twenties, wore a see-through blouse that surrendered transparency at the last possible point of decency; at the center she had pinned a Made-in-Taiwan red plastic rose, which matched another stuck into a pair of black lace underpants nailed to the wall. She stood looking forlorn, I thought, twisting a highball glass on stacks of joke napkins, turning them into little ziggurats.

In the dimness, the bar mirror, only a few feet away, returned no reflection, and I checked to see if I had on sunglasses. I didn't, but she wore hers. Perfume stuck to the wet bottle of beer she set down. "What's with the sign outside?" I said. "Wasn't sure this was a bar."

"Can't advertise bar or liquor in the city. About the most you can get away with is 'cold beverages of all kinds.' "

Four new, antiqued Pabst Blue Ribbon wall lamps behind the bar were mounted upside down with the name smeared over. "What's with the lights?"

"That's advertisin'."

"I can read 'Pabst' on the bottle in my hand but not on the wall?"

"You catch on fast. Where you from? Chicago?"

I told her. She took off her sunglasses to get or give a better look, then put them on again when a man came in for a bottle of beer to go. She rolled it carefully in a paper sack, but the outline was unmistakable. It looked like a little mummy.

"Where are *you* from?"

"Right here," she said. "Selma, everlovin' Alagoddamnbama, Heart of D-I-X-I-E." I smiled. "Don't laugh, Chicago. Here's the only place I ever been ceptin' Montgomery. And Biloxi once as a baby. But I'm headin' for New Orleans soon. This little number is on the move. Look away, Dixieland!" She removed her sunglasses. "So, what's Mr. Chicago doin' in Selma?"

"Mr. Chicago was encouraged to come to see what the march changed."

"What march?"

"King's march."

She lowered her voice. "Touchy shit, Chicago. You're two blocks from Brown's Chapel. That's where it all started."

"Still touchy? How long's it been?"

"Don't know. I was just a little kid."

"Do blacks come in here now?"

"*Here?* They got their clubs, we got ours."

"Doesn't sound like much has changed."

She turned to a sharp-edged man who had just sat down. He loudly said, "Can I get me a Tom and Collins or is lollygaggin' all that gets done in here?" She mixed his drink and talked with him. Every so often he turned on me his small, round eyes. She walked back up the bar.

"Thirteen years ago Ray says the march was. Want another?"

"Sure, if you mean a beer."

"Why don't you talk to Ray? He saw it both times."

"Ray doesn't look like the chummy sort."

"He's all right, usually. I cain't tell you anything." She looked down the bar. "Hey, Ray. I was tellin' Chicago about that night those dudes came in here and saw there wasn't any of their kind and left."

"So?"

"So, like he wanted to know if things changed."

Ray, a jagged man, sat down beside me and looked hard at the woman. He said, "How's it his concern?" Still talking to her, he turned to me and in my face opened a smile like a jackknife. "All these Northern boys wanna know is 'How's your nigger problem?' Don't they think we get sick of that? Won't they let us rest? Ain't they got nothin' new to say?"

"I got accused last night of ignoring it."

"Okay, sonny-jim. I'll tell you about change." It came out like a threat. "Change ruined this town. Bar I just come from, three of them sittin' in there big as sin. Fifteen years ago you couldna hired a nigger to go in there. You talk about change, and I say to you, 'Go to hell.' "

170

I let it pass. Headline: YANKEE HALF-BREED KNIFED.

He waited, then said, "I'll tell you this too. Problems we got ain't so much from niggers. They're more likely from Northern jacks comin' down here messin' where it ain't their concern. Tellin' us how to live. That's what's got everybody riled includin' niggers. You a reporter?"

"Just traveling through. Wanted to see what's changed in Selma."

"Way we do bidness what's changed. For the worse. But the thinkin' ain't. We live ever man like he wants. Take Bernita here. She wants to get on the bar and strip and show off her bidness, ain't no man gonna stop her."

"Would anybody stop a black man if he wanted a drink in here?"

"I'll be go to hell. Shit. I been all through this. I'm sick of it." He turned away and talked to Bernita. She left to serve a table, and he looked at me again. "Cain't figure what you're gettin' at."

"Just want to see how things are. All I know is from books or TV."

"There it is. That whole march was a TV stunt. Niggers knew what would happen here. That's why they came. Hardly none of them lived here. They knew the sheriff had himself a reputation. They picked him, not the town. Well, they got what they were lookin' for. I'm sick of goin' over and over it." He went to the toilet. When he came back, he had another drink. "Cain't figure what you're drivin' at."

I didn't answer. He kept turning to the topic as

if I were pushing him into it. He wanted to talk it through, and he blamed me for that.

"Those marchers rolled their own dice, and we got flammed. Course it ain't hard to flam George Wallace."

"What are you saying?"

"I'm tellin' you sickin' dogs and poundin' the niggers was a lack of ignorance. We shoulda paid no mind. Then the cameras woulda stayed in the bags. That's what ruined us—photographers and reporters. Like with the Klan. Some Grand Genie comes crawlin' outa his rotten stump, and there go the cameras and the tongue-cluckin' over the poor South." He stared into the dark mirror. "Used to be everybody stayed in their place. That's what's got all mixed round. I'm sick of talkin' about it."

"Don't get the wrong idea," Bernita said. "Selma's a nice town. We got Coloreds in city hall and places. Only thing I don't like is people are two-faced—friendly at first, then you see the truth."

Ray said, "Don't know what he's tryin' to get at. Hell, I got niggers workin' for me over at the dealership. I hire them, but they up and quit."

"What kind of work?"

"Washin' cars."

"They ever get to sell a car?"

"You know anything? I'd lose ever one of my customers."

"Looks like you've got each other by the balls. Somebody needs to let go."

He leaned back on the stool. "Well, well, well. Got a lot of advice, don't you now? You don't know a damn thing. Come in for a day and got the answers. No use explainin' to you. Tell me, you talk with any niggers?"

"Not here."

"Not here. You got a picture in your brain all made up like a bed. Know all about it. We never burned our cities."

"Who said it was a Southern problem? It's a world problem."

"You finally come up with somethin'."

As we talked, he said *nigger* less, as if he'd drained the poison for a while. He didn't soften; he just expressed himself in other terms, although at no time did he try to hide where he stood. But he held more sorrow and regret than hatred. He was more empty than malicious.

Martin Luther King, Jr., Drive used to be Sylvan Street. Some whites in Selma still called it Sylvan Street. It's the main route through the so-called project—a typical federally sponsored housing district—and the street the Southern Christian Leadership Conference assembled the marchers on, using the block under the high steeple of Brown's Chapel as the starting point. The first marchers walked down Sylvan (as it was then), up Water Avenue, turned left, and started across Pettus Bridge. About half a mile. At the other end of the bridge, deputies and troopers, shouting to the people they had no permit to march, forced them back to Water Street. But for once, chants and signs and feet were better weapons than anything the state could summon. Whitman, the egalitarian, said it a century before:

I will make a song for the ears of the President,
full of weapons with menacing points,
And behind the weapons countless dissatisfied
faces.

When King assembled the marchers again two weeks later, he had not only a permit, he had also the protection—albeit spotty—of federal troops called out by President Johnson, the man with the big ears. People gathered at Brown's Chapel and walked fifty miles to Montgomery. The two marches roused Washington as none of the other SCLC confrontations had, and a few months later the Congress passed the Federal Voting Rights Act.

It was dark and moonless when I started looking for Brown's Chapel. I planned just to drive by, but I stopped near a big brick church that fit the description to ask a black man if it was the chapel. "That's it," he said. "What difference does it make?"

Without knowing it, he had asked me the question I'd come to Selma to answer. "Isn't this where King started the march?"

"What they say. So who cares?"

I stood on the step of the van. "I'm trying to find out if things have changed since the march."

"Tell you in three words. *Ain't nothin' changed.*"

"Let me ask another question. Can you get a drink in Mickey's tonight?"

"Go ask me if I *want* in there, because I'll tell you they don't gotta keep this man out because he don't want in."

"I hear you, but *could* you?"

"Minute I do it's membership time."

"I just went in and nobody said anything about membership."

"Your membership's got a way of standin' out—just like mine."

Several teenagers gathered around. I was the wrong color on the wrong street, but no one said anything. The man talking to me was James Walker, born and raised in the Selma project and just discharged from four years in the Air Force. "Been almost ten years to the day since King got shot," he said, "and the movement's been dead that long. Things slippin'. Black man's losin' ground again. My momma's afraid to talk to a white, and my grandmomma don't care. She just worries about the kids."

"Didn't the march do anything you can see?"

"Say what? Last week I went to get my driver's license. Twelve-thirty, Lunchtime. Sign on the door says they open again at one. I wanted to wait inside, so I pulled on the door. Trooper comes out and says, 'What's wrong, fool? Can't read? Get off that door less you want me next time comin' out shootin'.' There's your change."

"Where?"

"Ten years ago he would come out shootin' the first time."

"What happened?"

"Nothin', dude. This man's not stupid. I know when to shut up and I know when to talk. This man knows when he's got a chance."

A police car cruised by. A teenager said, "That's twice." A Buick pulled up and Walker got in. He said, "You're makin' people nervous comin' in

175

down here. You ain't the right color, you know. Better watch your ass tonight." The car jumped forward then backed out. "If you ain't jivin' about the church, come round the basketball court in the mornin'."

I drove out to George Corley Wallace Community College, one of three new schools by that name in the state. Sometime after midnight, the Ghost shook a little and I woke up. It shook again. I crept to the front curtain. A man standing on the bumper played a light over the seats. Just as I opened the door, he got into a squadcar. 'What's wrong?" I called out.

"Only checking, neighbor." He drove off quickly.

I closed up again and went back to bed. Checking? What the hell for?

At ten the next morning, I was back on King Drive, a block south of where it crosses Jefferson Davis Avenue. On the basketball court, Walker was alone, juking and shooting. "Hey! You showed up." For the first time I saw him smile. "Just workin' on my game till school starts. Didn't get out of the Air Force in time to make spring term."

"What school?"

"Alabama Lutheran here in Selma. All-black, which is what I want. I'm tired of hasslin' with whites. Got enough in the Force."

"You don't want to go North or West?"

"And be a minority? That ain't my land."

"What you do here?"

"Study guidance counselin'. I'm stayin' where I can do some good. Fifty-five percent of Selma's black. We got potential. First, though, brothers gotta see what's on the other side of Pettus Bridge, see where to go from here."

"What do you mean?"

"I mean figurin' a new course. King said turn the other cheek. Malcolm X said fight fire with fire. I don't want that. But we gotta show the brothers they can do more than just hang cool like meat in a locker."

"Maybe things haven't changed because of apathy in the project."

"I ain't lettin' nobody off that easy. A man shouldn't gotta care so much about gettin' a fair game. *You* gotta worry ever day about a fair game?"

"Not usually."

"So why should this man? Sure, the brothers could do more, and they would if they didn't spend so much time gettin' and keepin' a job. Wearies a man out. It never quits. If a brother gets hired and then gets active—there goes the job he worked his ass off to get."

"Can't legally let a man go if he's not talking around on company time."

"They don't fire him—ain't that clean. They hassle him. Get him thinkin' new ideas ain't worth it. Stay on him till he quits. A mover gets to stay only if boss-man's under quota. Otherwise, carry your hat in your hand."

A friend of Walker's came up. "Saw you down here last night," he said. "We doan get many calls from your people." His name was Charles Davis. He worked the middle shift at a battery factory. "I'll tell you about jobs. If I quit mine and go over to the job office, they'll hand me a shovel or send me to Florida to pick oranges. I can do more than dig a hole or cut a weed."

"Lotta people in the project feel like they cain't be nobody," Walker said. "Me? I feel I can be President of the United States."

"Sheeeit, man!" Davis said. "Force musta did your brain-housing group in."

"I know things ain't changed, but things gonna change."

"Young, and mad, and believe so much," Davis said.

"I'm twenty-four and he's thirty-one. So I *am* from nowhere. I'm talkin' future. Anyway, this man wants to know about the march."

"Think I was fifteen," Davis said. "Made both marches. People be sayin' we wasted our time, but things are better. Least a little bit."

"Ain't nothin' changed didn't have to change," Walker said.

"Some of those things be important, though. But lotta times it's like always. Take yesterday. I put a quarter in a sodapop machine at the gas station. Money keeps comin' down. Two honkies sit watchin'. I ask if the machine was broke, and one honker says it takes thirty cents now. Machine says twenty-five on it. Then he says, 'Wondered how long fore you figured it out.' He couldn't tell me they changed it. I said, 'Don't take long to figure you,' and walked off. Other honker says, 'Want me to whup the nigger?' Five years ago I'da fought him. Now I try to ignore it. But hey, I used to follow Malcolm X."

"I'll tell you one," Walker said. "Alabama state

motto is 'Defendin' Our Rights.' And that's all we're doin'. All the time."

"Motto doan have you in mind, James."

"Better start."

"Hey, we finally got a black Santa Claus at the mall. Only thing, he scared hell out of the little black kids. They be dreamin' of a white Christmas."

"That's just education," I said.

"Yeah, but you see how far it goes. Littlest thing's work and worry. Gotta always have your back in the air, and that wears you down, just like they want. Here's another one. Six people killed in the project last year, and nobody's gone uptown for murder yet. If a white dude gets it, somebody goes uptown inside three weeks. Maybe the wrong man, but somebody's goan. Law don't care what we do to ourself. Black on black's outside their law."

"No black police?"

"They be worsen a honkey pig. Those black motherheads'll manhandle you. Nothin' but Oreos —black out, white in."

"All honkey law wants is get a man in jail so's they know where he's at."

"But whiteys that run things here don't mind a little black poontang now and then. That's their contribution to equality—hump a nigger."

"Yeah, but let a black dude even walk down the street next to a white woman, and in six months they goan frame you. Goan plant some dope in your ride or your house. Put a white bitch on you and pay her to yell rape. They come up with somethin'. They want our best women, but they

179

take you uptown if you say 'hey' to a honkey woman none of them would touch with a fence rail."

We walked around to a small, windowless, brick sweetshop run by a blindman named Louis. Davis bought three cigarettes, lit one, and put two under his hat. A white candy vendor came in. Louis asked how many of each item he was leaving. They conducted the transaction on trust.

Davis said, "Saw whitey rip you, Louie."

"Naw, you didn't. Candyman ain't rippin' off old Louie."

Walker and I drank grape Nehi. He said, "Louis, tell the man here what it was like when we all did the march."

"Louie done a business like he never seen."

"Just business to you, ain't that right, Louie?"

"Business be business."

Outside the shop, Davis said, "I'll tell you a funny one. Last week watchin' at the ballgame. A couple of us sittin' on the fender of some Pontiac. Litty bitty white dude comes up draggin' a base-ball bat. He's just learnin' to talk. He says, 'You niggers get off my daddy's car!' Couldn't hardly pronounce *nigger*. We laughed. Then daddy comes up and moves the car and never says nothin'. We never blamed the kid. We know where it's comin' from."

A uniformed man drove by in a Bell Telephone truck. Walker nudged Davis. "That's four today. Two last night."

"What's going on?" I said.

"Sheriff's deputy. That's their undercover truck."

"Great undercover to wear a uniform," I said. "Why are they watching you?"

"They ain't watchin' us, my man—they be watchin' you."

"Me? Why me? They think I'm agitating?"

Walker and Davis laughed derisively. "They doan give a shit about that. They think you the dope man."

"A dealer? How do they come up with that?"

"Eyeballs, man. White dude in the project at night, drivin' a van, Northern license. Yeah, man, you be dealin' all right."

"If you ain't, they gonna put some stuff on you if you look like trouble."

"A cop checked the truck over last night."

"Pickin' information. Figurin' how to handle you. When they pull you in, you goan be surprised they know the size of your jockstrap."

"You got any stuff, hide it good or dump it. Don't try to sell now."

"I've got beer and some bourbon. Clean as a whistle."

"Until they stop you and look your ride over."

"Stay long enough, and they goan get you—two miles over the speed limit, forgettin' to signal, somethin'."

"To them, you be worsen a nigger now."

Davis had to go to work, and Walker had someone to see. I headed up Broad Street—clean, orderly Broad Street. I'd gone into the project for a few hours, and already I felt marked. I was suspicious. Just paranoia, of course.

On the way out of town, I passed three police cars stationed at intersections. They must have only been waiting for traffic to clear because no one followed me. But I drove under the speed limit, came to absolute stops at every light and sign, signaled turns a block ahead. And I hardly took my eyes off the rearview mirror. What a way to go.

Uniontown, Demopolis. The Tombigbee River and blue highway 28. I missed the turnoff to Sucarnochee, Mississippi, and had to enter the state by way of Scooba on route 16, a road of trees and farmhouses. The farmhouses weren't the kind with large, encircling porches and steeply pitched roofs and long windows you used to see, but rather new houses indistinguishable from wet-bar, walkout basement, Turfbuilder-Plus suburban models.

Then Philadelphia, Mississippi. Here, too, the old, sad history. The town, like others in the area, was built over the site of a Choctaw village. The Choctaw, whose land once covered most of Mississippi, earned a name from their skill in horticulture and diplomacy; they were a sensible people whose chieftains attained position through merit. In the early nineteenth century, they learned from white men and began building schools and adding livestock to their farms. Later, whites would refer to them as one of the "five civilized tribes." Nevertheless, as pressure from white settlement increased, the Choctaw had to cede to the government one piece of land (in million-acre increments) after another. Federal agents pressured tribes to sign treaties through mixed-bloods bribed with whiskey and trinkets; they promised Indians annuities, land grants, and reparations, almost none

182

of which the Congress ever paid. To President Andrew Jackson, it made no difference that Choctaw officers like Ofahoma had fought with him against rebellious Creeks; Jackson pushed on with land-gobbling compacts. With the Treaty of Dancing Rabbit Creek, held in the woods northeast of Philadelphia, the Choctaw gave up the last of their land and reluctantly agreed to leave Mississippi forever. They walked to the arid Indian Territory where they set up their own republic modeled after the government that had just dispossessed them.

It's a sad history not because of the influx of settlers—after all, Indians had encroached upon each other for thousands of years. It's a sad history because of the shabby way the new people dealt with tribal Americans: not just the lies, but the utter unwillingness to share an enormous land.

Yet, a thousand or so Choctaw secretly stayed in Mississippi to claim land promised, although few ever saw a single acre returned. That afternoon their descendants were shopping along the square on Philadelphia, eating a hotdog at the Pow Wow drive-in, taking a few hours away from the reservation west of town. Holding to the token parcel now theirs, they could watch towns white men had built wither: Improve, Enterprise, Increase, Energy, Progress. As for what the land around the towns produced, they could watch that too.

Highway 16 passed through green fields, blue ponds, clumps of pine; it crossed the earthy Yokahockana River, a name that stands with other rivers of strong name in Mississippi: the Yazoo, Yalobusha, Little Flower, Noxubee, Homochitto,

Bogue Chitto, Chickasawhay, Skuna, the Singing River.

At Ofahoma, I drove onto the Natchez Trace Parkway, a two-lane running from Natchez to near Nashville, which follows a five-hundred-mile trail first opened by buffalo and Indians. Chickasaws called it the "Path of Peace." In 1810, the Trace was the main return route for Ohio Valley traders who, rather than fight the Mississippi currents, sold their flatboats for scrap in Natchez and walked home on the Trace. The poor sometimes traveled by a method called "ride and tie": two men would buy a mule; one would ride until noon, then tie the animal to a tree and walk until his partner behind caught up on the jack that evening. By mid-century, steamboats made the arduous and dangerous trek unnecessary, and the Trace disappeared in the trees.

Now new road, opening the woods again, went in among redbuds and white blossoms of dogwood, curling about under a cool evergreen cover. For miles no powerlines or billboards. Just tree, rock, water, bush, and road. The new Trace, like a river, followed natural contours and gave focus to the land; it so brought out the beauty that every road commissioner in the nation should drive the Trace to see that highway does not have to outrage landscape.

Northeast of Tougaloo, I stopped to hike a trail into a black-water swamp of tupelo and bald cypress. The sun couldn't cut through the canopy of buds and branches, and the slow water moved darkly. In the muck pollywogs were starting to squirm. It was spring here, and juices were getting

184

up in the stalks; leaves, terribly folded in husks, had begun to let loose and open to the light; stuff was stirring in the rot, water bubbled with the froth of sperm and ova, and the whole bog lay rank and eggy, vaporous and thick with the scent of procreation. Things once squeezed close, pinched shut, things waiting to become something else, something greater, were about ready.

I had a powerful sense of life going about the business of getting on with itself. Pointed phallic sprouts pressed up out of the ooze, green vegetable heads came up from the mire to sniff for vegetation of kin. Staminate and pistillate, they rose to the thrall of the oldest rhythms. Things were growing so fast I could almost feel the heat from their generation: the slow friction of leaf against bud case, petal against petal. For some time I stood among the high mysteries of being as they consumed the decay of old life.

Then I went back to the Trace and followed dusk around the spread of Jackson highways that had broken open like aneurisms and leaked out strawberry-syrup pancakes, magic-finger motel beds, and double-cheese pizzas. Across the Pearl River and into Clinton, a hamlet that Sherman pillaged but decided not to burn. The place was shut down. Near the campus of old Mississippi College, I parked for the night and ate a tin of tuna and three soft carrots. Rejected the chopped liver. I ate only because I didn't know what else to do. I'd got uppity about multilane America and was paying the price. Secretly, I hungered for a texturized patty of genetically engineered cow.

A century and a half ago, the founders of Mississippi College hoped the school would become the state university. But that didn't work out, so they gave it to the Presbyterians; that didn't work out either, and the Presbyterians gave it back. The Baptists had a go at it, and the college got on in its own quiet way, eventually turning out three governors. Actually, all the changing around may have made little difference. A student told me that everyone in town was a Baptist anyway, even the Presbyterians.

I was eating breakfast in the cafeteria. A crewcut student wearing mesh step-in casuals sat down to a tall stack of pancakes. He was a methodical fellow. After a prayer running almost a minute, he pulled from his briefcase a Bible, reading stand, clips to hold the book open, a green felt-tip, a pink, and yellow; next came a squeeze-bottle of liquid margarine, a bottle of Log Cabin syrup wrapped in plastic, a linen napkin, and one of those little lemony wet-wipes. The whole business looked like the old circus act where twelve men get out of a car the size of a trashcan.

A woman with a butter-almond smile sat down across from me. Her hair, fresh from the curling wand, dropped in loose coils the color of polished pecan, and her breasts, casting shadows to her waist, pressed full against a glossy dress that looked wet. A golden cross swung gently between, and high on her long throat was a small PISCES amulet. Her dark, musky scent brought to mind the swamp. We nodded and she said in soft Mississippian, "You were very interested in Jerry's pancakes."

"It was the briefcase. I thought he was going to pull out a Water-Pik and the Ark of the Covenant next."

"He's a nice boy. His parameters just aren't yours." She couldn't have surprised me more had she said floccinaucinihilipilification. "The bottom line is always parameters no matter what the input."

"Let me make a crazy guess. You're in computer programming."

"I'm in business, but my brother is the computer programmer in Jackson. He's got me interested in it. He plays with the computer after hours. Made up his Christmas cards on an IBM three-sixty-one-fifty-eight last year and did his own wedding invitations two years ago. But we're channelized different. I want to use the computer to enrich spiritual life. Maybe put prayers on a computer like that company in California that programs them. For two dollars, they run your prayer through twice a day for a week. They send up ten thousand a month."

"What if God doesn't know Fortran?"

"Come on, you! People are critical, but they don't ridicule prayer wheels or rosaries and those are just prayer machines."

"Does God get a printout?"

"Quit it! You get the printout. Suitable for framing. Quit smiling!"

"Sorry, but you said they send the prayers 'up,' and I just wondered what kind of hard copy we're dealing with here."

"You're a fuddydud! It's all just modalities. The prayer still has to come from the heart. Japa-

187

nese write prayers on slips of paper and tie them to branches so the wind sort of distributes them. Same thing—people just try to maximize the prayer function."

"You're a Pisces?"

"Would a Sagittarius wear a Pisces necklace?"

"How can you believe in astrology and wear a cross?"

"What a fuddydud! Who made the stars? Astrology's just another modality too." She took a computer card from her notebook. "I've got to get to class, but here's one more modality. In India, people pray when they eat—like each chew is a prayer. Try it sometime. Even grumpy fuddyduds like it."

She handed me the card and hurried off. Here it is, word for word:

SCRIPTURE CAKE

2 cups Proverbs 30:33	1 cup Genesis 43:11
3 ½ cups Exodus 29:2	6 Isaiah 10:14
3 cups Jeremiah 6:20	2 tbsp I Corinthians 5:6
2 cups I Samuel 30:12	1 tbsp I Samuel 14:25
2 cups Nahum 3:12	Season with I Kings
½ cup Judges 4:19	10:10
	Follow Leviticus 24:5

SERVE WITH LOVE
. . . SALLY

I went to the Trace again, following it through pastures and pecan groves and tilled fields; wildflowers and clover pressed in close, and from trees, long purple drupes of wisteria hung like grape clusters; in one pond a colony of muskrats. I turned off near Learned and drove northwest to cross the Mississippi at Vicksburg. South of town, I ate a sandwich where Civil War earthworks stuck out on a bluff high above the river. From these aeries, cannoneers had lobbed shells onto Union gunboats running the river. Anything—a rock, a stick—falling from that height must have hit with a terrible impact.

The western side of the river was Louisiana, and the hills of Mississippi gave way to low and level cotton fields where humid heat waves boiled up, turning dusty tractors into shimmering distortions. The temperature climbed to eighty-six. Once, a big oak or gum grew in the middle of each of these fields, and under them, the farmer ate dinner, cooled the team, took an afternoon nap. Now, because they interfered with air-conditioned powerhouse tractors plowing the acres, few of the tall trees remained.

The traffic on U.S. 80 had gone to I-20, and the two-lane carried only farm trucks and tractors pulling big canisters of liquid fertility. The federal highway, like most I'd driven, was much rougher than state or county highways, so we all went slowly, just trundling along in the heat.

A traveler who leaves the journey open to the road finds unforeseen things come to shape it. "The fecundity of the unexpected," Proudhon called it. The Cajun Fried Chicken stand in Monroe (accent the first syllable), where I'd stopped for gas, determined the direction of the next several days. I wasn't interested in franchise chicken, but the word *Cajun* brought up the scent of gumbo, hot boudin, and dirty rice. Monroe is a long way from Cajunland, but while the tank filled, I decided to head south for some genuine Cajun cooking.

On the other side of the pump, a man with arms the size of my thighs waited for the nozzle. He said, "You drive through or what?"

"On my way south."

"You want some meat?" It sounded aggressive, like, "Want a knuckle sandwich?"

"Pardon me?"

"You want meat? I'm flying out of Shreveport this afternoon. Can't carry the steaks with me. Just got called to Memphis. If you're cooking out, might as well take them. It's you or the garbage can."

He had a way with words.

"Get him the steaks, Roger." A boy, about ten, came around and handed me four nice flank cuts still frozen. I thanked the man.

"What'd you pay for your Ford?" the boy said.

"Three thousand in round numbers."

"How much to build the insides?"

"Couple hundred dollars."

"How about that homemade bed? Could I try it?" I opened the door, he jumped on the bunk, stretched out, and made a loud snoring noise. Dreaming of far places. His eyes popped open. "Inflation's added about twelve percent. These models run higher now. How's the gas mileage?"

"Around twenty-five to the gallon."

"Can't be."

"Can be and is. Straight stuff, no factory options except highback seats, lightweight, and I drive around fifty." That short man of a boy depressed me. Ten years old and figuring the rate of interest and depreciation instead of the cost of adventure. His father handed me a loaf of bread.

"Thanks very kindly," I said, "but I'm not much for white bread."

"Just have to leave it along the interstate for possums and niggers."

He did it again.

With the steaks and white bread (would go well with chopped liver) I drove south toward the flat, wet triangle of gulf-central Louisiana that is Cajunland. The highway clattered Ghost Dancing and shook me so that my head bounced like one of those plastic dogs in car rear windows. The beat made me groggy, and I couldn't shake it, and I didn't want to stop. After a while, the road seemed a continuum of yellow-lined concrete, a Möbius strip where I moved, going neither in nor out, but around and up and down to all points of the compass, yet always rolling along on the same plane.

My eyes were nearly closed. Then a dark face staring in. My head snapped back, and I pulled the truck out of the left lane. A hitchhiker. I stopped. His skin tone shone like wet delta mud, and his smile glittered like a handful of new dimes. He was heading home to Coushatta after spending two days thumbing along I-20 from Birmingham, where he'd looked for work as a machinist. He'd found nothing. Usually he got long rides on freeways if he could manage one, but it was easier for a black man to get a lift on the small roads where

191

there were more Negro drivers. Sometimes the ride included a meal and bed, but last night he'd slept in a concrete culvert. I asked where he learned his trade. "In the Army. I was a Spec Four."

"Were the jobs filled in Birmingham?"

"They said they were. I don't know."

"Was it a racial question, do you think?"

He moved warily in his seat. "Can't always tell. It's easy to say that."

"What will you do now?"

"Go home and wait for something to open up." We rode quietly, the even land green and still. He was a shy man and appeared uncertain about what to say. I filled some silence, and then he said, "Seems things I wait for don't come along, and the ones I want to see pass on by, stop and settle in."

"I'm between jobs myself. Waiting for something to open up too."

"I hope I'm just between jobs. I went in the Army to learn a trade. Figured I'd found a good one for civvy life. Now I'm looking like my uncle. He only had one good job in his life. Good for his time anyway. Ran an elevator at the Roosevelt Hotel in New Orleans. Then they put in push-button elevators. He said he drove his old elevator a hundred thousand miles. He came back to Coushatta and did a little field work, then went hunting a better job in Dallas and got shot dead. I used to think he musta been a bum. Don't see it like that now."

The rest of the way was mostly quiet. "I'll get out here," he said at last.

"A man gave me some steaks. My cooler won't

keep them in this heat. Why don't you take a couple?" I pulled out a steak and handed him the rest. "Gave me this bread too. Take it if you like."

He put the steaks in his plaid suitcase but had to carry the bread in his hand. "Can I ask you a question? Why did you give me a ride?"

"I was dozing off. Owed you for waking me up."

He shook his head. "Maybe. It'll be a good night at home. Mama loves steak."

Up the road he went, thumb out, smiling into the tinted windshields. Home is the hunter, home from the hill; home the sailor, home from the sea. And what about the Specialist Four home from Birmingham?

All the way to Opelousas, I thought of the machinist whose name I never learned. He had gone out and come back only to find a single change: he was older. Sometimes a man's experience is like the sweep second hand on a clock, touching each point in its circuit but always the arcs of movement repeating.

Near Ville Platte a scene of three colors: beside a Black Angus, in a green pasture, a white cattle egret waited for grubbings the cow stirred up. The improbable pair seemed to know each other well, standing close yet looking opposite directions. I don't know what the egret did before white men brought it fields and cattle; I suppose it took its long, reedy legs to shallow water and picked in the bayous for a couple of million years, each bird repeating until the new way of life came to it.

I switched on the radio and turned the dial. Somewhere between a shill for a drive-up savings and loan and one for salvation, I found a raucous music, part bluegrass fiddle, part Texas guitar, part Highland concertina. Cajun voices sang an old, flattened French, part English, part undecipherable.

Looking for live Cajun music, I stopped in Opelousas at the Plantation Lounge. Somebody sat on every barstool; but a small man, seeing a stranger, jumped down, shook my hand, and insisted I take his seat. In the fast roll of Cajun English, he said it was the guest stool and by right belonged to me. The barmaid, a woman with coiled eyes, brought a Jax. "Is there Cajun music here tonight?" I asked.

"Jukebox is our music tonight," she snapped.

A man called Walt, with dark hair oiled and slicked back in the style of an older time, squeezed in beside me. "If you're lookin' for French music, you need to get yourself to laugh yet."

"What's that mean?"

"Means haul your butt to laugh yet. Biggest Coonass city in the world."

"Lafayette?" I made it three syllables.

"You got it, junior, but we don't say Lah-fay-et."

"Where should I go in Laughyet?"

He drew a map so detailed I could almost see chuckholes in the streets. "Called Eric's. That's one place. In Laughyet they got whatever you want: music, hooch, girls, fights, everything." He passed the bar peanuts. "By the way, junior," he said casually, "ever had yourself a Cajun woman?"

194

His question silenced the bar. "Don't think I have."

"Got some advice for you then—if you find you ever need it."

It was the quietest bar I'd ever been in. I answered so softly no sound came out, and I had to repeat. "What advice?"

"Take off your belt before you climb on so you can strap your Yankee ass down because you'll get taken for a ride. Up the walls and around."

Now the whole bar was staring, I guess to surmise whether my Yankee ass was worth strapping down. One rusty geezer said, "Junior ain't got no belt."

Walt looked at my suspenders and pulled one, letting it snap back. "My man," he said, "tie on with these and you'll get zanged out the window like in a slingshot."

The men pounded the bar and choked on their Dixie beer. One began coughing and had to be slapped on the back. Two repeated the joke.

Walt shouted to the barmaid, "Let's get junior another Jax." To me he said, "Don't never take no offense at a Coonass. We're all fools in God's garden. Except for bettin'. Now that's serious. These boys'll bet on anything that moves or scores points and even some things that don't do neither. Charles, here, for example, will bet he can guess to within four how many spots on any Dalmatian dog. I bet on movement because I don't know dogs and not too many things score points. But everything moves—sooner or later. Even hills. Old Chicksaw taught me that."

If you've read Longfellow, you can't miss Cajunland once you get to the heart of it: Evangeline Downs (horses), Evangeline Speedway (autos), Evangeline Thruway (trucks), Evangeline Drive-in, and, someone had just said, the Sweet Evangeline Whorehouse.

I found my way among the Evangelines into an industrial area of Lafayette, a supply depot for bayou and offshore drilling operations. Along the streets were oil-rig outfitters where everything was sections of steel: pipes, frames, ladders, derricks, piles, cables, buoys, tanks. Crude oil opened Acadian Louisiana as nothing in the past three centuries had, and it seemed as if little could be left unfound in Cajun hamlets once quite literally backwaters.

Eric's, on the edge of the outfitters' district, was a windowless concrete-block box with a steel door and broken neon and a parking lot full of pickups, Cadillacs, and El Caminos ("cowboy Cadillacs"). But no French music.

I drank a Dixie and ate bar peanuts and asked the bartender where I could hear "chanky-chank," as Cajuns call their music. She, too, drew a map, but her knowledge gave out before she got to the destination. "It's called Tee's. It's down one of these roads, but they all look alike to me out there."

"Out there?"

"It's in the country. Follow my map and you'll be within a couple miles."

When I left she said good luck. The traveler should stand warned when he gets wished good luck. I followed her map until the lights of

Lafayette were just a glowing sky and the land was black. I wound about, crossing three identical bridges or crossing one bridge three times. I gave up and tried to find my way back to town and couldn't do that either.

Then a red glow like a campfire. A beer sign. Hearty music rolled out the open door of a small tavern, and a scent of simmering hot peppers steamed from the stovepipe chimney. I'd found Tee's. Inside, under dim halos of yellow bug lights, an accordion (the heart of a Cajun band), a fiddle, guitar, and ting-a-ling (triangle) cranked out chanky-chank. The accordionist introduced the numbers as songs of *amour* or *joie* and the patrons cheered; but when he announced *"un chanson de marriage,"* they booed him. Many times he cried out the Cajun motto, *"Laissez les bons temps rouler!"*

While the good times rolled, I sat at the bar next to a man dying to talk. My Yankee ass and his were the only ones in the place. His name was Joe Seipel and his speech Great Lakes. I asked, "You from Wisconsin?"

"Minnesota. But I have been here seven years working for P.H.I."

"What's P.H.I.?"

He put down his bottle and gave me an exaggerated, wide-eyed, open-mouthed look to indicate my shocking ignorance. "You gotta be kidding!"

"About what?"

"Petroleum Helicopters Incorporated!" He shook his head. "Jees!"

"Oh, that's right. What kind of helicoptering do

197

you do?" I tried to talk between numbers, but he talked through it all.

"I don't fly. I'm a mechanic. But Stoney here flies out to the offshore rigs. Delivers materials, crews. You know."

The pilot, in his fifties, wore cowboy boots and a jaunty avocado jumpsuit. He was applying a practical *Bridges-at-Toko-Ri* machismo to a hugely mammaried woman who had painted on a pair of arched, red lips the likes of which the true face of womankind has never known.

Seipel said, "I was just like you when I came here—dumb as hell. But I've read about Louisiana. Learned about Coonasses from that yellow book."

"What yellow book is that?"

"That one comes out every month."

"*National Geographic?*"

"That's it. They had a story on Coonasses."

"Did they explain the name 'Coonass'?"

"I think they missed that."

A small, slue-footed Gallic man wearing a silky shirt with a pelican on it dragged an upturned metal washtub next to the band and climbed on. I think he'd taken out his dentures. A mop handle with baling twine tied to it projected from the tub, and he thrust the stick about in rhythm with the music, plucking out the sound of a double bass.

"That's DeePaul on the gut bucket," Seipel said. "He's not with the band."

After a couple of numbers on the tub, the small man hopped down and waltzed around the floor, quite alone, snapping his wrists, making sharp

198

rapid clacks with four things that looked like big ivory dominoes.

"Those are the bones," Seipel said. "Sort of Cajun castanets."

When the band folded for the night, the little fellow sashayed to the lighted jukebox, drawn to it like a moth, and clacked the bones in fine syncopation, his red tongue flicking out the better to help him syncopate, his cropped orb of a head glowing darkly. Seipel hollered him over.

He showed how to hold the bones one on each side of the middle fingers, then flung out his wrist as if throwing off water and let loose a report like the crack of a bullwhip. "Try dem in you hands."

The bones were smooth like old jade. I laboriously inserted the four-inch counters between my fingers and snapped my wrist. *Cluk-cluk.* "Lousy," Seipel said. I tried again. *Cluk-cluk.* Wet sponges had more resonance. Seipel shook his head, so I handed them to him. He got them mounted, lashed out an arm, and a bone sailed across the room.

"You boys don't got it," DeePaul said, his words loopin in the old Cajun way. DeePaul's name was in fact Paul Duhon. He had cut the clappers from a certain leg bone in a steer and carved them down to proper shape and a precise thickness. "You got to have da right bone, or da sound she muffle. And da steer got to be big for da good ringin' bones."

I tried again. *Cluk-cluk.* "I work at dis forty years," Duhon said, "and just now do I start gettin' it right. Look at me, gettin' old and just now gettin' good. Dat's why only ole, ole men play da good bones."

"Where'd you learn to make them?"

"Ole color man, he work on da rayroad. He got nuttin' but he love music so he play da bones. He play dem in da ole minstrel shows. He da one day call 'Mister Bones,' and it Mister Bones hisself he show me carvin'. Now people say, 'Come play us da bones in Shrevepoat.' But da bones just for fun."

"DeePaul flies kites," Seipel said. "Wants in the *Guinness Book*."

"My kites day fly for time in da air, not how high. Someday I want people to be rememberin' Duhon. I want 'Duhon' wrote down."

"I can play the musical saw," Seipel said and called to the barmaid, "Got a saw here?" She pushed him a saltshaker. "What's this?"

"That's the salt you're yellin' for." Seipel and I laughed, holding on to the bar. Duhon went home. Everybody went home. The barmaid watched us wearily. "Okay," she said, "come on back for some hot stuff."

"Is that where we find out why they call themselves 'Coonasses'?" I said, and we laughed again, holding on to each other.

"All right, boys. Settle down." She led us not to a bedroom but to a large concrete-floor kitchen with an old picnic table under a yellow fluorescent tube. We sat and a young Cajun named Michael passed a long loaf of French bread. The woman put two bowls on the oil cloth and ladled up gumbo. Now, I've eaten my share of gumbo, but never had I tasted anything like that gumbo: the oysters were fresh and fat, the shrimp succulent, the spiced sausage meaty, okra sweet, rice soft, and the roux—the essence—the roux was right. We could almost stand our spoons on end in it.

The roots of Cajun cookery come from Brittany and bear no resemblance to Parisian cuisine and not even much to the Creole cooking of New Orleans. Those are *haute cuisines* of the city, and Cajun food belongs to the country where things got mixed up over the generations. No one even knows the source of the word *gumbo*. Some say it derives from an African word for okra, *chinggombo*, while others believe it is a corruption of a Choctaw word for sassafras, *kombo*, the key seasoning.

The woman disappeared, so we ate gumbo and dipped bread and no one talked. A gray cat hopped on the bench between Seipel and me to watch each bite of both bowls we ate. Across the room, a fat, buffy mouse moved over the stove top and browsed for drippings from the big pot. The cat eyed it every so often but made no move away from our bowls. Seipel said, "I've enjoyed the hell out of tonight," and he laid out a small shrimp for the cat. Nothing more got spoken. We all went at the gumbo, each of us. Minnesotan, Cajun, cat, mouse, Missourian.

Sometime in the darkness of morning, the rain started. It pecked, then pelted, then fell in a steady, soft patter on the steel roof of Ghost Dancing, and my sleep was without shadows.

At six-thirty the sky was still dark, the rain falling steadily. An hour later: rain. Two hours later: no change. I got up, washed, ate some fruit and cheese. I draped across the bunk and read, occasionally looking into the gray obscuring rain, listening to thunder (puts the sugar in the cane), watching Spanish moss (a relative of the pineapple) hang still in the trees like shredded, dingy bedsheets. At ten-thirty the rain dropped straight down as if from a faucet; I was able to leave the front windows half open. I didn't know then, but in April in coastal Louisiana you don't wait for the rain to stop unless you have all day and night. Which I did.

Reading my notes of the trip—images, bits of conversations, ideas—I hunted a structure in the events, but randomness was the rule. Outside, sheltered by a live oak, a spider spun a web. Can an orb weaver perceive the design in its work, the pattern of concentric circles lying atop radiation lines? When the mystical young Black Elk went to the summit of Harney Peak to see the shape of things, he looked down on the great unifying hoop of peoples. I looked down and saw fragments. But later that afternoon, a tactic returned to me from night maneuver training in the Navy: to see in deep darkness you don't look directly at an object—you look to the left; you look at something else to see what you really want to see. Skewed vision.

At five-thirty the rain stopped; it didn't ease, it just stopped. I walked through the west side of Lafayette where I'd parked for the night—and day as it turned out. The wetness deepened the tones of things as if the rain had been droplets of color. Azaleas dripped blood-red blossoms, camellias oozed carmine. The puddly ground squelched under me. The overcast moved east like a gray woolen blanket being pulled back, and the sun came in low beneath a wrinkling of clouds. Then a sunset happened, a gaudy polychrome sky—mauve, cerise, puce—so garish I couldn't take my eyes away.

On a front porch threatened with a turbulence of blooming vegetation, a man stood before his barbecue grill, the ghostly blue smoke rising like incense. His belly a drooping bag, his face slack, he watched the coals burn to a glow. He'd built many briquette fires. The man's numb stasis disturbed me.

Got to get moving, I thought, and hurried to my rig and drove to Breaux Bridge, "the crawfish capital of the world." I was looking for a crawdad supper. Breaux Bridge, on the Bayou Teche, stirred slowly with an awakened sense of Acadianism. Codofil, an organization working to preserve Cajun traditions and language, had placed signs in the dusty shop windows, things like SOYONS FIERS DE PARLER FRANÇAIS or PARLEZ FRANÇAIS—C'EST DE L'ARGENT EN POCHE. I asked a man locking his store where to eat crawfish. He sent me east across the bayou, through banks of willow and hanging moss, past little fencepost signs advertising Evangeline Maid bread, past front-yard shrines to the Virgin, past lots piled with fishing gear. At Henderson I found a wooden building hanging over Bayou Peyronnet just below the massive west levee of the Atchafalaya River basin; the heavy air of increase smelled of marine creatures and mud and hot peppers. On the roof of Pat's restaurant sat a six-foot, red plastic model of the Cajun totem: a boiled crawdad.

The menu claimed the catfish were fresh because they had slept the night before in the Atchafalaya. All well and good, but it was little crustaceans I was after. As journalist Calvin Trillin once said, the Atchafalaya swamp is to crawfish as the Serengeti to lions. The waitress wore threads of wrinkles woven like Chantilly lace over her forehead and spoke her English in quick, rounded Cajun measures. She brought a metal beer tray piled with boiled, whole crawfish glowing the color of Louisiana hot sauce. I worked my way down through the stack. The meat was soft and piquant, sweeter than shrimp, but I had no stomach for the buttery, yellow fat the Cajuns were sucking from the shells.

The waitress said, "Did they eat lovely like mortal sin?" and winked a lacy eyelid. "You know, the Cajun, he sometime call them 'mudbugs.' But I never tell a customer that until he all full inside. But the crawfish, he live smilin' in the mud, he do."

"They're just miniature lobsters. Are you Cajun?"

"Don't you know that now, *cher?*"

"Do you use your French?"

"Time to time, but not like my old aunt. She don't speak English except death's at the door, and then it sound like her French. People you age understand but don't speak it much, no. And the kids? They don't tell French from Eskimo. Schools, they hire a hundred teachers to give little ones French. But teachers they teach Paris people's French. Hell, we speak Cajun, us. The teachers, they look down at their noses on Cajun, so we don't care. I'm afraid for Cajun. Us, we're the last. But when I was a girl on the schoolyard, when they open the day with raisin' Old Glory, we sing the Marseillaise—we thought it was America's song."

In the warm night that come on to relieve the colors of the day, I went down through the rockless, liquid land, down along the Bayou Teche to St. Martinville, a crumbling hamlet where the past was the future.

Talk about your three-persons-in-one controversies. In St. Martinville a bronze statue of a seated young woman in wooden shoes, hands folded peacefully, head turned toward the Bayou Teche, commemorates—at one and the same time— Emmeline Labiche, Evangeline Bellefontaine, and Dolores Del Rio. The monument sits in the Poste de Attakapas Cemetery behind the great Catholic church of Saint Martin de Tours. After the bayou, the cemetery and church are the oldest things in town. The cruciform building, full of flickering candles, bloodied crucifixes, anguished representations of the Stages of the Cross, and plaster saints with maces and drawn swords, contains in one wing a twelve-foot-high replica of the Grotto of Lourdes. Although mass is now celebrated in English, the place, with its ancient torments, remains quite French in the old manner.

The bronze woman sits, literally, above the eighteenth-century grave of Emmeline Labiche, who, Cajuns say, wandered primitive America in search of her lover, Louis Arcenaux, whom she was separated from during the forced Acadian exodus (*Le Grand Dérangement*) out of British Nova

Scotia. At the army outpost on the Teche, she finally found Louis—engaged to another. Emmeline, exhausted from her wanderings, went mad from the shock of his faithlessness and died shortly after. They buried her behind the church. That's history.

But the name on the statue above Emmeline's tombstone is Evangeline. Cajuns believe Longfellow patterned his wandering heroine on Emmeline, and probably he did, although the poet never visited Louisiana, relying instead on information furnished by Nathaniel Hawthorne and a St. Martinville lawyer once Longfellow's student at Harvard. To visualize the land, he went to Banvard's "Moving Diorama" of the Mississippi—a three-mile-long canvas painting of a boat-level view. Longfellow said the river came to him. He filled in with details from Darby's *Geographical Description of Louisiana* and his own imagination, changing the outcome so that in old age Evangeline at last finds her love on his deathbed in a Philadelphia almshouse. That's the poetry.

Then there's Hollywood. The face on the statue, smooth and beautiful and untouched by madness or years of wandering the wilderness, is that of Dolores Del Rio, the Mexican-born actress who completed the trinity by playing Evangeline in the 1929 movie filmed nearby at Lake Catahoula. To thank the townspeople, the cast presented a statue of Evangeline-Emmeline that Miss Del Rio posed for. The actress, cynics said, saw a chance to have her beauty immortalized in something more durable than celluloid. If many citizens no longer know the name, they all know the face.

St. Martinville was pure Cajun bayou, distinctive and memorable in a tattered way. Wood and iron galleries were rickety, brick buildings eroded, corrugated metal roofs rusting. The church stood on the square, the courthouse down Main Street. On the upper side of the square that morning, Maurice Oubre's bakery turned out the last of the day's pastry, and on the west side at Thibodeaux's Cafe & Barbershop, Mr. Thibodeaux had been cutting hair since five A.M. Across the street, taverns got swept out, and the smell of last night's beer mixed with Thibodeaux's thick *café noir*, Oubre's croissants, and the damp air off the Teche.

In the *Petit Paris de l'Amerique* Museum gift shop next to the church, a powdery old lady asked the priest to bless a souvenir candle she'd just bought; he waved his hand over it and said, "May God bless this candle and all who use it, in the name of the Father, Son, and Holy Spirit." Above his head, on the Coke machine, a sign: SHOPLIFTING IS A CRIME AND SIN. GOD SEES ALL AND REMEMBERS!!!! Sin was underlined three times.

Because of a broken sealed-beam headlight and Zatarain's Creole Mustard, an excellent native mustard, I met Barbara Pierre. I had just come out of Dugas' grocery with four jars of Zatarain's, and we almost collided on the sidewalk. She said, "You're not from St. Martinville, are you? You can't be."

"I'm from Missouri."

"What in the world are you doing here? Got a little Huck Finn in you?"

"Just followed the bayou. Now I'm looking for the Ford agency."

"Coincidences. I work there. I'll show you the way."

She was a secretary at the agency and took classes at the University of Southwestern Louisiana in Lafayette when she could. I asked about St. Martinville, but she had to start working before we could say much.

"Here's an idea," she said. "Come by at noon and we can have lunch at my place. I live in the project on the other side of the bayou."

I picked her up at twelve. She asked about the trip, especially about Selma and how things were as I saw them. "A white man griped about changes, and a black said there weren't enough changes to gripe about."

"That's us too. What we want is slow coming—if it's coming at all. Older blacks here are scared of whites and won't do much for change if it means risk. Others don't care as long as everything gets smothered over with politeness by whites. Young blacks see the hypocrisy—even when it's not there. But too many of them are junked on drugs, and that's where some of this town wants us."

"Don't the whites here try to help?"

"A few, but if a white starts helping too much, they get cut off or shut down by the others and end up paying almost the price we do. Sure, we got good whites—when they're not scared out of showing sympathy."

On Margaret Street, she pointed to her apartment in a small one-story brick building. Standard federal housing. As we went to the door, a shadowy face watched from behind a chintz curtain in another apartment.

"See that? Could be the start of bad news," she said.

"Maybe I should leave. I don't want to cause trouble for you."

"Too late. Besides, I live my own life here. I won't be pushed. But it'll come back in some little way. Smart remark, snub. One old white lady kicks me at the library. Swings her feet under the table because she doesn't want my kind in there. I could break her in two, she's so frail. She'll be kicking like a heifer if she gets wind of this."

Barbara Pierre's apartment was a tidy place but for books on the sofa. "You can see I use the library even with the nuisances. The kicking bitch hides books I return so I get overdue notices and have to go prove I turned the book in. I explain what's going on, but nothing changes. Simplest thing is trouble."

"That's what I heard in Selma."

"I'm not alone, but sometimes it seems like a conspiracy. Especially in little towns. Gossip and bigotry—that's the blood and guts."

"Was that person who just looked out the window white?"

"Are you crazy? Nobody on this end of Margaret Street is white. That's what I mean about us blacks not working together. Half this town is black, and we've only got one elected black official. Excuse my language, but for all the good he does this side of the bayou, he's one useless black mofo."

209

"Why don't you do something? I mean you personally."

"I do. And when I do, I get both sides coming down on me. Including my own family. Everywhere I go, sooner or later, I'm in the courtroom. Duplicity! That's my burning pot. I've torn up more than one court of law."

We sat down at her small table. A copy of *Catch-22* lay open.

"Something that happened a few years ago keeps coming back on me. When I was living in Norristown, outside Philadelphia, I gained a lot of weight and went to a doctor. She gave me some diet pills but never explained they were basically speed, and I developed a minor drug problem. I went to the hospital and the nuns said if I didn't sign certain papers they couldn't admit me. So I signed and they put me in a psychiatric ward. Took two hellish weeks to prove I didn't belong there. God, it's easy to get somebody adjudicated crazy."

"Adjudicated?"

"You don't know the word, or you didn't think I knew it?"

"It's the right word. Go on."

"So now, because I tried to lose thirty pounds, people do a job on my personality. But if I shut up long enough, things quiet down. Still, it's the old pattern: any nigger you can't control is crazy."

As we ate our sandwiches and drank Barq's rootbeer, she asked whether I had been through Natchitoches. I said I hadn't.

"They used to have a statue up there on the main street. Called the 'Good Darkie Statue.' It was an old black man, slouched shoulders, big possum-eating smile. Tipping his hat. Few years ago, blacks made them take it down. Whites couldn't understand. Couldn't see the duplicity in that statue—duplicity on *both* sides. God almighty! I'll promise them one thing: ain't gonna be no more gentle darkies croonin' down on the levee."

I smiled at her mammy imitation, but she shook her head. "In the sixties I wanted that statue blown to bits. It's stored in Baton Rouge now at LSU, but they put it in the wrong building. Ought to be in the capitol reminding people. Preserve it so nobody forgets. Forgives, okay—but not forgets."

"Were things bad when you were a child?"

"Strange thing. I was born here in 'forty-one and grew up here, but I don't remember prejudice. My childhood was warm and happy—especially when I was reading. Maybe I was too young to see. I don't know. I go on about the town, but I love it. I've put my time in the cities—New Orleans, Philly. Your worst Southern cracker is better than a Northern liberal, when it comes to duplicity anyway, because you know right off where the cracker crumbles. With a Northerner, you don't know until it counts, and that's when you get a job done on yourself."

"I'd rather see a person shut up about his prejudices."

"You haven't been deceived. Take my job. I was pleased to get it. Thought it was a breakthrough for me and other blacks here. Been there three weeks, and next Wednesday is my last day."

"What happened?"

"Duplicity's what happened. White man in the shop developed a bad back, so they moved him inside. His seniority gets my job. I see the plot—somebody in the company got pressured to get rid of me."

"Are you going to leave town?"

"I'm staying. That's my point. I'll take St. Martinville over what I've seen of other places. I'm staying here to build a life for myself and my son. I'll get married again. Put things together." She got up and went to the window. "I don't know, maybe I'm too hard on the town. In an underhanded way, things work here—mostly because old blacks know how to get along with whites. So they're good darkies? They own their own homes. They don't live in a rat-ass ghetto. There's contentment. Roots versus disorder." She stopped abruptly and smiled. "Even German soldiers they put in the POW camp here to work the cane fields wanted to stay on."

We cleared the table and went to the front room. A wall plaque:

OH LORD, HELP ME THIS DAY
TO KEEP MY BIG MOUTH SHUT.

On a bookshelf by the window was a two-volume microprint edition of the *Oxford English Dictionary*, the one sold with a magnifying glass.

"I love it," she said. "Book-of-the-Month Club special. Seventeen-fifty. Haven't finished paying for it though."

"Is it the only one in town?"

"Doubt it. We got brains here. After the aristocracy left Paris during the French Revolution, a lot of them settled in St. Martinville, and we got known as *Le Petit Paris*. Can you believe this little place was a cultural center only second to New Orleans? Town started slipping when the railroad put the bayou steamers out of business, but the church is proof of what we had."

"When you finish the college courses, what then?"

"I'd like to teach elementary school. If I can't teach, I want to be a teacher's aide. But—here's a big 'but'—if I can make a living, I'll write books for children. We need black women writing, and my courses are in journalism and French. Whatever happens, I hope they don't waste my intelligence."

She went to wash up. I pulled out one of her books: *El Señor Presidente* by Guatemalan novelist Miguel Asturias. At page eighty-five she had underlined two sentences: "The chief thing is to gain time. We must be patient."

On the way back to the agency, she said, "I'll tell you something that took me a long time to figure out—but I know how to end race problems."

"Is this a joke?"

"Might as well be. Find a way to make people get bored with hating instead of helping. Simple." She laughed. "That's what it boils down to."

The Corps of Engineers calls it the Atchafalaya Basin Floodway System. Some Acadians call it a boondoggle in the boondocks. The Atchafalaya River, only one hundred thirty-five miles long, has an average discharge more than twice as great as that of the Missouri River although the area it drains is less than a fifth of the Missouri's and the Big Muddy is nearly twenty times as long. Yet, the Atchafalaya forms the biggest river basin swamp in North America, and before it became an overflow drain, its swamp was at least as biologically rich and varied as the Everglades. Maybe it still is, despite claims by older Cajuns that wildlife isn't what it was a generation ago. Nevertheless, some ornithologists believe the swamp might hold the last ivory-billed woodpecker.

After the great flood of 1927, the Corps built hundreds of miles of "protection levees" around the upper Atchafalaya and down the length of the basin to create an "emergency discharge" route for the Mississippi and Red rivers. The Corps said had it done nothing to the Atchafalaya, the Mississippi—always trying to change course—would eventually open a new channel about sixty miles north of St. Martinville and leave New Orleans on a backwater oxbow.

The problem is that the engineers built so injudiciously, the swamp is filling with some of the one million tons of silt the big rivers carry in daily; and those Cajuns who traditionally make a living from the wetlands by fishing, frogging, mudbugging, trapping, and mosspicking are having to leave their fastness and take work in industry. The Corps altered not just the Atchafalaya and a great swamp but also one of the distinctive ethnic peoples in America.

Maybe the swamp is doomed anyway, what with bayous being dredged and channels dug so oil and

gas drilling equipment can get in, what with pipe-
lines being laid, and wipe-out logging of cypress
and tupelo. To be sure, dry-land farmers—a minority—are happy. At the north end of the basin,
they have cleared sixty thousand acres of swamp
hardwoods for pasturage and soybeans.

Now, to rectify their errors, the Corps wants
permanent control of the basin, and, of all things,
many environmentalists support the plan. Everyone believes what the dredge and bulldozer can
do, they can also undo; but a Cajun named Cassie
Hebert told me he had yet to see a bush-hog make
a mink.

Some Cajuns believe in only one thing—the
Mississippi. Herbert said: "The Atchafalaya's a
shorter way to the Gulf than the Missippi take.
Big river gonna find us down here, Corps be
damned. One day rain gonna start and keep on
like it do sometimes. When the rainin' stop, the
Missippi gonna be ninety miles west of N'Orleans
and St. Martinville gonna be a seaport. And it
won't be the firstest time the river go runnin' from
Lady N'Orleans."

Indian legend tells of a serpent of fabulous dimension living in the Atchafalaya basin; when
Chitimacha braves slew it, its writhing throes
gouged out Bayou Teche. *Teche* may be an Indian
word for "snake," and Cajuns say the big river
will one day avenge the serpent. We have only to
wait.

The Teche, at the western edge of the basin and
paralleling the Atchafalaya, has been spared the
salvation wreaked on the river, even though, before roads came, the little Teche—not the

Atchafalaya—was the highway from the Gulf into the heart of Louisiana. Half of the eighteenth-century settlements in the state lay along or very near the Teche: St. Martinville, Lafayette, Opelousas, New Iberia. The Teche was navigable for more than a hundred miles. Indians put dugouts on it; Spanish adventurers and French explorers floated it in cypress-trunk pirogues (some displacing fifty tons); settlers rode it in keelboats pulled by mules or slaves; merchandise arrived by paddlewheelers; and during the Civil War, Union gunboats came up the Teche to commandeer the fertile cane fields along its banks. All of this on a waterway no wider than the length of a war canoe, no deeper than a man, no swifter than mud turtles that swim it.

Blue road 31, from near Opelousas, follows the Teche through sugarcane, under cypress and live oak, into New Iberia. St. Martinville had dozed on the bayou for two hundred years. Not so New Iberia. A long strip of highway businesses had cropped up to the west, and the town center by the little drawbridge was clean and bright. No dozing here. Bayouside New Iberia gave a sense of both the new made old and the old made new: contemporary architecture interpreting earlier designs rather than imitating them; a restored Classic Revival mansion, Shadows on the Teche; a society whose members are hundred-year-old live oaks; and the only second-century, seven-foot marble statue of the Emperor Hadrian in a savings and loan. New Iberia suggested Cajun history, but St. Martinville lived it.

I took Louisiana 14; roadsides of pink thistle,

cemeteries jammed with aboveground tombs, cane fields under high smokestacks of sugar factories, then salt-dome country, then shrimp trawlers at Delcambre. My last chance at Cajun food was Abbeville, a town with two squares: one for the church, one for the courthouse. On the walk at Black's Oyster Bar a chalked sign: FRESH TOPLESS SALTY OYSTERS. Inside, next to a stuffed baby alligator, hung an autographed photo of Paul Newman, who had brought the cast of *The Drowning Pool* to Black's while filming near Lafayette. Considering that a recommendation, I ordered a dozen topless ("on the halfshell") and a fried oyster loaf (oysters and hot pepper garnish heaped between slices of French bread.) Good enough to require a shrimp loaf for the road.

On the highway, I wished the British had exiled more Acadians to America if only for their cooking. Somewhere lives a bad Cajun cook, just as somewhere must live one last ivory-billed woodpecker. For me, I don't expect ever to encounter either one.

The rice fields began near Kaplan, where the land is less than twenty feet above the sea only thirty miles south, and kept going all the way to Texas. The Lake Arthur bridge made a long, curvilinear glide into space as it rose above the water; passage was like driving the chromium contours of Louisianan Jose de Rivera's famous "Construction 8." At Lake Charles, another sinuous parabola of bridgeway, an aerial thing curving about so I could see its underside as I went up.

The city stretched below in a swelter of petrochemical plants and wharves. I got through only with effort and pressed north to state 27. When I had left home, I announced a stop, sooner or later, at a cousin's in Shreveport. I hoped for mail. U.S. 171 was traffic, fumes, heat, grim faces. I became a grim face and drove. Rosepine, Anacoco, Hornbeck, and Zwolle—alphabetically, the last town in the Rand-McNally *Road Atlas* (Abbeville, just south, is the first).

A yellow simmer of glaring haze sat on Shreveport like a pot lid. I pulled in at a honky-tonk called Charlie's to telephone my cousin. No one home. I took a seat at the bar. Charlie's was built-in-spare-time-after-bowling-league construction, the ceilings so low I could almost touch them flatfooted. After ten minutes I regained my vision in the cool darkness. Near the bar hung one of those pictures of dogs playing poker and cheating in a multitude of cleverly canine ways. The west fire exit unexpectedly opened and sunlight poured in; like Draculas before the cross, we cried out and covered our eyes.

Next to me, a lady nearing her seventh decade kept between us a white purse big enough for a mugger to hide in. She wore a black wig. Her devil-may-care red lipstick had come unhitched and slipped a notch; her layers of nail polish were chipped like paint on an old dory; and her hands lay in two piles on the bar, the slack skin taken up by plumpness. As for the Jungle Gardenia perfume, it was only a question of time before tsetse flies hit.

She reached over and lifted my can of Jax as if to test the weight. Then she turned, saw me, and jumped. "Oh! Gracious! You've scared me! I'm sorry! I thought you went off and left your beer. Gracious!"

"May I buy you one?"

"Oh! Gracious, no! Beer does things to me. I just look after the girls."

"Are you related?"

"Goodness, no! Only a friend. I worry about them with these cowboys."

The "girls" were the bartender and a pool player, both of whom looked quite capable of handling any of the spinstool cowboys (Shreveport is more Dallas than New Orleans). The bartender was, in the lingo, one tough broad. A snake fits its skin no tighter than she fit her bluejeans. The pool player, a woman of sleek legs, wore a tank top and cut-offs that had seen the absolute maximum of strategic cutting. The game she played was, nominally, eight ball, but the real purpose was to make spectacular shots—never mind if the cue ball ended up in someone's Schlitz.

After each shot, she groaned and took a long, hard stretch out of her hustler's crouch and said, "Ah cain't shoot worth a damn today." Who had noticed her shooting, watching as we were her form? She kept a beercan on a stack of damp dollar bills. As lousy as she played, she managed to beat the Louisiana cowboys who laughed with beer commercial heartiness. They knew a good entertainment value when they saw it.

The overripe lushness of Jungle Gardenia enveloped me again. "Who's your favorite picture-show actor?" she said.

"I don't know. Alan Bates. Jimmy Stewart. Chief Dan George."

"Mine's Franchot Tone."

There followed a long recital of movie titles, bits of plot, pieces of dialogue. As she talked, she laid a soft curl of fingers over my wrist; it wasn't a gesture of friendship so much as an ascertaining of my presence, a holding of her audience. Once she had heard that Mr. Tone wore a stomach corset in his later years, but she knew that couldn't have been true. The lady must have known more about Franchot Tone than anyone else in the world. Whatever empty spaces had opened in her life she filled with dreams of a flickering vision. As Jesus or Mozart or Crazy Horse fills hollows in others, so Franchot Tone had come to his lady moist in her Jungle Gardenia.

I called my cousin again, got directions, and drove to her house. The sun was gone when the family sat down to dinner. A pair of heavy moths bumped the screen, and we took barbecued chicken from the platter. It had been a long time since I'd eaten among faces I'd seen before, and I knew it would be hard leaving.

Departure from Memphis

FANNY TROLLOPE

Fanny Trollope (1776–1861) is remembered mainly for her book about America (and for her son Anthony, the novelist). It was the most famous travel book of its age, offending the Americans but delighting the English. Dickens thought it the best of hundreds written about America and Mark Twain said "She did not gild us; neither did she whitewash us." Her writing was controversial because she believed the American ideal of equality destroyed prospects for culture and manners. In this passage, she colorfully describes a trip by steamboat on the Ohio River from Memphis to Cincinnati.

On the 1st of February, 1828, we embarked on board the Criterion, and once more began to float on the "father of waters", as the poor banished Indians were wont to call the Mississippi. The company on board was wonderfully like what we had met in coming from New Orleans; I think they must have all been first cousins; and what was singular, they, too, had all arrived at high rank in the army. For many a wearisome mile above the Wolfe River the only scenery was still forest—forest—forest; the only variety was produced by the receding of the river at some points, and its encroaching on the opposite shore. These changes are continually going on, but from what cause none could satisfactorily explain to me. Where the river is encroaching, the trees are seen growing in water many feet deep; after some time, the water undermines their roots, and they become the easy victims of the first hurricane that blows. This is one source of the immense quantities of drift wood that float into the Gulf of Mexico. Where the river has receded, a young growth of cane-brake is soon seen starting up with the rapid vegetation of the climate; these two circumstances in some degree relieve the sameness of the thousand miles of vegetable wall. But we were now approaching the river which is emphatically called "the beautiful", La Belle Rivière of the New Orleans French; and a few days took us, I trust for ever, out of that murky stream which is as emphatically called "the deadly": and well does it seem to merit the title; the air of its shores is mephitic, and it is said that nothing that ever sank beneath its muddy surface was known to rise again. As truly does "La Belle Rivière" deserve its name; the Ohio is bright and clear; its banks are continually varied as it flows through what is called a rolling country, which seems to mean a district that cannot show a dozen paces of level ground at a time. The primeval forest still occupies a considerable portion of the ground, and hangs in solemn grandeur from the cliffs; but it is broken by frequent settlements, where we were cheered by the sight of herds and flocks. I imagine that this river presents almost every variety of river scenery; sometimes its clear wave waters a meadow of level

222

turf; sometimes it is bounded by perpendicular rocks; pretty dwellings, with their gay porticoes are seen, alternately with wild intervals of forest, where the tangled bear-brake plainly enough indicates what inhabitants are native there. Often a mountain torrent comes pouring its silvery tribute to the stream, and, were there occasionally a ruined abbey, or feudal castle, to mix the romance of real life with that of nature, the Ohio would be perfect.

So powerful was the effect of this sweet scenery, that we ceased to grumble at our dinners and suppers; nay, we almost learnt to rival our neighbours at table in their voracious rapidity of swallowing, so eager were we to place ourselves again on guard, lest we might lose sight of the beauty that was passing away from us.

Yet these fair shores are still unhealthy. More than once we landed, and conversed with the families of the wood-cutters, and scarcely was there one in which we did not hear of some member who had "lately died of the fever".—They are all subject to ague; and though their dwellings are infinitely better than those on the Mississippi, the inhabitants still look like a race that are selling their lives for gold.

Louisville is a considerable town, prettily situated on the Kentucky, or south side of the Ohio; we spent some hours in seeing all it had to show; and had I not been told that a bad fever often rages there during the warm season, I should have liked to pass some months there for the purpose of exploring the beautiful country in its vicinity. Frankfort and Lexington are both towns worth visiting; though from their being *out of the way* places, I never got to either. The first is the seat of the state government of Kentucky, and the last is, I was told, the residence of several independent families, who, with more leisure than is usually enjoyed in America, have its natural accompaniment, more refinement.

The falls of the Ohio are about a mile below Louisville, and produce a rapid too sudden for the boats to pass, except in the rainy season. The passengers are obliged to get out below them, and travel by land to Louisville, where they find other vessels ready to receive them for the remainder of the voyage. We were spared this inconvenience by the water being too high for the rapid to be much felt, and it will soon be altogether removed by the Louisville canal coming into operation, which will permit the steam-boats to continue their progress from below the falls to the town.

The scenery on the Kentucky side is much finer than on that of Indiana, or Ohio. The state of Kentucky was the darling spot of many tribes of Indians, and was reserved among them as a common hunting-ground; it is said, that they cannot yet name it without emotion, and that they have a sad and wild lament that they still chant to its memory. But their exclusion thence is of no recent date; Kentucky has been longer settled than the Illinois, Indiana, or Ohio; and it appears not only more highly cultivated, but more fertile and more picturesque than either. I have rarely seen richer pastures than those of Kentucky. The forest-trees, where not too crowded, are of magnificent growth; and the crops are gloriously abundant, where the thriftless husbandry has not worn out the soil by an unvarying succession of exhausting crops. We were shown ground which had borne abundant crops of wheat for twenty successive years; but a much shorter period suffices to exhaust the ground, when it is made to produce tobacco without the intermission of some other crop.

We reached Cincinnati on the 10th of February. It is finely situated on the south side of a hill that rises gently from the water's edge: yet it is by no means a city of striking appearance—it wants domes, towers, and steeples; but its landing-place is noble, extending for more than a quarter of a mile. It is well paved, and surrounded by neat, although not handsome, buildings. I have seen fifteen steam-boats lying there at once, and still half the wharf was unoccupied.

On arriving we repaired to the Washington Hotel, and thought ourselves fortunate when we were told that we were just in time for dinner at the table d'hôte; but when the dining-room door was opened, we retreated with a feeling of dismay at seeing between sixty and seventy men already at table. We took our dinner in another room with the females of the family, and then went forth to seek a house for our permanent accommodation.

We went to the office of an advertising agent, who professed to keep a register of all such information, and described the dwelling we wanted. He made no difficulty, but told us his boy should be our guide through the city, and show us what we sought; we accordingly set out with him, and he led us up one street and down another, but evidently without any determinate object; I therefore stopped, and asked him where-about the houses were which we were doing to see.

"I am looking for bills," was his reply.

I thought we could have looked for bills as well without him, and I told him so; upon which he assumed an air of great activity, and began knocking regularly at every door we passed, inquiring if the house was to be let. It was impossible to endure this long, and our guide was dismissed, though I was afterwards obliged to pay him a dollar for his services.

We had the good fortune, however, to find a dwelling before long, and we returned to our hotel, having determined upon taking possession of it as soon as it could be got ready. Not wishing to take our evening meal either with the threescore and ten gentlemen of the dining-room, nor yet with the half-dozen ladies of the bar-room, I ordered tea in my own chamber. A good-humoured Irish woman came forward with a sort of patronising manner, took my hand, and said: "Och, my honey, ye'll be from the old country. I'll see you will have your tay all to yourselves, honey." With this assurance we retired to my room, which was a handsome one as to its size and bed-furniture; but it had no carpet, and was darkened by blinds of paper such as rooms are hung with, strings very awkwardly attached to the window-frames, whenever light or air was wished for. I afterwards met with these same uncomfortable blinds in every part of America.

Our Irish friend soon reappeared, and brought us tea, together with the never-failing accompaniments of American tea-drinking, hung beef, "chipped up" raw, and sundry sweetmeats of brown-sugar hue and flavour. We took our tea, and were enjoying our family talk, relative to our future arrangements, when a loud sharp knocking was heard at our door. My "come in" was answered by the appearance of a portly personage, who proclaimed himself our landlord.

"Are any of you ill?" he began.

"No, thank you, sir; we are all quite well" was my reply.

"Then, madam, I must tell you, that I cannot accommodate you on these terms; we have no family tea-drinkings here, and you must live either with me and my wife, or not at all in my house."

This was said with an air of authority that almost precluded reply, but I ventured a sort of apologetic hint, that we were strangers, and unaccustomed to the manners of the country.

"Our manners are very good manners, and we don't wish any changes from England," rejoined our sturdy landlord, with an aspect that assuredly did not indicate any very affectionate partiality to the country he named.

I thought of mine host of the Washington afterwards, when reading Scott's *Anne of Geierstein;* he, in truth, strongly resembled the innkeeper therein immortalised, who made his guests eat, drink, and sleep, just where, when, and how he pleased. I made no further remonstrance, but determined to hasten my removal. This we achieved the next day to our great satisfaction.

We were soon settled in our new dwelling, which looked neat and comfortable enough; but we speedily found that it was devoid of nearly all the accommodation that Europeans conceive necessary to decency and comfort. No pump, no cistern, no drain of any kind, no dustman's cart, or any other visible means of getting rid of the rubbish, which vanishes with such celerity in London, that one has no time to think of its existence; but which accumulated so rapidly at Cincinnati, that I sent for my landlord to know in what manner refuse of all kinds was to be disposed of.

"Your Help will just have to fix them all into the middle of the street; but you must mind, old woman, that it is the middle. I expect you don't know as we have got a law what forbids throwing such things at the sides of the streets; they must all just be cast right into the middle, and the pigs soon takes them off."

In truth the pigs are constantly seen doing Herculean service in this way through every quarter of the city: and though it is not very agreeable to live surrounded by herds of these unsavoury animals, it is well they are so numerous, and so active in their capacity of scavengers; for without them the streets would soon be choked up with all sorts of substances in every stage of decomposition.

We had heard so much of Cincinnati, its beauty, wealth, and unequalled prosperity, that when we left Memphis, to go thither, we almost felt the delight of Rousseau's novice, *"un voyage à faire, et Paris au bout!"*—As soon, therefore, as our little domestic arrangements were completed, we set forth to view this "wonder of the West," this "prophet's gourd of magic growth"—this "infant Hercules"; and surely no travellers ever paraded a city under circumstances more favourable to their finding it fair to the sight. Three dreary months had elapsed since we had left the glories of London behind us; for nearly the whole of that time we had beheld no other architecture than what our ship and steam-boats had furnished; and, excepting at New Orleans, had seen hardly a trace of human habitations. The sight of bricks and mortar was really refreshing, and a house of three stories looked splendid. Of this splendour we saw repeated specimens, and moreover a brick church, which, from its two little peaked spires, is called the two-horned church. But, alas! the flatness of reality after the imagination has been busy! I hardly know what I expected to find in this city, fresh risen from the bosom of the wilderness, but certainly it was not a little town, about the size of Salisbury, without even an attempt at beauty in any of its edifices, and with only just enough of the air of a city to make it noisy and bustling. The population is greater than the appearance of the town would lead one to expect. This is partly owing to the number of free negroes who herd together in an obscure part of the city, called little Africa; and partly to the density of the population round the paper-mills and other manufactories. I believe the number of inhabitants exceeds twenty thousand.

We arrived in Cincinnati in February, 1828, and I speak of the town as it was then; several small churches have been built since, whose towers agreeably relieve its uninteresting mass of buildings. At that time I think Main Street, which is the principal avenue (and runs through the whole town, answering to the High Street of our old cities) was the only one entirely paved. The *trottoir* is of brick, tolerably well laid, but it is inundated by every shower, as Cincinnati has no drains whatever. What makes this omission the more remarkable is, that the situation of the place is calculated both to facilitate their construction and to render them necessary. Cincinnati is built on the side of a hill that begins to rise at the river's edge; and were it furnished with drains of the simplest arrangement, the heavy showers of the climate would keep them constantly clean: as it is, these showers wash the higher streets, only to deposit their filth on the first level spot; and this happens to be in the street second in importance to Main Street, running at right-angles to it, and containing most of the large warehouses of the town. This deposit is a dreadful nuisance, and must be productive of miasma during the hot weather.

The town is built, as I believe most American towns are, in squares, as they call them; but these squares are the reverse of ours, being solid instead of hollow. Each consists, or is intended to consist, when the plan of the city is completed, of a block of buildings fronting north, east, west, and south; each house communicating with an alley, furnishing a back entrance. This plan would not be a bad one, were the town properly drained; but as it is, these alleys are horrible abominations, and must, I conceive, become worse with every passing year.

To the north Cincinnati is bounded by a range of forest-covered hills, sufficiently steep and rugged to prevent their being built upon, or easily cultivated, but not sufficiently high to command from their summits a view of any considerable extent. Deep and narrow water-courses, dry in summer, but bringing down heavy streams in winter, divide these hills into many separate heights, and this furnishes the only variety the landscape offers for many miles round the town. The lovely Ohio is a beautiful feature wherever it is visible; but the only part of the city that has the advantage of its beauty, is the street nearest to its bank. The hills of Kentucky, which rise at about the same distance from the river, on the opposite side, form the southern boundary to the basin in which Cincinnati is built.

On first arriving, I thought the many tree-covered hills around very beautiful; but long before my departure, I felt so weary of the confined view, that Salisbury Plain would have been an agreeable variety. I doubt if any inhabitant of Cincinnati ever mounted these hills so often as myself and my children; but it was rather for the enjoyment of a freer air, than for any beauty of prospect, that we took our daily climb. These hills afford neither shrubs nor flowers, but furnish the finest specimens of millepore in the world; and the water-courses are full of fossil productions.

The forest-trees are neither large nor well grown, and so close as to be nearly knotted together at top: even the wild vine here loses its beauty; for its graceful festoons bear leaves only when they reach the higher branches of the tree that supports them, both air and light being too scantily found below to admit of their doing more than climbing with a bare stem till they reach a better atmosphere. The herb we call pennyroyal was the only one I found in abundance, and that only on the brows, where the ground has been partially cleared; vegetation is impossible elsewhere, and it is this circumstance which makes the "eternal forests" of America so detestable. Near New Orleans the undergrowth of palmetto and pawpaw is highly beautiful; but in Tennessee, Indiana, and Ohio, I never found the slightest beauty in the forest-scenery. Fallen trees in every possible stage of decay, and congeries of leaves that have been rotting since the flood, cover the ground and infect the air. The beautiful variety of foliage afforded by evergreens never occurs; and in Tennessee, and that part of Ohio that surrounds Cincinnati, even the sterile beauty of rocks is wanting. On crossing the water to Kentucky the scene is greatly improved; beech and chestnut, of magnificent growth, border the beautiful river; the ground has been well cleared, and the herbage is excellent: the pawpaw grows abundantly, and is a splendid shrub, though it bears neither fruit nor flowers so far north. The noble tulip-tree flourishes here, and blooms profusely.

The river Licking flows into the Ohio nearly opposite Cincinnati; it is a pretty winding stream, and two or three miles from its mouth has a brisk rapid dancing among white stones, which, in the absence of better rocks, we found very picturesque.

MIDWESTERN
UNITED STATES

Hospitality in the Woods

JAMES AUDUBON

James Audubon (1785–1851): The famous ornithologist and artist of the Birds of America *folios did much casual exploring of the Ohio River country from his Kentucky homestead. Any traveler who has lost the way on a stormy night will be heartened by the memorable experience Audubon recounts here of a trip through the forests of Illinois.*

Hospitality is a virtue, the exercise of which, although always agreeable to the stranger, is not always duly appreciated. The traveller who has acquired celebrity, is not unfrequently received with a species of hospitality, which is so much alloyed by the obvious attention of the host to his own interest, that the favour conferred upon the stranger must have less weight, when it comes mingled with almost interminable questions as to his perilous adventures. Another receives hospitality at the hands of persons who, possessed of all the comforts of life, receive the way-worn wanderer with pomposity, lead him from one part of their spacious mansion to another, and bidding him good night, leave him to amuse himself in his solitary apartment, because he is thought unfit to be presented to a party of *friends*. A third stumbles on a congenial spirit, who receives him with open arms, offers him servants, horses, perhaps even his purse, to enable him to pursue his journey, and parts from him with regret. In all these cases, the traveller feels more or less under obligation, and is accordingly grateful. But, kind reader, the hospitality received from the inhabitant of the forest, who can offer only the shelter of his humble roof, and the refreshment of his homely fare, remains more deeply impressed on the memory of the bewildered traveller than any other. This kind of hospitality I have myself frequently experienced in our woods, and now proceed to relate an instance of it.

I had walked several hundred miles, accompanied by my son, then a stripling, and, coming upon a clear stream, observed a house on the opposite shore. We crossed in a canoe, and finding that we had arrived at a tavern, determined to spend the night there. As we were both greatly fatigued, I made an arrangement with our host to be conveyed in a light Jersey wagon a distance of a hundred miles, the period of our departure to be determined by the rising of the moon. Fair Cynthia, with her shorn beams, peeped over the forest about two hours before dawn, and our conductor, provided with a long twig of hickory, took his station in the fore-part of the wagon. Off we went at a round trot, dancing in the cart like pease in a sieve. The road, which was just wide enough to allow us to pass, was full of deep ruts, and covered here and there with trunks and stumps, over all which we were hurried. Our conductor, Mr. Flint, the landlord of the tavern, boasting of his perfect knowledge of the country, undertook to drive us by a shortcut and we willingly confided ourselves to his management. So we jogged along, now and then deviating to double the fallen timber. Day commenced with the promise of fine weather, but several nights of white frost having occurred, a change was expected. To our sorrow, the change took place long before we got to the road again. The rain fell in torrents; the thunder bellowed; the lightning blazed. It was now evening, but the storm had brought perfect night, black and dismal. Our cart had no cover. Cold and wet, we sat silent and melancholy, with no better expectation than that of passing the night under the little shelter the cart could afford us.

To stop was considered worse than to proceed. So we gave the reins to the horses, with some faint hope that they would drag us out of our forlorn state. Of a sudden the steeds altered their course, and soon after we perceived the glimmer of a faint light in the distance, and almost at the same moment heard the barking of dogs. Our horses stopped by a high fence, and fell a-neighing, while I hallooed at such a rate, that an answer was speedily obtained. The next moment, a flaming pine torch crossed the gloom, and advanced to the spot where we stood. The Negro boy who bore it, without waiting to question us, enjoined us to follow the fence, and said that Master had sent him to show the strangers to the house. We proceeded, much relieved, and soon reached the gate of a little yard, in which a small cabin was perceived.

A tall, fine-looking young man stood in the

open door, and desired us to get out of the cart and walk in. We did so, when the following conversation took place. "A bad night this, strangers; how came you to be along the fence? You certainly must have lost your way, for there is no public road within twenty miles." "Aye," answered Mr. Flint, "sure enough we lost our way; but, thank God! we have got to a house, and thank *you* for your reception." "Reception!" replied the woodsman, "no very great thing after all; you are all here safe, and that's enough. Eliza," turning to his wife, "see about some victuals for the strangers, and you, Jupiter," addressing the Negro lad, "bring some wood and mend the fire. Eliza, call the boys up, and treat the strangers the best way you can. Come, gentlemen, pull off your wet clothes, and draw to the fire. Eliza, bring some socks and a shirt or two."

For my part, kind reader, knowing my countrymen as I do, I was not much struck at all this; but my son, who had scarcely reached the age of fourteen, drew near to me, and observed how pleasant it was to have met with such good people. Mr. Flint bore a hand in getting his horses put under a shed. The young wife was already stirring with so much liveliness, that to have doubted for a moment that all she did was not a pleasure to her would have been impossible. Two Negro lads made their appearance, looked at us for a moment, and going out, called the dogs. Soon after the cries of the poultry informed us that good cheer was at hand. Jupiter brought more wood, the blaze of which illuminated the cottage. Mr. Flint and our host returned, and we already began to feel the comforts of hospitality. The woodsman remarked that it was a pity we had not chanced to come that day three weeks; "for," he said, "it was our wedding-day, and father gave us a good house-warming, and you might have fared better; but, however, if you can eat bacon and eggs, and a broiled chicken, you shall have that. I have no whisky in the house, but father has some capital cider, and I'll go over and bring a keg of it." I asked how far off his father lived. "Only three miles, Sir, and I'll be back before Eliza has cooked your supper." Off he went accordingly, and the next moment the galloping of his horse was heard. The rain fell in torrents, and now I also became struck with the kindness of our host.

To all appearance the united age of the pair under whose roof we had found shelter did not exceed two score. Their means seemed barely sufficient to render them comfortable, but the generosity of their young hearts had no limits. The cabin was new. The logs of which it was formed were all of the tulip-tree, and were nicely pared. Every part was beautifully clean. Even the coarse slabs of wood that formed the floor looked as if newly washed and dried. Sundry gowns and petticoats of substantial homespun hung from the logs that formed one of the sides of the cabin, while the other was covered with articles of male attire. A large spinning-wheel, with rolls of wool and cotton, occupied one corner. In another was a small cupboard, containing the little stock of new dishes, cups, plates, and tin pans. The table was small also, but quite new, and as bright as polished walnut could be. The only bed that I saw was of domestic manufacture, and the counterpane proved how expert the young wife was at spinning and weaving. A fine rifle ornamented the chimney-piece. The fire-place was of such dimensions that it looked as if it had been purposely constructed for holding the numerous progeny expected to result from the happy union.

The black boy was engaged in grinding some coffee. Bread was prepared by the fair hands of the bride, and placed on a flat board in front of the fire. The bacon and eggs already murmured and spluttered in the frying-pan, and a pair of chickens puffed and swelled on a gridiron over the embers, in front of the hearth. The cloth was laid, and every thing arranged, when the clattering of hoofs announced the return of the husband. In he came, bearing a two-gallon keg of cider. His eyes sparkled with pleasure as he said, "Only think, Eliza, father wanted to rob us of the strangers, and was coming here to ask them to his own house, just as if we could not give them enough ourselves; but here's the drink. Come gentlemen, sit down and help yourselves." We did so, and I, to enjoy the repast, took a chair of the husband's making in preference to one of those called *Windsor*, of which there were six in the cabin. This chair was bottomed with a piece of deer's skin tightly stretched, and afforded a very comfortable seat.

The wife now resumed her spinning, and the husband filled a jug with sparkling cider, and, seated by the blazing fire, was drying his clothes. The happiness he enjoyed beamed from his eye, as at my request he proceeded to give us an account of his affairs and prospects, which he did in the following words:—"I will be twenty-two next Christmas-day," said our host; "My father came from Virginia when young, and settled on the large tract of land where he yet lives, and where with hard working he has done well. There were nine children of us. Most of them are married and settled in the neighbourhood. The old man has divided his lands among some of us, and bought others for the rest. The land where I am he gave me two years ago, and a finer piece is not easily to be found. I have cleared a couple of fields, and planted an orchard. Father gave me a stock of cattle, some hogs, and four horses, with two Negro boys. I camped here for most of the time when clearing and planting; and when about to marry the young woman you see at the wheel, father helped me in raising this hut. My wife, as luck would have it, had a Negro also, and we have begun as well off as most folks, and, the Lord willing, may——but, gentlemen, you don't eat; do help yourselves—Eliza, maybe the strangers would like some milk." The wife stopped her work, and kindly asked if we preferred sweet or sour milk; for you must know, reader, that sour milk is by some of our farmers considered a treat. Both sorts were produced, but, for my part, I chose to stick to the cider.

Supper over, we all neared the fire, and engaged in conversation. At length our kind host addressed his wife as follows:—"Eliza, the gentlemen would like to lie down, I guess. What sort of bed can you fix for them?" Eliza looked up with a smile, and said: "Why, Willy, we will divide the bedding, and arrange half on the floor, on which we can sleep very well, and the gentlemen will have the best we can spare them." To this arrangement I immediately objected, and proposed lying on a blanket by the fire; but neither Willy nor Eliza would listen. So they arranged a part of their bedding on the floor, on which, after some debate, we at length settled. The Negroes were sent to their own cabin, the young couple went to bed, and Mr. Flint lulled us all asleep, with a long story intended to show us how passing strange it was that he should have lost his way.

"Tired nature's sweet restorer, balmy sleep,"—and so forth. But Aurora soon turned her off. Mr. Speed, our host, rose, went to the door, and returning assured us that the weather was too bad for us to attempt proceeding. I really believe he was heartily glad of it; but anxious to continue our journey, I desired Mr. Flint to see about his horses. Eliza by this time was up too, and I observed her whispering to her husband, when he immediately said aloud, "To be sure the gentleman will eat breakfast before they go, and I will show them the way to the road." Excuses were of no avail. Breakfast was prepared and eaten. The weather brightened a little, and by nine we were under way. Willy on horseback headed us. In a few hours, our cart arrived at a road, by following which we at length got to the main one, and parted from our woodsman with the greater regret that he would accept nothing from any of us. On the contrary, telling Mr. Flint with a smile, that he hoped he might some time again follow the longest track for a short cut, he bade us adieu, and trotted back to his fair Eliza and his happy home.

Return to Cincinnati

CHARLES DICKENS

Charles Dickens (1812–70): When Dickens visited America in 1842, the novelist was first received with ovations but was soon criticized for supporting abolition. He replied with articles sharply critical of the country. The following less contentious piece describes with great feeling a ride by stagecoach and ferry from Cincinnati to Niagara Falls, which impressed him deeply with its grandeur.

As I had a desire to travel through the interior of the State of Ohio, and to "strike the lakes," as the phrase is, at a small town called Sandusky, to which that route would conduct us on our way to Niagara, we had to return from St. Louis by the way we had come, and to retrace our former track as far as Cincinnati.

The day on which we were to take leave of St. Louis being very fine; and the steamboat, which was to have started I don't know how early in the morning, postponing, for the third or fourth time, her departure until the afternoon; we rode forward to an old French village on the river, called properly Carondelet, and nicknamed Vide Poche, and arranged that the packet should call for us there.

The place consisted of a few poor cottages and

two or three public houses; the state of whose larders certainly seemed to justify the second designation of the village, for there was nothing to eat in any of them. At length, however, by going back some half a mile or so, we found a solitary house where ham and coffee were procurable; and there we tarried to await the advent of the boat, which would come in sight from the green before the door, a long way off.

It was a neat, unpretending village tavern, and we took our repast in a quaint little room with a bed in it, decorated with some old oil-paintings, which in their time had probably done duty in a Catholic chapel or monastery. The fare was very good, and served with great cleanliness. The house was kept by a characteristic old couple, with whom we had a long talk, and who were perhaps a very good sample of that kind of people in the West.

The landlord was a dry, tough, hard-faced old fellow (not so very old either, for he was but just turned sixty, I should think), who had been out with the militia in the last war with England, and had seen all kinds of service—except a battle; and he had been very near seeing that, he added: very near. He had all his life been restless and locomotive, with an irresistible desire for change; and was still the son of his old self: for, if he had nothing to keep him at home, he said (slightly jerking his hat and his thumbs towards the window of the room in which the old lady sat, as we stood talking in front of the house), he would clean up his musket, and be off to Texas to-morrow morning. He was one of the very many descendants of Cain proper to this continent, who seemed destined from their birth to serve as pioneers in the great human army: who gladly go on from year to year extending its outposts, and leaving home after home behind them; and die at last, utterly regardless of their graves being left thousands of miles behind, by the wandering generation who succeed.

His wife was a domesticated, kind-hearted old soul, who had come with him "from the queen city of the world," which, it seemed, was Philadelphia; but had no love for this Western country, and, indeed, had little reason to bear it any; having seen her children, one by one, die here of fever, in the full prime and beauty of their youth. Her heart was sore, she said, to think of them; and to talk on this theme, even to strangers, in that blighted place, so far from her old home, eased it somewhat, and became a melancholy pleasure.

The boat appearing towards evening, we bade adieu to the poor old lady and her vagrant spouse, and, making for the nearest landing-place, were soon on board the Messenger again, in our old cabin, and streaming down the Mississippi.

If the coming up this river, slowly making head against the stream, be an irksome journey, the shooting down it with the turbid current is almost worse; for then the boat, proceeding at the rate of twelve or fifteen miles an hour, has to force its passage through a labyrinth of floating logs, which, in the dark, it is often impossible to see beforehand or avoid. All that night the bell was never silent for five minutes at a time; and after every ring the vessel reeled again, sometimes beneath a single blow, sometimes beneath a dozen dealt in quick succession, the lightest of which seemed more than enough to beat in her frail keel, as though it had been pie-crust. Looking down upon the filthy river after dark, it seemed to be alive with monsters, as these black masses rolled upon the surface, or came starting up again, head first, when the boat, in ploughing her way among a shoal of such obstructions, drove a few among them, for the moment, under water. Sometimes the engine stopped during a long interval, and then before her and behind, and gathering close about her on all sides, were so many of these ill-favored obstacles that she was fairly hemmed in; the centre of a floating island; and was constrained to pause until they parted somewhere, as dark clouds will do before the wind, and opened by degrees a channel out.

In good time next morning, however, we came again in sight of the detestable morass called Cairo: and, stopping there to take in wood, lay alongside a barge, whose starting timbers scarcely held together. It was moored to the bank, and on its side was painted "Coffee House;" that being, I suppose, the floating paradise to which the people fly for shelter when they lose their houses for a month or two beneath the hideous waters of the Mississippi. But, looking southward from this point, we had the satisfaction of seeing that intolerable river dragging its slimy length and ugly freight abruptly off towards New Orleans; and, passing a yellow line which stretched across the current, were again upon the clear Ohio, never, I trust, to see the Mississippi more, saving in troubled dreams and nightmares. Leaving it for the company of its sparkling neighbor was like the transition from pain to ease, or the awakening from a horrible vision to cheerful realities.

We arrived at Louisville on the fourth night, and gladly availed ourselves of its excellent hotel. Next day we went on in the Ben Franklin, a beautiful mail steamboat, and reached Cincinnati shortly after midnight. Being by this time nearly tired of sleeping upon shelves, we had remained awake to go ashore straightway; and, groping a passage across the dark decks of other boats, and among labyrinths of engine machinery and leaking casks of molasses, we reached the streets, knocked up the porter at the hotel where we had stayed before, and were, to our great joy, safely housed soon afterwards.

We rested but one day at Cincinnati, and then resumed our journey to Sandusky. As it comprised two varieties of stage-coach travelling, which, with those I have already glanced at, comprehend the main characteristics of this mode of transit in America, I will take the reader as our fellow-passenger, and pledge myself to perform the distance with all possible despatch.

Our place of destination, in the first instance, is Columbus. It is distant about a hundred and twenty miles from Cincinnati, but there is a macadamized road (rare blessing!) the whole way, and the rate of travelling upon it is six miles an hour.

We start at eight o'clock in the morning, in a great mail-coach, whose huge cheeks are so very ruddy and plethoric that it appears to be troubled with a tendency of blood to the head. Dropsical it certainly is, for it will hold a dozen passengers

247

inside. But, wonderful to add, it is very clean and bright, being nearly new; and rattles through the streets of Cincinnati gayly.

Our way lies through a beautiful country, richly cultivated, and luxuriant in its promise of an abundant harvest. Sometimes we pass a field where the strong bristling stalks of Indian corn look like a crop of walking-sticks, and sometimes an enclosure where the green wheat is springing up among a labyrinth of stumps; the primitive worm-fence is universal, and an ugly thing it is; but the farms are neatly kept, and, save for these differences, one might be travelling just now in Kent.

We often stop to water at a roadside inn, which is always dull and silent. The coachman dismounts and fills his bucket, and holds it to the horses' heads. There is scarcely ever any one to help him; there are seldom any loungers standing round; and never any stable company with jokes to crack. Sometimes, when we have changed our team, there is a difficulty in starting again, arising out of the prevalent mode of breaking a young horse: which is to catch him, harness him against his will, and put him in a stage-coach without further notice: but we get on somehow or other, after a great many kicks and a violent struggle; and jog on as before again.

Occasionally, when we stop to change, some two or three half-drunken loafers will come loitering out with their hands in their pockets, or will be seen kicking their heels in rocking-chairs, or lounging on the window-sill, or sitting on a rail within the colonnade: they have not often anything to say, though, either to us or to each other, but sit there idly staring at the coach and horses. The landlord of the inn is usually among them, and seems, of all the party, to be the least connected with the business of the house. Indeed, he is, with reference to the tavern, what the driver is in relation to the coach and passengers: whatever happens in his sphere of action, he is quite indifferent, and perfectly easy in his mind.

The frequent change of coachmen works no change or variety in the coachman's character. He is always dirty, sullen, and taciturn. If he be capable of smartness of any kind, moral or physical, he has a faculty of concealing it which is truly marvelous. He never speaks to you as you sit beside him on the box, and if you speak to him, he answers (if at all) in monosyllables. He points out nothing on the road, and seldom looks at anything: being, to all appearance, thoroughly weary of it, and of existence generally. As to doing the honors of his coach, his business, as I have said, is with the horses. The coach follows because it is attracted to them and goes on wheels: not because you are in it. Sometimes, towards the end of a long stage, he suddenly breaks out into a discordant fragment of an election song, but his face never sings along with him: it is only his voice, and not often that.

He always chews and always spits, and never encumbers himself with a pocket-handkerchief. The consequences to the box passenger, especially when the wind blows towards him, are not agreeable.

Whenever the coach stops, and you can hear the voices of the inside passengers; or whenever any bystander addresses them, or any one among them;

or they address each other; you will hear one phrase repeated over and over and over again to the most extraordinary extent. It is an ordinary and unpromising phrase enough, being neither more nor less than "Yes, sir;" but it is adapted to every variety of circumstance, and fills up every pause in the conversation. Thus:

The time is one o'clock at noon. The scene, a place where we are to stay to dine on this journey. The coach drives up to the door of an inn. The day is warm, and there are several idlers lingering about the tavern, and waiting for the public dinner. Among them is a stout gentleman in a brown hat, swinging himself to and fro in a rocking-chair on the pavement.

As the coach stops, a gentleman in a straw hat looks out of the window.

STRAW HAT (to the stout gentleman in the rocking-chair). I reckon that's Judge Jefferson, ain't it?

BROWN HAT (still swinging; speaking very slowly; and without any emotion whatever). Yes, sir.

STRAW HAT. Warm weather, Judge.

BROWN HAT. Yes, sir.

STRAW HAT. There was a snap of cold last week.

BROWN HAT. Yes, sir.

STRAW HAT. Yes, sir.

A pause, they look at each other very seriously.

STRAW HAT. I calculate you'll have got through that case of the corporation, Judge, by this time, now?

BROWN HAT. Yes, sir.

STRAW HAT. How did the verdict go, sir?

250

BROWN HAT. For the defendant, sir.

STRAW HAT (interrogatively). Yes, sir?

BROWN HAT (affirmatively). Yes, sir.

BOTH (musingly, as each gazes down the street). Yes, sir.

Another pause. They look at each other again, still more seriously than before.

BROWN HAT. This coach is rather behind its time to-day, I guess.

STRAW HAT (doubtingly). Yes, sir.

BROWN HAT (looking at his watch). Yes, sir; nigh upon two hours.

STRAW HAT (raising his eyebrows in very great surprise). Yes, sir!

BROWN HAT (decisively, as he puts up his watch). Yes, sir.

ALL THE OTHER INSIDE PASSENGERS (among themselves). Yes, sir.

COACHMAN (in a very surly tone). No, it ain't.

STRAW HAT (to the coachman). Well, I don't know, sir. We were a pretty tall time coming that last fifteen mile. That's a fact.

The coachman making no reply, and plainly declining to enter into any controversy on a subject so far removed from his sympathies and feelings, another passenger says, "Yes, sir;" and the gentleman in the straw hat, in acknowledgment of his courtesy, says, "Yes, sir," to him in return. The straw hat then inquires of the brown hat whether that coach in which he (the straw hat) then sits is not a new one? To which the brown hat again makes answer, "Yes, sir."

STRAW HAT. I thought so. Pretty loud smell of varnish, sir?

BROWN HAT. Yes, sir.

ALL THE OTHER INSIDE PASSENGERS. Yes, sir.

BROWN HAT (to the company in general). Yes, sir.

The conversational powers of the company having been by this time pretty heavily taxed, the straw hat opens the door and gets out; and all the rest alight also. We dine soon afterwards with the boarders in the house, and have nothing to drink but tea and coffee. As they are both very bad, and the water is worse, I ask for brandy; but it is a Temperance Hotel, and spirits are not to be had for love or money. This preposterous forcing of unpleasant drinks down the reluctant throats of travellers is not at all uncommon in America, but I never discovered that the scruples of such wincing landlords induced them to preserve any unusually nice balance between the quality of their fare and their scale of charges: on the contrary, I rather suspected them of diminishing the one and exalting the other, by way of recompense for the loss of their profit on the sale of spirituous liquors. After all, perhaps, the plainest course for persons of such tender consciences would be, a total abstinence from tavern-keeping.

Dinner over, we get into another vehicle which is ready at the door (for the coach has been changed in the interval), and resume our journey; which continues through the same kind of country until evening, when we come to the town where we are to stop for tea and supper; and having delivered the mailbags at the Post Office, ride through the usual wide street, lined with the usual stores and houses (and drapers always having hung up at their door, by way of sign, a piece of bright red cloth), to the hotel where this meal is prepared. There being many boarders here, we sit down a large party, and a very melancholy one as usual. But there is a buxom hostess at the head of the table, and opposite, a simple Welsh schoolmaster with his wife and child; who came here, on a speculation of greater promise than performance, to teach the classics: and they are sufficient subjects of interest until the meal is over, and another coach is ready. In it we go on once more, lighted by a bright moon, until midnight; when we stop to change the coach again, and remain for half an hour or so in a miserable room, with a blurred lithograph of Washington over the smoky fireplace, and a mighty jug of cold water on the table: to which refinement the moody passengers do so apply themselves that they would seem to be, one and all, keen patients of Doctor Sangrado. Among them is a very little boy, who chews tobacco like a very big one; and a droning gentleman who talks arithmetically and statistically on all subjects, from poetry downwards; and who always speaks in the same key, with exactly the same emphasis, and with very grave deliberation. He came outside just now, and told me how that the uncle of a certain young lady who had been spirited away and married by a certain captain lived in these parts; and how this uncle was so valiant and ferocious that he shouldn't wonder if he were to follow the said captain to England, "and shoot him down in the street, wherever he found him;" in the feasibility of which strong measure I, being for the moment rather prone to contradiction, from feeling half asleep and very tired, declined to acquiesce: assuring him that if the uncle did resort to it, or gratified any other little whim of the like nature, he would find himself one morning prematurely throttled at the Old Bailey; and that he would do well to make his will before he went, as he would certainly want it before he had been in Britain very long.

On we go all night, and by and by the day begins to break, and presently the first cheerful rays of the warm sun, come slanting on us brightly. It sheds its light upon a miserable waste of sodden grass, and dull trees, and squalid huts, whose aspect is forlorn and grievous in the last degree. A very desert in the wood, whose growth of green is dank and noxious like that upon the top of standing water: where poisonous fungus grows in the rare footprint on the oozy ground, and sprouts like witches' coral from the crevices in the cabin wall and floor; it is a hideous thing to lie upon the very threshold of a city. But it was purchased years ago, and as the owner cannot be discovered, the State has been unable to reclaim it. So there it remains, in the midst of cultivation and improvements, like ground accursed, and made obscene and rank by some great crime.

We reached Columbus shortly before seven o'clock, and stayed there, to refresh, that day and night: having excellent apartments in a very large unfinished hotel called the Neill House, which were richly fitted with the polished wood of the black walnut, and opened on a handsome portico and stone veranda, like rooms in some Italian mansion. The town is clean and pretty, and of course is "going to be" much larger. It is the seat of the State legislature of Ohio, and lays claim, in consequence, to some consideration and importance.

There being no stage-coach next day upon the road we wished to take, I hired "an extra," at a reasonable charge, to carry us to Tiffin; a small town from whence there is a railroad to Sandusky. This extra was an ordinary four-horse stage-coach, such as I have described, changing horses and drivers, as the stage-coach would, but was exclusively our own for the journey. To insure our having horses at the proper stations, and being incommoded by no strangers, the proprietors sent an agent on the box, who was to accompany us the whole way through; and thus attended, and bearing with us, besides, a hamper full of savory cold meats, and fruit, and wine; we started off again, in high spirits, at half-past six o'clock next morning, very much delighted to be by ourselves, and disposed to enjoy even the roughest journey.

It was well for us that we were in this humor, for the road we went over that day was certainly enough to have shaken tempers that were not resolutely at Set Fair down to some inches below Stormy. At one time we were all flung together in a heap at the bottom of the coach, and at another we were crushing our heads against the roof. Now one side was down deep in the mire, and we were holding on to the other. Now the coach was lying on the tails of the two wheelers; and now it was rearing up in the air, in a frantic state, with all four horses standing on the top of an insurmountable eminence, looking coolly back at it, as though they would say, "Unharness us. It can't be done." The drivers on these roads, who certainly get over the road in a manner which is quite miraculous, so twist and turn the team about in forcing a passage, corkscrew fashion, through the bogs and swamps, that it was quite a common circumstance, on looking out of the window, to see the coachman, with the ends of a pair of reins in his hands, apparently driving nothing, or playing at horses, and the leaders staring at one unexpectedly from the back of the coach, as if they had some idea of getting up behind. A great portion of the way was over what is called a corduroy road, which is made by throwing trunks of trees into a marsh, and leaving them to settle there. The very slightest of the jolts with which the ponderous carriage fell from log to log was enough, it seemed, to have dislocated all the bones in the human body. It would be impossible to experience a similar set of sensations in any other circumstances, unless, perhaps, in attempting to go up to the top of St. Paul's in an omnibus. Never, never once, that day, was the coach in any position, attitude, or kind of motion to which we are accustomed in coaches. Never did it make the smallest approach to one's experience of the proceedings of any sort of vehicle that goes on wheels.

Still, it was a fine day, and the temperature was delicious, and though we had left Summer behind us in the west, and were fast leaving Spring, we were moving towards Niagara and home. We alighted in a pleasant wood towards the middle of the day, dined on a fallen tree, and leaving our best fragments with a cottager, and our worst with the pigs (who swarm in this part of the country like grains of sand on the seashore, to the great comfort of our commissariat in Canada), we went forward again gayly.

As night came on, the track grew narrower and narrower, until at last it so lost itself among the trees, that the driver seemed to find his way by instinct. We had the comfort of knowing, at least, that there was no danger of his falling asleep, for every now and then a wheel would strike against an unseen stump with such a jerk, that he was fain to hold on pretty tight and pretty quick, to keep himself upon the box. Nor was there any reason to dread the least danger from furious driving, inasmuch as over that broken ground the horses had enough to do to walk; as to shying, there was no room for that; and a herd of wild elephants could not have run away in such a wood with such a coach at their heels. So we stumbled along, quite satisfied.

These stumps of trees are a curious feature in American travelling. The varying illusions they present to the unaccustomed eye, as it grows dark, are quite astonishing in their number and reality. Now there is a Grecian urn in the centre of a lonely field; now there is a woman weeping at a tomb; now a very commonplace old gentleman in a white waistcoat, with a thumb thrust into each armhold of his coat; now a student poring on a book; now a crouching Negro; now a horse, a dog, a cannon, an armed man; a hunchback throwing off his cloak and stepping forth into the light. They were often as entertaining to me as so many glasses in a magic lantern, and never took their shapes at my bidding, but seemed to force themselves upon me, whether I would or no; and, strange to say, I sometimes recognized in them counterparts of figures once familiar to me in pictures attached to childish books, forgotten long ago.

It soon became too dark, however, even for this amusement, and the trees were so close together that their dry branches rattled against the coach on either side, and obliged us all to keep our heads within. It lightened, too, for three whole hours; each flash being very bright, and blue, and long; and as the vivid streaks came darting in among the crowded branches, and the thunder rolled gloomily above the tree-tops, one could scarcely help thinking that there were better neighborhoods at such a time than thick woods afforded.

At length, between ten and eleven o'clock at night, a few feeble lights appeared in the distance, and Upper Sandusky, an Indian village, where we were to stay till morning, lay before us.

They were gone to bed at the log-inn, which was the only house of entertainment in the place, but soon answered to our knocking, and got some tea for us in a sort of kitchen or common room, tapestried with old newspapers, pasted against the wall. The bedchamber to which my wife and I were shown was a large, low, ghostly room; with a quantity of withered branches on the hearth, and two doors without any fastening, opposite to each other, both opening on the black night and wild country, and so contrived that one of them always blew the other open: a novelty in domestic architecture which I do not remember to have seen before, and which I was somewhat disconcerted to have forced on my attention after getting into bed, as I had a considerable sum in gold, for our travelling expenses, in my dressing-case. Some of the luggage, however, piled against the panels, soon settled this difficulty, and my sleep would not have been very much affected that night, I believe, though it had failed to do so.

My Boston friend climbed up to bed somewhere in the roof, where another guest was already snoring hugely. But, being bitten beyond his power of endurance, he turned out again, and fled for shelter to the coach, which was airing itself in front of the house. This was not a very politic step as it turned out, for the pigs scenting him, and looking upon the coach as a kind of pie with some manner of meat inside, grunted round it so hideously, that he was afraid to come out again, and lay there shivering till morning. Nor was it possible to warm him when he did come out, by means of a glass of brandy; for in Indian villages, the legislature, with a very good and wise intention, forbids the sale of spirits by tavern-keepers. The precaution, however, is quite inefficacious, for the Indians never fail to procure liquor of a worse kind, at a dearer price, from travelling peddlers.

It is a settlement of the Wyandot Indians who inhabit this place. Among the company at breakfast was a mild old gentleman, who had been for many years employed by the United States Government in conducting negotiations with the Indians, and who had just concluded a treaty with these people by which they bound themselves, in consideration of a certain annual sum, to remove next year to some land provided for them west of the Mississippi, and a little way beyond St. Louis. He gave me a moving account of their strong attachment to the familiar scenes of their infancy, and in particular to the burial-places of their kindred; and of their great reluctance to leave them. He had witnessed many such removals, and always with pain, though he knew that they departed for their own good. The question whether this tribe should go or stay had been discussed among them a day or two before, in a hut erected for the purpose, the logs of which still lay upon the ground before the inn. When the speaking was done, the ayes and noes were ranged on opposite sides, and every male adult voted in his turn. The moment the result was known, the minority (a large one) cheerfully yielded to the rest, and withdrew all kind of opposition.

We met some of these poor Indians afterwards, riding on shaggy ponies. They were so like the meaner sort of gypsies, that if I could have seen any of them in England, I should have concluded, as a matter of course, that they belonged to that wandering and restless people.

Leaving this town directly after breakfast, we pushed forward again, over a rather worse road than yesterday, if possible, and arrived about noon at Tiffin, where we parted with the extra. At two o'clock we took the railroad; the travelling on which was very slow, its construction being indifferent, and the ground wet and marshy; and arrived at Sandusky in time to dine that evening. We put up at a comfortable little hotel on the brink of Lake Erie, lay there that night, and had no choice but to wait there next day, until a steamboat bound for Buffalo appeared. The town, which was sluggish and uninteresting enough, was something like the back of an English wateringplace out of the season.

Our host, who was very attentive and anxious to make us comfortable, was a handsome middleaged man, who had come to this town from New England, in which part of the country he was "raised." When I say that he constantly walked in and out of the room with his hat on; and stopped to converse in the same free-and-easy state; and lay down on our sofa, and pulled his newspaper out of his pocket, and read it at his ease; I merely mention these traits as characteristic of the country: not at all as being matter of complaint, or as having been disagreeable to me. I should undoubtedly be offended by such proceedings at home, because there they are not the custom, and where they are not, they would be impertinences; but, in America, the only desire of a good-natured fellow of this kind is to treat his guests hospitably and well; and I had no more right, and I can truly say no more disposition, to measure his conduct by our English rule and standard, than I had to quarrel with him for not being of the exact stature which would qualify him for admission into the Queen's Grenadier Guards. As little inclination had I to find fault with a funny old lady who was an upper domestic in this establishment, and who, when she came to wait upon us at any meal, sat herself down comfortably in the most convenient chair, and, producing a large pin to pick her teeth with, remained performing that ceremony, and steadfastly regarding us meanwhile with much gravity and composure (now and then pressing us to eat a little more), until it was time to clear away. It was enough for us that whatever we wished done was done with great civility and readiness, and a desire to oblige, not only here, but everywhere else; and that all our wants were, in general, zealously anticipated.

We were taking an early dinner at this house, on the day after our arrival, which was Sunday, when a steamboat came in sight, and presently touched at the wharf. As she proved to be on her way to Buffalo, we hurried on board with all speed, and soon left Sandusky far behind us.

She was a large vessel of five hundred tons, and handsomely fitted up, though with high-pressure engines; which always conveyed that kind of feeling to me which I should be likely to experience, I think, if I had lodgings on the first floor of a powder-mill. She was laden with flour, some casks of which commodity were stored upon the deck. The captain coming up to have a little conversation, and to introduce a friend, seated himself astride of one of these barrels, like a Bacchus of private life; and pulling a great clasp-knife out of his pocket, began to "whittle" it as he talked, by paring thin slices off the edges. And he whittled with such industry and hearty good-will, that but for his being called very soon, it must have disappeared bodily, and left nothing in its place but grist and shavings.

After calling at one or two flat places, with low dams stretching out into the lake, whereon were stumpy lighthouses, like windmills without sails, the whole looking like a Dutch vignette, we came at midnight to Cleveland, where we lay all night, and until nine o'clock next morning.

I entertained quite a curiosity in reference to this place, from having seen at Sandusky a specimen of its literature in the shape of a newspaper, which was very strong indeed upon the subject of Lord Ashburton's recent arrival at Washington, to adjust the points in dispute between the United States Government and Great Britain: informing its readers that as America had "whipped" England in her infancy, and whipped her again in her youth, so it was clearly necessary that she must whip her once again in her maturity: and pledging its credit to all True Americans, that if Mr. Webster did his duty in the approaching negotiations, and sent the English Lord home again in double-quick time, they should, within two years, sing "Yankee Doodle in Hyde Park, and Hail Columbia in the scarlet courts of Westminster!" I found it a pretty town, and had the satisfaction of beholding the outside of the office of the journal from which I have just quoted. I did not enjoy the delight of seeing the wit who indited the paragraphs in question, but I have no doubt he is a prodigious man in his way, and held in high repute by a select circle.

There was a gentleman on board, to whom, as I unintentionally learned through the thin partition which divided our stateroom from the cabin in which he and his wife conversed together, I was unwittingly the occasion of very great uneasiness. I don't know why or wherefore, but I appeared to run in his mind perpetually, and to dissatisfy him very much. First of all I heard him say: and the most ludicrous part of the business was, that he said it in my very ear, and could not have communicated more directly with me, if he had leaned upon my shoulder, and whispered me: "Boz is on board still, my dear." After a considerable pause he added, complainingly, "Boz keeps himself very close:" which was true enough, for I was not very well, and was lying down, with a book. I thought he had done with me after this, but I was deceived; for a long interval having elapsed, during which I imagine him to have been turning restlessly from side to side, and trying to go to sleep, he broke out again with, "I suppose *that* Boz will be writing a book by and by, and putting all our names in it!" at which imaginary consequence of being on board a boat with Boz, he groaned, and became silent.

We called at the town of Erie at eight o'clock that night, and lay there an hour. Between five and six next morning we arrived at Buffalo, where we breakfasted; and, being too near the Great Falls to wait patiently anywhere else, we set off by the train, the same morning at nine o'clock, to Niagara.

It was a miserable day; chilly and raw; a damp mist falling; and the trees in that northern region quite bare and wintry. Whenever the train halted, I listened for the roar; and was constantly straining my eyes in the direction where I knew the Falls must be, from seeing the river rolling on towards them; every moment expecting to behold the spray. Within a few minutes of our stopping, not before, I saw two great white clouds rising up slowly and majestically from the depths of the earth. That was all. At length we alighted: and then, for the first time, I heard the mighty rush of water, and felt the ground tremble underneath my feet.

The bank is very steep, and was slippery with rain and half-melted ice. I hardly know how I got down, but I was soon at the bottom, and climbing, with two English officers who were crossing and had joined me, over some broken rocks, deafened by the noise, half-blinded by the spray, and wet to the skin. We were at the foot of the American Fall. I could see an immense torrent of water tearing headlong down from some great height, but had no idea of shape, or situation, or anything but vague immensity.

When we were seated in the little ferry-boat, and were crossing the swollen river immediately before both cataracts, I began to feel what it was: but I was in a manner stunned, and unable to comprehend the vastness of the scene. It was not until I came on Table Rock, and looked—Great Heaven, on what a fall of bright green water!— that it came upon me in its full might and majesty.

Then, when I felt how near to my Creator I was standing, the first effect, and the enduring one— instant and lasting—of the tremendous spectacle, was Peace. Peace of Mind, tranquility, calm recollections of the Dead, great thoughts of Eternal Rest and Happiness: nothing of gloom or terror. Niagara was at once stamped upon my heart, an Image of Beauty; to remain there, changeless and indelible, until its pulses cease to beat, forever.

Oh, how the strife and trouble of daily life

receded from my view, and lessened in the distance, during the ten memorable days we passed on that Enchanted Ground! What voices spoke from out the thundering water; what faces, faded from the earth, looked out upon me from its gleaming depths; what Heavenly promise glistened in those angels' tears, the drops of many hues, the gorgeous arches which the changing rainbows made!

I never stirred in all that time from the Canadian side, whither I had gone at first. I never crossed the river again; for I knew there were people on the other shore, and in such a place it is natural to shun strange company. To wander to and fro all day, and see the cataracts from all points of view; to stand upon the edge of the Great Horseshoe Fall, marking the hurried water gathering strength as it approached the verge, yet seeming, too, to pause before it shot into the gulf below; to gaze from the river's level up at the torrent as it came streaming down; to climb the neighboring heights and watch it through the trees, and see the wreathing water in the rapids hurrying on to take its fearful plunge; to linger in the shadow of the solemn rocks three miles below; watching the river as, stirred by no visible cause, it heaved and eddied and awoke the echoes, being troubled yet, far down beneath the surface, by its giant leap; to have Niagara before me, lighted by the sun and by the moon, red in the day's decline, and gray as evening slowly fell upon it; to look upon it every day, and wake up in the night and hear its ceaseless voice: this was enough.

I think in every quiet season now, still do those

waters roll and leap, and roar and tumble, all day long; still are the rainbows spanning them, a hundred feet below. Still, when the sun is on them, do they shine and glow like molten gold. Still, when the day is gloomy, do they fall like snow, or seem to crumble away like the front of a great chalk cliff, or roll down the rock like dense white smoke. But always does the mighty stream appear to die as it comes down, and always from its unfathomable grave arises that tremendous ghost of spray and mist, which is never laid: which has haunted this place with the same dread solemnity since Darkness brooded on the deep, and that first flood before the Deluge—Light—came rushing on Creation at the word of God.

The River

JONATHAN RABAN

Jonathan Raban, born in Norfolk, England, in 1924, is a magazine writer whose earlier book, Arabia: A Journey through the Labyrinth, *prompted* New York Times *reviewer Anatole Broyard to declare "Raban a brilliant tragicomedian of traveling." Here, he confronts the Mississippi and measures that reality against a thirty-year-old dream.*

It is as big and depthless as the sky itself. You can see the curve of the earth on its surface as it stretches away for miles to the far shore. Sunset has turned the water to the color of unripe peaches. There's no wind. Sandbars and wooded islands stand on their exact reflections. The only signs of movement on the water are the lightly scratched lines which run in parallel across it like the scores of a diamond on a windowpane. In the middle distance, the river smokes with toppling pillars of mist which soften the light so that one can almost reach out and take in handfuls of that thickened air.

A fish jumps. The river shatters for a moment, then glazes over. The forest which rims it is a long, looping smudge of charcoal. You could make it by running your thumb along the top edge of the water, smearing in the black pines and bog oaks, breaking briefly to leave a pale little town of painted clapboard houses tumbling from the side of a hill. Somewhere in the picture there is the scissored silhouette of a fisherman from the town, afloat between the islands in his wooden pirogue, a perfectly solitary figure casting into what is left of the sun.

It is called the Mississippi, but it is more an imaginary river than a real one. I had first read *Huckleberry Finn* when I was seven. The picture on its cover, crudely drawn and colored, supplied me with the raw material for an exquisite and recurrent daydream. It showed a boy alone, his face prematurely wizened with experience. (The artist hadn't risked his hand with the difficulties of bringing off a lifelike Nigger Jim.) The sheet of water on which he drifted was immense, an enameled pool of lapis lazuli. Smoke from a half-hidden steamboat hung over an island of Gothic conifers. Cut loose from the world, chewing on his corncob pipe, the boy was blissfully lost in this stillwater paradise.

For days I lay stretched out on the floor of my attic room, trying to bring the river to life from its code of print. It was tough going. Often I found Huck's American dialect as impenetrable as Latin, but even in the most difficult bits I was kept at it by the persistent wink and glimmer of the river. I was living inside the book. Because I was more timid and less sociable than Huck, his and my adventures on the Mississippi tended to diverge. He would sneak off in a disguise to forage in a riverside town, or raid a wrecked steamboat; I would stay back on the raft. I laid troutlines for catfish. I floated alone on that unreal blue, watching for "towheads" and "sawyers" as the forest unrolled, a mile or more across the water.

I found the Mississippi in the family atlas. It was a great ink-stained Victorian book, almost as big as I was. "North Africa" and "Italy" had come loose from its binding, from my mother's attempt to keep up with my father's campaigns in the Eighth Army. North America, though, was virgin territory: no one in the family had ever thought the place worth a moment of their curiosity. I looked at the Mississippi, wriggling down the middle of the page, and liked the funny names of the places that it passed through. Just the sounds of Minneapolis . . . Dubuque . . . Hannibal . . . St. Louis . . . Cairo . . . Memphis . . . Natchez . . . Baton Rouge . . . struck a legendary and heroic note to my ear. Our part of England was culpably short of Roman generals, Indians and Egyptian ruins, and these splendid names added even more luster to the marvelous river in my head.

The only real river I knew was hardly more than a brook. It spilled through a tumbledown mill at the bottom of our road, opened into a little trout pool, then ran on through water meadows over graveled shallows into Fakenham, where it slowed and deepened, gathering strength for the long drift across muddy flatlands to Norwich and the North Sea. All through my Huckleberry Finn summer, I came down to the mill to fish for roach and dace, and if I concentrated really hard, I could see the Mississippi there. First I had to think it twice as wide, then multiply by two, then two again . . . The rooftops of Fakenham went under. I sank roads, farms, church spires, the old German prisoner-of-war camp, Mr. Banham's flour mill. I flooded Norfolk, silvering the landscape like a mirror, leaving just an island here, a dead tree there, to break this lonely, enchanted monotony of water. It was a heady, intensely private vision. I hugged the idea of the huge river to myself. I exulted in the freedom and solitude of being afloat on it in my imagination.

Year by year I added new scraps of detail to the picture. I came across some photographs of the Mississippi in a dog-eared copy of the *National Geographic* in a doctor's waiting room. Like inefficient pornography, they were unsatisfying because they were too meanly explicit. "Towboat *Herman Briggs* at Greenville" and "Madrid Bend, Missouri" gave the river a set of measurements that I didn't at all care for. I didn't want to know that it was a mile and a quarter wide, or that its ruffled water wasn't blue at all but dirty tan. The lovely, immeasurable river in my head was traduced by these artless images, and when the doctor called me in to listen to the noises in my asthmatic chest I felt saved by the bell.

Then I saw a painting by George Caleb Bingham. It showed the Missouri, not the Mississippi, but I recognized it immediately as my river. Its water had a crystalline solidity and smoothness, as if it had been carved from rosy quartz. The river and the sky were one, with cliffs and forest hanging in suspension between them. In the foreground, the ruffianly trapper and his son drifted in a dugout

271

canoe, their pet fox chained to its prow. The water captured their reflections as faithfully as a film. Alone, self-contained, they moved with the river, an integral part of the powerful current of things, *afloat* on it in exactly the way I had been daydreaming for myself. The French fur trader and his half-caste child joined Huck Finn—the three persons of the trinity which presided over my river.

Crouched under the willow below the mill, I lobbed my baited hook into the pool and watched the water spread. The Mississippi was my best invention; a dream that was always there, like a big friendly room with an open door into which I could wander at will. Once inside it, I was at home. I let the river grow around me until the world consisted of nothing except me and that great comforting gulf of water where catfish rooted and wild fruit hung from the trees on the towhead islands. The river was completely still as the distant shore went inching by. I felt my skin burn in the sun. I smelled sawn timber and blackberries and persimmons. I didn't dare move a muscle for fear of waking from the dream.

Now, thirty years later, the river was just a hundred miles ahead.

The road was empty—not a truck or a car in miles. If it hadn't been for the bodies of the dead raccoons, I might have taken my rented mustard Ford for the only thing on the move in the whole of Wisconsin. The coons had the dissolute repose of sleeping tramps, their splayed limbs hidden under rumpled coverlets of greasy fur. Poor coons.

Supremely talented, in a schoolboy way, at night exercises, at noisy raids on garbage cans, at climbing trees, they had no gift at all for crossing roads. Bright lights mesmerized them, and they died careless hobos' deaths on the wooded edges of tiny unincorporated towns.

Hunting for company, I twiddled my way through the burble on the radio.

"Good afternoon to all you Labor Day weekenders out there in northern Wisconsin. . . ." The announcer sounded like a naval captain in a 1950s movie, a honey-bass throbbing with authority and inner calm. "This is WWID, Ladysmith. Your Good News station."

The road sliced through a broken, hilly landscape of forest, corn and cattle. It had been like this for hours: the white-painted farms set back behind good fences, each one with its grain silo topped by an aluminum cone like a witch's hat, the long sweep of freshly harvested valleys reduced to hog's bristle, the slaughtered coons. No one about. In Goodrich and Antigo, Ruby, Bloomer and Cornell, there'd been the same Sunday somnolence in the standing heat.

At Goodrich I'd stopped for gas, and had had to wake the station's owner, who was asleep under the funnies section, framed between his ice chest and his Coke machine. "Shit," he'd said; then "Where you going?"—as if my presence on the highway were a violation of some Sunday blue law.

From the hillbilly fiddles, electric harmoniums and tabernacle choirs on the radio, a girl's voice broke through with manic brightness and clarity.

A song of peace, a song of joy,
A song for every little girl and boy,
A song that says, "God loves you!"

She dropped to a bedtime whisper. "God loves you," she crooned, while the strings and triangles went *hushabye, hushabye* in the background. "He really loves you." Stroking and snuggling her way into the hearts of the Labor Day weekenders, she said, "This isn't just a song for children, darling. Adults need love just as much, too." I squirmed in my car seat while she went on murmuring, *He loves you, He really loves you, He loves you,* and faded out, leaving the airwaves full of breathed kisses.

"Carol Lawrence," the announcer said. "Born-again Christian lady. 'Tell All the World About Love.' The love of God. That's what we're here to share on WWID, twenty-four hours a day, except for Monday mornings. Telling the Good News. And we tell everybody because faith comes by hearing it. We have to get it out. It's twenty-two before six."

Swaddled and babied by the Good News station, I drove on west. I was full of that receptive good humor which marks the beginnings of journeys—a time when everything is coated with the bloom of newness, and one's eyes and ears skitter like minnows, seizing excitedly on every humdrum scrap. A sleeping dog! They have sleeping dogs in Wisconsin! A pile of cut wood! They cut wood here! Look, cows! Look, a water tower! Look, a gas station! Everything shapes up to the same astonishing size. The Falcons had beaten the Saints, the Bears had beaten the Packers, a hurricane called David was making its way up the Florida coast. Key Biscayne had been evacuated. In Dominica, four hundred people sheltering in a church had been swept to death when a river changed its course. And a group called the Lonstroms were singing:

Well, I've found something that money can't buy,
I've found a gold mine beyond the blue sky,
I've found the land where I'll live when I die,
I've found the Lord—a rich man am I.

The cows were casting longer shadows now, and when the trees met over the road they formed a dark church nave. In the farmhouses, lights were coming on one by one, and their white barns were turning black against the sun. Connorsville. Forest. Somerset. New Richmond. Then the steep climb down into the valley of the St. Croix River.

"Christian witness. . . ." said the announcer. "Here's Len Mink." Len Mink was a sobbing tenor backed by a choir of lady angels.

I have returned to the God of my childhood,
To the same simple things as the child I once
knew;
Like the Prodigal Son, I long for my loved ones,
For the comforts of home and the God I outgrew.

He returned and returned and returned. He went back to the God of his father. He went back to the God of his mother. After half a dozen stanzas he was returning to "the Yahweh of Judah," his voice breaking down in the effort to recapture that lost Eden of the spirit. Finally he was shouting, "I have returned! I have returned! I have returned!" in an exultant, if implausible, carol from the womb.

Well, I was returning too. I had never quite given up dreaming of the river and still found comfort in the idea of that lovely, glassy sweep of open water. The rivers I fished, on weekend escapes from the city, were always shadowed by another, bigger river, broad and long enough to lose oneself on. Once, I'd actually seen the Mississippi, but it was from the window of a jet thirty thousand feet up, and the river looked as remote and theoretical as the twisty black thread in the family atlas. One sip of a Pan American highball, and it was gone.

Its afterimage lodged obstinately at the back of my head. In London, I had gone stale and dry. I felt that I'd run out of whatever peculiar reserves of moral capital are needed for city life. I couldn't write. For days on end I woke at five, confused and panicky, as the tranquilizers that I'd taken lost their grip. I listened to the jabbering sparrows in the yard and to the restless surf of overnight traffic on the road beyond. I lay clenched, struggling to get to sleep, and found myself thinking of the river, the great good place of my childhood. It was still just visitable. The dream was heavily overgrown now, and there were prohibitive signs and stretches of barbed wire to pass before one could get back to the old spot where the water spread away for miles, then dissolved into sky. Here, already half asleep, I let myself drift out into the current and watched the rising sun loom like a gigantic grapefruit through the mist.

Going down the river turned into an obsessive ritual. I had to relearn the child's trick of switching instantly into an imagined world. Soon I could work the magic with a few bare talismanic symbols—a curling eddy, a reedbed, an island, and a canister of photographer's smoke. It wasn't long before these daily dawn voyages began to suggest a real journey and a book.

The book and the journey would be all of a piece. The plot would be written by the current of the river itself. It would carry me into long deep pools of solitude, and into brushes with society on the shore. Where the river meandered, so would the book, and when the current speeded up into a narrow chute, the book would follow it. Everything would be left to chance. There'd be no advance reservations, no letters of introduction. I would try to be as much like a piece of human driftwood as I could manage. Cast off, let the Mississippi take hold, and trust to whatever adventures or longueurs the river might throw my way. It was a journey that would be random and haphazard; but it would also have the insistent purpose of the river current as it drove southward and seaward to the Gulf of Mexico.

It's hard to make travel arrangements to visit a dream. The voyage I was planning was on a river which existed only in my head. The real Mississippi was an abstraction. I studied it with impatience, feeling that the facts were just so many bits of grit in my vision of a halcyon river. I learned, without enthusiasm, about the construction of the lock-and-dam system. Figures began to swim in my head where the dream ought to be. In 1890, thirty million tons of freight had been carried downriver; in 1979, after a long and catastrophic decline in river trade, business was up again to forty million tons. The Civil War and the coming of the railroads had almost smashed the river as a commercial highway, but the oil crisis of the 1970s had brought the Mississippi back to life. A river barge, I read, "can move 400 tons of grain a mile on a gallon of fuel, compared with only 200 tons for a locomotive"; and a lot of people were now wanting to move a lot of tons of grain, because the United States had raised its quota of grain exports to Russia. So the port of New Orleans was busy with ships carting Midwestern wheat and corn and soybeans off to Murmansk and Archangel. To someone somewhere, I suppose, this kind of information has the ring of industrial piety; it didn't to me. It was reassuring to find that the river was important again, a central artery linking north and south in a drifting procession of towboats and barge fleets, but I found the details of its renascence grindingly dull. They threatened to contaminate that great, wide-open stretch of level water which was far more actual for me than these tawdry scraps of intelligence from the real world.

I went for long walks by the Thames, following the ebb tide as it ran out through Kew, Chiswick, Barnes, Putney, watching the way it piled against the bridges and came to the boil over deep muddy holes in the river bottom. It was the simple movement of the water that I liked, and its capacity to make the city which surrounded it look precarious and makeshift. The pastel cottages on the bank, with their bookshelves, net curtains, standing lamps and potted plants, stood on the lip of a real and dangerous wilderness. A freak tide, a careless shift in the current, and they could be swept away. The river, as it sluiced past their doorsteps, carried plenty of evidence of its deadliness. There were dead dogs in it, and shoved-in boats, and the occasional bloated human corpse. Once I found the body of a drowned woman. She was spread-eagled on the shore; her coat, of sodden leopard skin, had ridden up over her torso and covered her head. There were runs in her tights. Her boots were very new. At the coroner's inquest on her death, I heard that she'd left a note. It was rambling, disjointed, full of resentment and depression, but it didn't actually say that she intended to kill herself. It seemed rather that she had come to the river without knowing what she was going to do. Perhaps she believed that the mess and tangle of her life would somehow resolve itself if she could put it in perspective beside the bleak placidity of all that drifting water. It was probable, said the coroner, that she'd thrown herself into the river without premeditation; not really meaning to commit suicide, merely trying to assuage her misery and confusion in the comforting void of the Thames. He announced his verdict: death by misadventure.

I felt I understood what had drawn the woman to the river. I wanted to lose myself too. I had no intention of landing up in some small Midwestern city morgue, but I ached to run away from the world for a while, to put myself in the grip of a powerful current which would make my choices for me, to be literally adrift. The woman had gone to the river for solace, and had ended up drowning in it; I was going for much the same motive, but meant to stay afloat.

I hardly gave a thought to the mechanics of the voyage. It was, after all, a dream journey, and like a dream it was supposed to unfold spontaneously without effort on my part. Obviously I would need a craft of some kind, but I knew almost nothing at all about boats. A raft would turn the trip into a piece of quaint playacting; canoes capsized. I vaguely assumed that somewhere on the top end of the river I'd come across a leaky tub with a pair of oars, and cast off in that.

To make the voyage come true, I began to talk about it. At a party in London I met a man who had seen the Mississippi at St. Louis and had gone on a half-day tourist cruise up the river.

"It was amazingly depressing," he said. "Totally featureless. An awful lot of mud. You couldn't see anything over the top of the banks except dead trees. The only bearable thing about the entire afternoon was the ship's bar. It was full of people getting dead drunk so that they didn't have to look at the sheer bloody boredom of the Mississippi."

"That was just around St. Louis, though."

"Oh, it's all like that, I gather. That's what it's famous for, being very long and very boring. The only reason people ever go on the Mississippi at all is because after you've spent a couple of hours looking at that horrendous bloody river, even a dump like St. Louis starts to look moderately interesting. I think God made the Mississippi as a sort of warning, to prove that things really can be worse than you think."

He had an air of mighty self-satisfaction, having delivered me at a stroke from the lunatic fantasy with which I'd been possessed. Actually, I'd been rather excited by his description of the river. It had given it something of the melodramatic awfulness of a landscape by John Martin, a touch of *Sadek in Search of the Waters of Oblivion* with its dwarfish hominid scrambling into the world of treeless crags and dead seas.

"I suppose you thought you were going to do it in a *rowing* boat," the man said, snuffling with amusement at the notion. I didn't like the way he had consigned my trip to the past subjunctive tense.

"No, no. I'll have a . . . an outboard motor." I had had one experience with an outboard motor. I had driven myself from one end of a small Scottish loch to the other, where it had coughed and died. It had taken me three hours to row back through a rainstorm.

"You'd get swamped. Or be run down by one of those tow-things. When we were in St. Louis, people were always getting drowned in the river. Went out fishing, never came back, bodies recovered weeks later, or never recovered at all. So bloody common that it hardly ever made the local news."

Some days afterward, I ran into the man again.

"You're not still thinking of going down that river, are you?"

"I've written off about getting a motor."

"It'd cost you a hell of a lot less if you just swallowed a packet of razor blades. According to the Euthanasia Society, putting a plastic bag over your head is pretty much the best way to go." He introduced me to the woman he was with. "He's going to go down the Mississippi in a *dinghy*," he said.

"What a lovely thing to do," she said. "Just like Tom Sawyer—or was that Huckleberry Finn?"

The man smiled with exaggerated patience. It was the smile of a lonely realist stranded in the society of cloud-cuckoos.

That smile. I'd got used to it over the last few weeks. It said I was a jackanapes. Now, studying my route in the pale glow of the car map light, a scramble of lower-case names—*otisville, houlton, lakeland, hudson*—I imagined the smile broadening. In Minneapolis a boat was waiting for me. I was going to ride the river for as long and as far as I could go, and see whether it was possible to stitch together the imaginary place where I had spent too much of my time daydreaming and that other, real, muddy American waterway.

I was being interviewed by the radio pastor of WWID, Ladysmith.

"Have you said yes to Jesus yet?"

No.

"It's by His grace you're saved through faith. Exercise your faith and say, 'Lord, I'm receiving You as my Lord and Saviour.' "

My headlights picked out the twin marmalade eyes of a racoon in the road. I swerved just in time.

282

"Henry Slotter tells the news at nine, straight up, and then *Sunday Hymnsing* to follow, on this second of September, Labor Day Weekend. Now hear this. The Oklahoma Baptist Festival Choir. 'It Is Well with My Soul.' That says just about all that needs to be said, folks. It Is Well with My Soul . . ." The opening chords on an electric organ quivered with pious tremolo; then came the voices, the sopranos sounding as if they were crying for joy, the baritones and basses adding a counterpoint of moderation and common sense, as if getting on the right side of the Lord were just good business practice. I turned up the volume and joined the Interstate, singing my way into Minnesota along with the Oklahoma Baptist Festival Choir. After all, I was in no position to jeer at other people's dreams of personal salvation. I had my own hopes of becoming a born-again something, even if it wasn't a Christian. *It is well with my soul, pom, pom . . . well with my soul.*

I was jolted back into an America I recognized without affection. The bald glare of the sodium lights over the highway had flattened the landscape and robbed it of shadow and color. The exurban fringe of the twin cities of Minneapolis and St. Paul was the usual mess of neon doodles. Curlicues of mustard. Trails of ketchup. The motels, taco houses, Radio Shacks and Pizza Huts stretched away in a bilious blaze of American mock-Alpine. I remembered poring over the Victorian atlas, playing with the exotic syllables of Minneapolis as if they spelled Samarkand. Even now I wasn't quite prepared for the thoroughgoing charmlessness of this five-mile strip of junk food, porno movies and the kind of motels where you expect to find blood running down your shower curtain. There was a brief, merciful break of darkness. Then the illuminated crap began again.

It was only after I had gone on another mile or so that I realized I'd crossed the Mississippi. I had crossed the Mississippi. It had dropped through a crack in the lights of Minneapolis, and I hadn't even seen it go. The smile on the face of my London acquaintance would have been so superior that it would have joined up with his eyebrows in a perfect oval. It was a jackanapes' way of ending a pilgrimage and starting an odyssey.

I pushed on deeper into Minneapolis until I found myself driving up a street that felt like the heart of something. Hennepin Avenue. Louis Hennepin had been a seventeenth-century Franciscan friar who had been chaplain to the La Salle expedition which had charted the upper Mississippi in 1680. I'd just been reading about him in Francis Parkman's *La Salle and the Discovery of the Great West,* and was interested to see how his name had been commemorated here. Hennepin Avenue was blocked solid with gay bars, massage parlors, bright little boutiques with vibrators and dildos displayed in their windows, and the offices of pawnbrokers and bail bondsmen, now shuttered and padlocked for the night. Perhaps Father Hennepin had been an altogether merrier priest than Parkman had made him sound. Or perhaps the ruderies of Hennepin Avenue were intended to convey what Protestant Minnesota thought of foreign papists.

I stopped at a bar that looked and sounded

rather more straight than its neighbors: MOBY
DICK'S—FOR A WHALE-SIZED DRINK. Having just
missed out on one American epic by oversight,
I had better catch up with whatever classics I
could find. A few doors down the street, no doubt,
there'd be a sex shop called "The Scarlet Letter."

In the three-quarters dark, the walls of Moby
Dick's were bright with sweat. It was the kind of
place where all the loose ends of a city tend to
shake down together. A glazed-looking Indian in a
booth had a pitcher of beer for company. Two
blacks, wearing enviably sharp hats and suits with
lapels as narrow as switchblades, were feeding the
jukebox with quarters. At the bar, a drunk was
getting nowhere with the barmaid as he tried to
sweet-talk her into betting on the outcome of the
New England–Pittsburgh football game.

"Come on, honey. Just a little bet . . . a
gennelman's bet . . . Whaddaya say?"

On the TV screen above his head, someone
dressed up in medieval armor was running for a
touchdown.

"A *dollar*."

The barmaid squirted whiskey from a tube into
my glass.

"I said a *gennelman's* bet. One dollar. What's a
dollar between friends?" He sprawled across the
bar toward the girl in a sudden access of inspiration. "Hey . . . you can take Pittsburgh."

"Straight up or soda?" said the girl to me.

"Go on, what's a dollar?"

"Food, clothing and a place to sleep," I said.
Bob Hope had said that in a movie once.

The girl faced the drunk for the first time in minutes. "It's too early in the season. I ain't into the teams yet."

Defeated, he settled on me, grabbing at my sleeve as I started to leave the bar. "Where you from, fella? Where you from? I can tell you ain't from around here," he said with the triumphant cunning of a man who has got the better of half a bottle and can still pull off feats of amazing detection.

I headed for the empty booth next to the pickled Indian's.

"Hey, where you going? Where you going, fella?"

Far away, I hoped. South with the Monarch butterflies. Downstream.

Stapleton, Nebraska

BERTON ROUECHÉ

Berton Rouché: Born in Kansas City in 1911, Rouché was a newspaper reporter before joining the staff of The New Yorker *in 1944, where he is noted for his long continuing series "Annals of Medicine" on medical mysteries. His travel books include* What's Left: Reports on a Diminishing America *and* Sea to Shining Sea, *which is available in a large print edition as well. In his search for small town America, he visits Stapleton, Nebraska, and a way of life not frequently seen by travelers today.*

Stapleton, where I lived for a month, the month of May, is a crossroads county seat in the Sand Hills country of western Nebraska. It was founded in 1912, and it has a population of three hundred and three. The Sand Hills are grassy dunes. They are great, oceanic waves of sand with a carpeting of the rich native grass that nourished the buffalo—sand bluestem, prairie sand reed, sand lovegrass, switch grass, needle and thread. Briefly green in the short prairie spring, then brown and dry and blowing in the perpetual prairie wind, the Sand Hills form the largest natural cattle range in the United States. They cover all or much of twenty Nebraska counties. One of these, Cherry County, is bigger than Connecticut and Rhode Island combined. Logan County, of which Stapleton is the seat, is the smallest of the Sand Hills counties. It is roughly twice the size of Cape Cod. The Sand Hills grasslands are the quiddity of Stapleton. They surround and contain and sustain it. They also isolate it. Stapleton is the only town in Logan County. Its nearest neighbor is the village of Arnold (population 755), twenty miles away to the east, in Custer County. North Platte (population 19,287), the metropolis of western Nebraska, is twenty-nine miles to the south. Thedford (population 293) is thirty-six miles to the north, and a roadside hamlet called Tryon (population 166) is twenty-seven miles to the west. There is nothing between Stapleton and its neighbors—nothing at all. No roadhouses, no driveins, not even a filling station. There is only the long, empty highway and the range. Sometimes, in the distance, one can see a clump of trees and a windmill and a ranch house. The population of rural Logan County—that is, the county exclusive of Stapleton—is six hundred and ninety-one.

Stapleton is linked to its neighbors by two highways. They are U.S. Highway 83, the main north-and-south route in the area, and Nebraska Highway 92, running east and west. Both are single-lane blacktop highways, and they intersect at a right-angle crossing about half a mile east of the village. Stapleton stands in a windbreak grove of cottonwoods and Chinese elms, and can be only glimpsed from the intersection. Except in winter, when the leaves are down, travelers often pass it unawares. Highway 92 runs through the middle of Stapleton and is one of its two main streets, but Stapleton is not a highway village. It was differently designed. It was laid out as a railroad town. Stapleton came into being (on a section—or square mile—of land provided by two pioneer cattlemen) as the terminus of a branch line of the Union Pacific Railroad, and its second main street is Main Street, which runs north and south. Main Street is eighty feet wide and a half mile long, and it runs from one end of town to the other. It begins at the yellow clapboard Union Pacific Depot, at the north end, and it ends at the red brick Stapleton Consolidated School. There is a parade on Main Street every weekday morning (weather permitting) during the school year. This is part of the training of the Stapleton High School Band. The band marches—flags flying and drum majorettes strutting—out from the school and up to the depot and back. People come out of the Main Street stores and offices and stand and watch it go by.

Stapleton has always been a village. It has never been much larger than it is today. Once, round 1930, its population climbed as high as five hundred and one. The village is now a little smaller than it was at the time of the First World War. But Stapleton has the look of a town—an urban look. There are no wandering, cowpath streets, no straggle out along the highway. It is plotted in the urban gridiron pattern, and its limits are clearly defined. The backyards of the outermost houses all end at a barbed-wire fence, and beyond the fence is the range. Stapleton has several urban amenities. It has a municipal park with a tennis court and picnic ovens and picnic tables and benches. It maintains the county ambulance (the nearest hospitals are St. Mary's Hospital and Memorial Hospital, in North Platte), and the drivers, members of the fire department, are trained in first aid. It has a municipal waterworks and a municipal sewer system. Its telephone system is fully automatic, and the lines are laid underground. Most of the streets are lighted and paved, and the paved streets all have sidewalks. The streets are named in the functional urban fashion. The north-south streets—the streets that parallel Main Street—are named for the letters of the alphabet. There are ten of these streets—A Street through J Street. (Main Street runs between F and G.) The other streets are numbered. They run from First Street, at the depot, to Sixth Street, at the school. Highway 92 is known formally as Third Street. There are, however, no street signs in Stapleton, and (except for Main Street) the street names are never used. The intersection of Main Street and Highway 92 is usually called the Corner.

Most Stapletonians are born in a North Platte hospital, and almost all of them are buried in one or another of three Logan County cemeteries— McCain, St. John's, and Loup Valley. Loup Valley Cemetery is the smallest and the most remote. It lies in a fold in the range about ten miles west of Stapleton, on the road to Tryon. St. John's, a Roman Catholic cemetery that was consecrated in 1915, and McCain are both just east of town, on the road that leads to Arnold. McCain is the largest of the three cemeteries, and by far the oldest. It was established (as the gift of the widow of a pioneer named Robert McCain) in 1884, and it occupies four acres on a hilltop planted with bushy box elders and big, spreading cedars. It offers a commanding view of the surrounding countryside, and also of the past. A majority of the early settlers (and the founders of the established local families) are buried there: Miller, Burnside, Hartzell, Clark, Wheeler, Smith, Wells, Bay, Perry, Erickson, Abrams, Joedeman, Salisbury, Loudon. Many of the pioneers were veterans of the Civil War, all having served with the Union Army. The notations on their headstones are geographically descriptive: "Co. C, 9 Ohio Calvary"; "Co. A, 81 Pa. Infantry"; "Co. H, 71 N.Y. Infantry"; "10 Indiana Cav."; "Co. F, 86 Ill. Inf."; "Co. D, 1st Iowa Calvary"; "Co. E, 5th Iowa Infantry." Except for an elaborate white marble shaft commemorating Robert McCain, and one or two other monumental monuments, the headstones are modest tablets. A few are inscribed with conventional pieties ("Though thou art done, fond mem'ry clings to thee"), but most of them carry only a name and a date. The given names of the men are equally conventional: Joseph, William, Richard, John, Edward. The given names of the women at McCain, and also at Loup Valley (though not, of course, at St. John's), are more imaginative. Some of them are wildly so: Melita, Alvirda, Glenola, Vernie Lynn, Tressa, Verla, Idara, Delma, Velna, Zetta, Uhleen, Berdie, Zella, Lesta, Verga, Lenna, Jacobina, Dalorus, Talitha, Caline, Mayden, Sedona, Orpha, Doralie, Urah. These names are not, as I at first supposed, the fancies of a vanished generation. Such names are still popular in Stapleton. A

291

high-school senior I met is named Vaneta. One of her classmates is named Wilda. A first grader, about whom I read, is named Jeanna. A second grader is named Tena. There is a sixth grader named Kerri. And the first name of Mrs. Robert A. Perry, the wife of a prominent Logan County rancher, is Alta May.

Practically everybody in Stapleton lives on the south side of town. There are only five families on the north side of the highway. The churches—Presbyterian, Catholic, and Assembly of God—all are in the residential area. The First Presbyterian Church—the largest and oldest of the Stapleton churches—and the fundamentalist Assembly of God are both on Main Street, south of the Corner, and St. John's Catholic Church is a block to the west. There is plenty of space in Stapleton (there are vacant lots on every block), but most of the homes are built on fifty-foot plots. "The Sand Hills is a big country," James Morey, a farmer who now lives in town, told me. "If you ever homesteaded up on the Dismal River, like I did, you'd know what I'm talking about. People like company. They like to have close neighbors." Some of the houses are brick, some are asbestos shingle, and some are clapboard painted white, but they are otherwise much alike. The usual house has one story, with a little stepped stoop and a low-pitched pyramidal roof. The chairman of the Board of Trustees, the governing body of Stapleton—a retired (and reputedly well-to-do) merchant and landowner named John Beckius—lives in such a house, and so does Mrs. Vivian Nelson, a laundress. The biggest house in town is the Catholic rectory. Most of the houses have flower and vegetable gardens, and the lawns are often strangely ornamented. Some people move old, axe-handled backyard pumps around to the front and paint them in bright colors. Many people cut openings in plastic Clorox bottles and hang them up as houses for purple martins. People also paint old coffeepots and teakettles and hang them in groups from poles and plant them with geraniums and petunias and marigolds. The garage of one house has a garden of cabbage-size pink roses and giant blue delphiniums painted on an outside wall. "That wall goes back to our painting fad," Mrs. Earl Glandon, an amateur artist and the wife of a former postmaster, told me. "A professional artist came to town for a while and gave painting lessons, and there were about fourteen ladies that joined the class. One of the ladies painted the garage wall. Another lady, a widow lady, heard about a famous old sod house out south of town somewhere, and she went there and painted a picture of it, and a little later the man who owned the sod house asked her about the picture, and she invited him over to see it, and he came and they got friendly and he married her. He moved her into his sod house, and the first thing she did was to paint it. She painted wisteria around the door and morning glories climbing up the walls of the house. It was like that garage. She made it look more cheerful."

The main business block in Stapleton is Main Street just north of the Corner. It is a sun-baked block in summer—the only block of Stapleton without a twilit canopy of trees—but the sidewalks in front of some of the buildings are shaded by metal awnings. Most of the buildings on the block are one-story buildings of red or yellow brick. About half of them have high false fronts. There are two vacant buildings on the block. One is an old store full of broken fixtures. The other is a boarded-up movie house. It went out of business in 1955, but there is a painted-over name still visible on the façade: "The New Theater." The block contains six stores. Three of them are grocery stores (Black's Thriftway Grocery, Denny's Market, and Ewoldt's Grocery & Locker), and there is a hardware store (Hanna's Supply), a feed store (Miller Ranch Supply), and a farm-equipment store (Salisbury Implement Company). All of them are more or less general stores. Ewoldt's is almost a department store. It occupies three rooms on the ground floor of a two-story building that was once the Hildenbrandt Hotel (there are twenty-one numbered rooms, including a bridal suite, on the second floor), and it sells—along with meats and groceries—drugs, cosmetics, notions, toys, memorial wreaths, school supplies, work clothes, boots, big hats, and ice. The other business buildings on the block are a laundromat (Bud's Holiday Laundry), a bowling alley (Bronco Bowl), the Stapleton *Enterprise* (a weekly paper), and the Bank of Stapleton. There is also a two-story (with a false front) Masonic Temple, and an American Legion Post. The bank is on the northwest corner of the Corner, and it is the most imposing building on the block. It is a square brick building with ornamental cornices and glass-brick windows and a high, pedimented roof. Along the highway side is a two-rail iron-pipe railing. On Saturday afternoons, there are usually a couple of cowboys sitting there with their heels hooked over the bottom rail and their hats tipped down on their noses.

The Stapleton Post Office, a red brick building that somewhat resembles the bank, is on the southwest corner of the Corner. Across Main Street from the post office is Chesley's Barber Shop. "I've only got one complaint," Everette C. Chesley, the barber, told me. "It isn't about long hair. The kids around here don't wear their hair what I would call short, but they do come in and get haircuts. My complaint is shaves. I used to shave maybe fifteen fellows of a Saturday. The last time I shaved a fellow was an old man two months ago. I might as well get rid of my razors. A razor is like an arm or a leg. It goes dead unless you use it." Next door to the barbershop is the Logan County Courthouse. The courthouse was built in 1963 and is the newest building in Stapleton. It is an L-shaped building faced with polished pink granite, with a flagpole in front and a parking lot and an acre of well-kept lawn. There is a little cluster of businesses up around the depot. The office and storage bins of the Stapleton Mill & Elevator Co. are there, and a feed lot, and two lumberyards —the S. A. Forest Lumber Company and the Greenslit Lumber Company. Their yards are stacked with big round metal water troughs and creosoted fence posts and spools of barbed wire. (In Stapleton, as everywhere else west of Pittsburgh, barbed wire is "bob wire"). Except for two living-room beauty parlors—one (Dotti's Beauty Salon) on the west side of town and the other

(Beauty Shop) in a house near the school—the other Stapleton businesses are all situated on the highway. Just west of the Corner are a beer bar and liquor store (Wagon Wheel Tavern) and a Rural Electrification Administration garage. East of the Corner are a farm-equipment store (Magnuson Implement Company), two filling stations (East Side Skelly Service and A. A. Gulf Service), the fire station, and the Whiteway Cafe & Motel.

"My wife and I took over the newspaper in nineteen sixty," Arthur French, the publisher of the *Enterprise*, told me. "We came over from Tryon. Tryon is pretty little, and it's also pretty staid. Stapleton is more like a town. When we first arrived here, there were maybe a few more business places than there are now. There was another cafe and a drugstore. But they were mostly run by older people with their money down deep in their pockets. They was just setting there. Now all the stores have younger people in charge. Dick Black at the Thriftway and Elwin Miller at the Ranch Supply and Dick Kramer at the Skelly station, they're just in their twenties, and Alfred Ewoldt isn't very much older. Neither is Dean Hanna, at the Gulf station. I'm still under forty myself. Even Ed Burnham—Edwin H. Burnham, the president of the bank and I guess you could say our leading citizen. He has the insurance agency there at the bank and he owns a lot of property and he has a big interest in the elevator and he's building himself a new fifty-thousand-dollar home out east of town. Even Ed is only about fifty. Ed believes in Stapleton, and he'll put up money to prove it. Ed gave me my start here with a very generous loan. We've also got a real nice Chamber of Commerce, with thirty-five members, and I think we've got a future. Our only problem is getting help. I could use another man in our printshop, and I had a fellow lined up down in the Platte. He drove up with his wife one day. They made a couple of passes around town and then came into the shop and the wife said, 'I didn't see the shopping center. Where is it?' I said we didn't have a shopping center here. 'Let's go,' she said."

The name of Edwin H. Burnham is often heard in Stapleton. He is not always in residence there (during my stay he was sojourning at a hunting lodge he has in Canada), but his presence is constantly felt. "Our banker is the pleasantest man you ever saw," Charles V. Greenslit, the owner of the lumberyard that bears his name, told me. "Hail fellow well met. Always smiling. Generous. Gave our village an ambulance. Gives to all the churches. Our old banker—the man who brought Ed Burnham here—he was just the opposite. He was conservative. He was the kind of banker who wouldn't think of making a loan unless you hardly needed the money. Burnham's happy to help anybody. And he's done well for himself. Real well. Everything he touches turns to money. I sometimes wonder how he does it. He's never here. But he's building himself a sixty-thousand-dollar home out east of town. So maybe he's planning to settle down." Everybody seems to think well of Burnham. "Ed Burnham is a real asset," Leslie M. Bay, the county judge, told me. "When we were getting ready to build the new courthouse, he got us a big bond break. He bid our building bonds down to three percent, and then stepped back and let somebody else bid them in at two point eight-five percent. One of our problems here is housing. Ed won't let a house fall down. He'll fix it up and put it back to work. He's always finding an old house out in the county somewhere and moving it into town. Right now, he's building himself a nice new home on some land he owns out east of here. I understand it's costing him in the neighborhood of seventy-five thousand dollars. Of course, Ed has improved himself. He's made a lot of money. But you'd never know he had a dime. He's a common as an old shoe. He'd just as soon set down and drink a bottle of beer as not. Wherever he's at, that's where he is. Ed's at home anywhere. He's a rancher out at your ranch. In Rome, he's a Roman."

The Whiteway was my home in Stapleton. I had a room (with a big springy bed and a rocking chair and a table) in the Motel, and I took my meals at the Cafe. The Cafe occupies the front end of a long, narrow, shingle-sided building with a low, overhanging roof all around and a gravelly unpaved parking lot on three sides. The Motel is in back, behind the kitchen, and overlooks a chicken yard patrolled by three excitable roosters. It consists of five rooms (with baths) and the apartment of the manager. The Whiteway is owned by a woman in Hooker County, and it is leased from her by a Logan County farmer named James Wonch. (Wonch is a powerful man with a shaven head and dark-brown eyes. I had been in Stapleton about a week before I met him, and I was strangely struck by his appearance. There was something unusual about his looks that I couldn't quite identify. I thought at first that is must be the shaven head— and then I realized. The unusual thing was his eyes. Almost everybody in Stapleton—everybody but Wonch and one or two others—has blue eyes.) The manager of the Whiteway is a plump, pretty, white-haired widow (with blue eyes) named Clarice Olson, and she also does most of the cooking and all of the baking at the Cafe. "I open up at about six-thirty, and we close at night when the last customer gets up and leaves," Mrs. Olson told me. "That's usually around ten o'clock. Our people come in for breakfast, for second breakfast, for midmorning coffee, for noon dinner, for afternoon coffee, for supper, and for evening coffee. There's usually somebody waiting when I open up in the morning. Most of the time, it's Red Black. Red and his wife both work for the county. He's a road grader, and she cleans at the courthouse. Red drives her to work and then comes around for his coffee. Half the time, he opens the door for me. Then he sits and watches me get my baking started. I bake two dozen cinnamon rolls every morning, and about a half a dozen pies. Always apple, always cherry, and either lemon or chocolate meringue. Sometimes I make a few doughnuts. Then I get dinner started. My first dinner customer is Vera Gragg, one of the tellers at the bank. She comes in at eleven-thirty, on the dot. They're my most regular customers—Vera and Red Black." Mrs. Olson's daughter, a divorcée named LaDonna Wisdom, is the regular Cafe waitress, and a young girl named Grace Young helps out when needed.

For much of my stay, I was the only traveler at the Motel, but the Cafe was almost always crowded. There were always a couple of cars pulled up in front (nobody in Stapleton ever walks anywhere), and usually a dusty pickup truck from one of the farms or ranches. The Cafe is the social center of Stapleton. Almost everybody in town drops in at some time almost every day. One Sunday afternoon, I counted a dozen cars parked there. Three of them were Cadillacs.

The Cafe is a clean and comfortable cafe. It is warm in cold weather and icily air-conditioned in summer, and the three outer walls are windows. There are six cream-and-gold Formica tables around the window walls, and a counter with five stools across the back. A door at one end of the counter opens into a private dining room that will accommodate about twenty diners. The Chamber of Commerce holds its monthly dinner meetings there. There is a soda fountain behind the counter (with a display of candy bars and chewing gum and foil-wrapped bandoleers of Alka-Seltzer), but the cooking is all done in the kitchen. There is a jukebox the size of an organ near the dining-room door, with an automated repertoire of "Lonesome Highway" and "Sugar Shack" and a hundred other country-and-Western tunes. There is a Coca-Cola machine and a Dr Pepper machine and a cigarette machine. There is a bulletin board on the wall near the jukebox with a calendar ("Compliments Central Nebraska Commission Co., Broken Bow, Nebr., Cattle Sale Every Saturday") and an assortment of bulletins ("Wanted: Write-in-Votes for Joe Klosen"; "Midwest Breeders Cooperative: Beef

& Dairy Semen, Liquid Nitrogen, A-I Supplies";
"The Last Pages—for booking, call Steven Myers,
Bill Dolan, Doug Wallace, N. Platte"; "Bull Sale,
Ogallala Sale Barn, Ogallala, Nebr.: 39 Angus, 2
Charolais, 45 Herefords, 5 Shorthorns") and a
motto ("No Man Is Good Enough to Govern Another Without the Other's Consent"). There is a
blackboard menu on the wall behind the counter
with one permanent entry: "Roast Beef, $1.40."
Other entries that appear on the board from time
to time are "Scalloped Potatoes & Ham, $1.25"
and "Salmon Loaf, $1.25." The roast beef is pot
roast. Steak is never listed on the menu but is
always available, and it is always cut thin and
always chicken-fried. There is a sign near the
blackboard: "Margarine Served Here." The bread
is Rainbo Bread.

One rainy morning, I lingered over breakfast at
the Cafe. I sat at a window table and ate fried eggs
and thick pancakes and watched the cars pull in
and out and the customers come and go. Several
of the cars had little decal American flags on the
windows, and one had a bumper sticker: "Trust
in Christ." Some sparrows were nesting under the
eaves of the Cafe, and they flew from car to car,
feeding on the insects shattered on the radiator
grilles. I knew some of the customers by name
and most of the others by sight. There were three
R.E.A. technicians in cowboy hats and boots.
There was Alfred Ewoldt in cowboy boots and a
hunting cap. There was a young cowboy in a
sweatshirt with lettering across the back: ". . . and
a Follower of Women." There was an elderly
farmer in bib overalls matching double or nothing

for coffee with the waitress, LaDonna Wisdom. There was the county judge, Judge Bay, with a lump of snuff under his lower lip, and Mrs. Thomas Mahoney, the village clerk and the wife of a Union Pacific conductor. There were two school-bus drivers (of a total of nine)—Mrs. Beverly Lehmkuhler, a widow, and Mrs. Norman Yardley, the wife of the high-school principal— eating a second breakfast; they rise early to circle the county and bring the students in to school. There was Mrs. Noma Wells, the widow of a merchant and landowner, who spends much of her time driving around town in a saffron-yellow Cadillac. (Her car is one of five Cadillacs in Stapleton, and there are also three new Lincoln Continentals.) There was a thin girl in jeans and a T-shirt. There was James Wonch. There was a tall, stooped, flat-bellied cowboy in a rodeo shirt with the sleeves cut off at the shoulders. There was James Morey, the former Dismal River home- steader, with an old black hat on the back of his head, talking to the other waitress, Grace Young. I sat and looked and listened.

James Morey: How about you and me having a date sometimes?
Grace Young: I don't go out with old whiskery men.
James Morey: I could shave. But have I got a chance? I ain't going to shave in the middle of the week unless there's at least a chance.

Mrs. Lehmkuhler: The first one I picked up this morning brought me an apple. And another one gave me some fudge. They're going to get me fat.

James Wonch: It's a funny thing. My dad used to walk to school. I rode a horse. But all my kids have to do is stand and wait for the bus.

LaDonna Wisdom: One week, I cut down eating and I gained five pounds. When I stepped on the scales, I was real disgusted. So I went back to eating.

Elderly Farmer: I'll match you for one of them rolls.

R.E.A. Man: Marijuana?

Second R.E.A. Man: They call it pot. It looks like it's moving this way. They say the kids have got it at Broken Bow.

Third R.E.A. Man: We used to call it Mary Jane.

Mrs. Mahoney: I don't know about the Platte. But they've never had to draft a boy from here. Or from Tryon. Or from Arnold, for that matter.

Girl in the T-Shirt: No, I've just got the two. But I was married at fifteen and I'm only eighteen now and I'm not going to have no more. For a while, anyway. I will say this. I never had no trouble having any of my kids. The girl next to me the last time, she had a Cesarean. My second baby, he's ten months now, but a couple of months ago he couldn't sit up or anything. He had the rickets. They started giving him lots of vitamins, and now he can sit and everything real good.

Mrs. Wells: I'm washing at Bud's this morning, so while I'm working I thought I'd have some coffee.

Mrs. Mahoney: LaDonna, I came away this morning without any matches. Have you got some?

LaDonna Wisdom: Here—can you catch?

Mrs Mahoney: I catch real good. When you've got a boy in the Boy Scouts working on merit badges, you can do a lot of things. I can tie knots and make a fire and talk in the Morse code. I can do a hundred things I never wanted to do.

Mrs. Yardley: Be glad you haven't got a daughter. Mine has been practicing for the 4-H cake demonstration, and she ended up in the kitchen last Saturday with eighteen sponge cakes.

Judge Bay: It don't blow every day, but then it blows twice the next day to make up for it.

Mrs. Mahoney: . . . sewing on Sunday. My mother would have said that I'll never get to Heaven until I stop and take those stitches out with my nose. She also used to say that you haven't learned to sew until you've learned to rip.

The cowboy in the sleeveless shirt got up to go, and stopped and looked at me, and then came over. "Excuse me," he said. "But you look mighty familiar to me. I wonder haven't I seen you someplace before. Where are you from?"

I told him that I lived in New York.

"That could be it," he said. "I could have seen you there. I used to travel—before and after the service. My feet have been on every soil in the continental United States and the world. Except only Russia. I used to speak fourteen different languages, but I didn't keep it up. Now I've only got but one. Well, *choco-chuco-mungo-mango-boola-mack*."

"What?" I said.

"That's Indian for 'see you later,' " he said.

I was ready to leave, too. I pushed back my chair and put a tip on the table ("You don't have to do that every time," LaDonna said), and paid my bill, and followed the cowboy out. My breakfast, including orange juice and coffee, cost sixty cents.

The Cafe is not exclusively an adult gathering place. It also serves as the corner drugstore for the teenage boys of Stapleton. There are a few boys hanging around nearly every evening, but their big night there is Friday night. They drift up after supper in their dress-up clothes—clean, faded bluejeans, two-toned high-heeled boots with fancy stitching, big hats (felt in winter, straw in summer), and brightly patterned shirts with double pockets and snaps for buttons. Most of the boys have cars (drivers are licensed at sixteen in Nebraska), and they lean against the parked cars in front of the Cafe and kick gravel and wrestle and yell to each other ("Hey Larry—where's Kramer and those guys?") and stomp inside and play the jukebox and get Cokes and come shoving out and trade arm punches, and the boys with dates drive up and the others flock around and make jokes ("Hey, is that a new shirt, or is that a new shirt?"), and the girls in the cars laugh and comb their hair and shriek back and forth, and every now and then a car with a couple in it will start up abruptly ("Watch him lay some rubber now. He's put fifty thousand miles on those tires and half of it is just in starts") and take off down the highway and after a while come roaring back and park again and sit and then suddenly charge off once more, with the radio thumping and twanging, and this time the car will head out toward U.S. 83 and Arnold, or west toward Tryon, and pretty soon all the couples are gone and the jukebox stops and the Cafe lights go out, and then the car doors begin to slam and the engines race and the remaining cars move off and up to the depot and down past the school and home.

The courthouse is the office building of Stapleton. It houses around a dozen village, county, state, and federal offices. The village clerk and the village marshal; the county clerk, the county treasurer, the county (or probate) judge, the county welfare director, the county Board of Commissioners (executive body concerned with taxes, roads, budgets, assessments), and the county sheriff; the state Agricultural Extension Service representative (or county agent); and two agencies of the United States Department of Agriculture—all have offices there. The building also houses a courtroom (with jury room and chambers for the visiting district judge at his quarterly sessions), a jail (with two cells), a local-history museum, and a public library.

The museum is an accretion of odds and ends (a wooden lemon press, an 1807 edition of the Bible, two shaving mugs, a pair of "Driving Gloves worn by E. R. Smith when he drove the second car in Logan County in 1907," a blue glass ball stamped "Harden's Hand Grenade Fire Extinguisher Pat. 1981") arranged in a case in the courtroom foyer, but the library is a substantial one. It has an annual budget for books of five hundred dollars, and an accessible collection of some thirty-four thousand books, including a shelf of standard Nebraska authors—Willa Cather, Mari Sandoz, John G. Neihardt, Bess Streeter Aldrich. It is an active library, and the children are introduced to it at an early age through a weekly story hour conducted by volunteer readers. Some women drive in with their children from distant ranches for the weekly reading. ("This is a real conservative community," Charles Hunnel, the superintendent of the Stapleton school, told me. "The people here believe very highly in education. Our annual budget at the school is over two hundred thousand dollars. That's almost half the total tax income of the county. We have a very high educational level. More than half of our high-school graduates go on to college, and we have practically no dropouts. In my seven years in this job, we've had just two—two girls dropped out to get married. We haven't produced any geniuses. It isn't an intellectual community. But there's a real respect for learning.") The librarian is a widow named Florence L. Brown. Mrs. Brown is also something of a local historian. "People are always asking me where Stapleton got its name," she told me. "Well, I finally found out. I found an editorial in a copy of the *Enterprise* for October 17, 1912, that explained everything. I made a copy for the library, and here it is. Sit down and read it." It read:

Mr. D. C. Stapleton has for the past thirty years felt an abiding interest and faith in the future of central western Nebraska, and while his larger interests have called him abroad for the greater part of the time, for several years past, he has never lost sight of the fact that out here in Nebraska was the place of all the rest he could call "home," for it was here he homesteaded in the year 1884 and it was in recognition of his high ideals of what western Nebraska ought to be and do, and his constant efforts toward that goal that this city was named "Stapleton" in his honor.

There is no crime in Stapleton. People leave the keys in their cars and the doors of their houses unlocked. Don Vetter, the village marshal, wears a policeman's blue cap, but he is only nominally a peace officer. His main job is operating the water plant, the sewage plant, and the dump. Law and order is formally represented in Stapleton by the Logan County sheriff. The sheriff is a big, comfortable man of sixty-two with a star on his shirt and a smile on his face and a revolver in a drawer of his desk. His name is Arthur Wiley, and he has been sheriff since 1954. "Order is no problem here," he told me. "This is a peaceable town.

Nobody crowds anybody. There's plenty of lee-way. A man has got the freedom to go out and holler if he wants to. Law is what I'm mostly concerned with. I mean summonses and traffic offenses and things like that. No local boy has ever got in serious trouble in my time in office. Once in a while, I break up a fight at the bar. That's usually August, when we have our fair and rodeo and some cowboy pours a glass of beer down some other guy's neck. We've never in history had a murder here. I did get shot up once. A couple of kids started out at Imperial—down south of Ogallala—breaking into places and stealing what they wanted. This was in 1961, in the wintertime, with snow on the ground. Well, they came into town here one night and broke into Ewoldt's store. Ewoldt lives upstairs, but they didn't know that, and he heard them messing around and called me at home, and I came driving up and caught them up by the depot. They were in their sock feet, trying on a bunch of cowboy boots they'd stole. Their car was full of fancy shirts and Stetson hats and forty-dollar boots—all kinds of cowboy stuff. I got them out of their car and had the driver standing with his hands on the roof in the regular way, and I was frisking him. Well, all of a sudden the other boy came around the car, and when I looked up he had a revolver in his hand. I slipped behind the driver. My gun was an old .351 auto-matic—what they call a riot gun. I told the boy to drop that revolver. But the driver gave a jump and pushed up my gun, and before I could get it back in position the other boy fired his revolver. I didn't know how he missed me, but he did. He hit the driver instead—hit him in the arm. My gun was ready then, and I fired and hit him at the belt, on the buckle, and staggered him against the car. I told him to drop his gun. But he didn't. He up and shot me. Shot me in the left side, and the bullet went through both lobes of my liver. All I felt was like a hot poker or something touching me there. But I dropped my gun and sat down in a snowdrift. The boys jumped back in their car and made to drive off. But before they more than got started I reached around and found my gun and fired and shot out their front tire. The driver jumped out yelling and put his hand up—his good hand. But the other one, he was still acting up. He called me a dirty s.o.b. and a lot worse, and started shooting at me again. So I did the same. He was leaning over the top of the car, and my first shot only hit the shoulder padding of his coat. Then I shot into the car and blew out the windows in his face. He couldn't see with all that glass flying, but I didn't feel like shooting anymore, and Don Vetter came running up, and that was it. They hauled the three of us off to the hospital at North Platte to get patched up. I was laid up there for quite a few weeks. One of the boys turned out to be fourteen years old, and the other one was fifteen. They both got something like eighteen months of correction. The boy that did all the shooting, he came out and turned into a pretty solid citizen. I understand he's never given anybody any more trouble. But the other boy—I don't know. I never heard."

The principal business of the courthouse is the

farms and ranches of Logan County. Their needs and responsibilities make up most of the routine work of the county clerk and the county treasurer and the county judge and the county commissioners, and they are the entire concern of the county agent and the two Department of Agriculture agencies. The Logan county agent is also the county agent of McPherson County, the neighboring county on the west. This gives him a district almost the size of Delaware. He is a crewcut young man with a faraway look, named Edmond A. Cook. "This is conservative country," he told me. "There are progressive people—people who adapt to the modern world—but the other kind are still around. 'Conservative' isn't really the right word. The people I mean are rigid. They're self-sufficient and individualistic. They still have the pioneer mentality. Their grandfathers *were* the pioneers out here. Well, a county agent is an educator. My job is to take the research information from the experimental stations and get it to the farmers in a form they can use. This means meetings and workshops, and the subjects are insect problems, crops—feed crops—and irrigation. We've got an interesting project going on now. It's a new way of growing corn in this dry country. Sod corn, we call it. There's no tillage—you plant rows of corn in the untouched sod. The growth of the grass is retarded chemically for about thirty days. That gives the corn a head start. Then the grass comes along in the normal way and holds the soil between the rows, and after the corn is harvested the grass is there for fall pasture and cover through the winter. The sod is precious here. The wind is the enemy. We have plenty of water, but it's all underground. There's an ocean of pure water, the sweetest in the world, under these Sand Hills. The trouble is we get only about eighteen inches of rain a year—about half of what you get back East—and the wind blows all the time. The sod is the only thing that keeps the land from blowing away. We almost lost it back in the thirties, you know. I don't know how our sod-corn project will work out. There are people who will give it serious attention. But there are also those who won't. They're still back there with the homesteaders who wouldn't change—who kept on plowing the dust and overgrazing the range. Nobody can tell them anything. They have to be in pretty bad trouble before they'll come to me for help."

The U.S.D.A. agencies that have offices in the courthouse are the Agricultural Stabilization and Conservation Service and the Soil Conservation Service. Each consists of a manager and a couple of women clerks. The Agricultural Stabilization and Conservation Service administers the federal crop-control (or production-adjustment) program, and it has been represented in Stapleton since 1959 by a native of Tryon (and a former rancher and Army officer) named William Griffith. "I'm a native and I'm prejudiced," he told me, "but I've observed a good many other places, and the Sand Hills country is hard to beat for good living. You can buy a half of beef that you've selected yourself, and Ewoldt's will butcher it and age it and keep it for you in their locker. Or a lamb or a hog. There's good pheasant shooting and good deer hunting—did you ever taste venison salami? The

312

people are friendly. Maybe they're too friendly—everybody knows everybody's business. We have very little changeover. People come here and they don't want to leave. Our teachers stay on forever. We have only one serious problem. It's the economic problem that's threatening all of rural and small-town America. We can't keep our young people. The farms and ranches are getting bigger and bigger and more and more mechanized, and the jobs are getting fewer and fewer. Not many of our local boys can hope to make a living here. They want to stay, but they can't—not unless they make a special effort. My youngest son is at the University of Nebraska, and his plan is to be a veterinarian so he can stay on here in the Sand Hills. Randy Joe Kramer, the salutatorian of the senior class at the high school this year, is another example. He's going to the university to study agriculture. He wants to be a county agent. On the other hand, there are John Beckius's two sons. They're more typical. There wasn't anything for them here. One of them is working down in Platte, and the other is out in Denver."

The manager of the Soil Conservation Service office is a broad, smiling, bespectacled man (with brown eyes) named John H. Sautter. Sautter is a former high-school teacher and an authority on the pasture grasses of western Nebraska, and his job is counseling the ranchers of Logan and McPherson Counties on how to preserve and improve their range. The experience has given him a view of human nature much like that of the county agent, Cook. "The better the rancher, the more apt he is to ask us for help," he told me. "The poor ones don't bother. It's like everything else—the less you know, the less you want to know." I spent an afternoon out in the field with Sautter. He had been asked by a prosperous rancher to draft an improvement program for some grassland a few miles north of town, and we drove out there together in a government pickup truck that was geared to riding the range.

It was a beautiful afternoon, with a high, blue sky and a horizon of great white clouds and a cooling flow of breeze. There was a meadowlark on almost every fencepost, and a ring of old automobile tires laid flat around the foot of every telephone pole. The meadowlark is the state bird of Nebraska, and it has the distinction, now rare among state birds (how often does one see a bluebird in New York?), of being ubiquitous in its state. The tires are a protective contrivance peculiar to the Sand Hills. "Cattle are one of the problems of the cattle range," Sautter told me. "Cattle like to scratch themselves, and they particularly like to scratch against a pole where they can circle around and around. Those tires keep them back and away. They don't like the feel of them underfoot. Otherwise, they'd go scratching around until they dug a trench in the ground and the pole got loose and fell out. Their trails are almost as bad. Cattle are great creatures of habit. They'll follow the same little track through a gap in the hills until they've dug a trench, and with the kind of wind we have out here it doesn't take long for a trench to grow into a gully."

We turned off the highway at an opening in the fence and went over a gridiron cattle guard. We headed across a range hub-deep in grass. There were cattle grazing on a slope in the distance, and off to the right was the long green wall of a windbreak. "This country was practically treeless in the Indian-and-buffalo days," Sautter told me. "The only trees were along the Platte and the Dismal River, up north, and some of the little creeks. The windbreaks are all man-made. The early settlers planted them with trees they hauled all the way up from the river bottoms. That's why you see so many cottonwoods. A cottonwood will grow from a slip, like a willow. Windbreaks are part of my job. A lot of the big ones around here were put in back in the thirties. Some of them are a mile long. Shelter belts, they called them then. Those were desperate years. People had the idea that trees would increase the humidity. It was a survival of the kind of wishful thinking that told the first settlers that rain followed the plow. In the thirties, they thought trees would bring rain. They thought they would break the drought. The design of a windbreak depends on the site, and also on what it's specifically for—to shelter your house or your livestock, or to protect a field or an orchard or a garden. We think a windbreak should be at least four rows deep. Five is better. The conventional design puts tall, broad-leaf trees, like ash or Chinese elm, in the middle and smaller, denser evergreens, like pines and cedars, in the outer rows. My own preference is for pine exclusively and cedar. That windbreak over there is one of the older ones. It's a mixture of various plantings—box elder, Chinese elm, Russian olive, cottonwood, cedar, and even some wild plum. And if you'll look up there—off near the end—do you see something moving? That's a little herd of antelope."

We bumped slowly on across the range. The range was not entirely grass. There were occasional scatterings of wild flowers—blue pentstemon, yellow wild mustard, orange gromwell. We cut around the side of a hill and labored up an easier slope and came out on a windy plateau. The range spread out below us. A tiny car crept along the faraway highway. Sautter stopped the truck and rolled down his window. "This is excellent range," he said. "It's in good condition, too. Predominantly sand bluestem. That little shrublike plant you see here and there is a legume we call leadplant. When you see it growing undisturbed like that, it's an indication of good range condition. It means the cattle have plenty of other things to eat. They'll eat leadplant, but generally not until they've grazed off the best of the grass. It's a different story down there in the valley. This is natural range up here. The valley has been farmed, and the native grasses are just about gone. What you see there is panic grass and six-week fescue and western ragweed. And a little buffalo grass. You probably can't see the buffalo grass. It's real short—never gets higher than four or five inches. I happen to know it's there. People are always talking and writing about buffalo grass. I guess it sounds romantic. Buffalo grass is a native grass, but that doesn't make it desirable. It probably came in wherever the buffalo overgrazed the range. It has one good use. It's tough and will stand a lot of traffic. We use it around here in the outfield in the ballparks. It's going to take work to bring that valley back. The homesteaders did just about everything they could to ruin this land. They never learned to understand it. They grew a lot of corn because corn was what they knew. That bared the soil at planting time in the spring, and then in the fall they turned the cows into the corn to graze. That kept the land open all through the winter. Corn exhausts the soil, and open soil blows. The only reason most of these people quit farming here was they had nothing left to farm. The people now know better—most of them, anyway. This is grazing land. And when it's maintained right, it's about the best there is."

Sautter rolled up his window and sat back in his seat. "The only thing we can't control is fire," he said. "Prairie fires are a constant threat, and they're almost always acts of God. Nobody in this country is crazy enough to drop a cigarette on the range. The usual cause of a prairie fire is lightning. Practically all the fires that the Stapleton fire department goes out on are prairie fires. And they can be bad—real bad. I don't know if you've noticed my hands and my neck and chin. That's all grafted skin. I got involved in a prairie fire a few years back—in March of nineteen seventy-seven. It was a windy day, and dry like it usually is, and the grass was about a foot high. I was driving out of town, and I saw some smoke in the hills out south. When a man sees a fire around here, he generally tries to do something about it. We all of us carry a shovel in our cars. Well, I headed that way, and there was a ranch house nearby and I stopped and asked if they had called the fire department, and the woman said she had. But I thought I could do a little something in the meantime. So I went on to the fire. I left my pickup truck on the road and got out my shovel and went through the fence to the range. The fire was burning northwest to southwest. I went down the west side of the fire line, digging and throwing dirt. I worked for about a quarter of a mile. I had it out except for a few stems and chips, and I started back to the pickup. It was then that the wind took a change. It swung around to blowing from the northeast, and it picked up to about sixty miles an hour, and a few smolderings blew into some fresh grass. It went up like a bomb. I was about forty feet from the new line, and it had me cut off from the pickup—it was a couple of hundred yards away. I saw that big wall of fire coming at me, and I knew I was up the creek. You can't get away from a grass fire. You can't outrun it. All you can do is hope for the best and go through it. People have done it and come out the other side. The trouble is a fire like that burns up all the oxygen in the air. It's hard to get a good breath, and I was half worn out from shoveling. Anyway, I ran, but I lost control and I tripped and fell and went down. I lay there—I couldn't move—and the fire burned over, under, and around me. I had on an insulated coat and boots and cap. But my pants, they were permanent-press synthetic—the kind that gets hot and stays hot. And my gloves were in my pocket. So my hands and my legs and part of my face got cooked. I don't know how long I lay there. I got to my feet somehow and got myself back to the pickup—the fire had left me far behind—and got it started and drove till I met the fire trucks coming out from town. The funny thing is it was only then that I started to hurt. They got me into the ambulance and we started for North Platte. Then I really began to hurt. I couldn't wait to get to the hospital, and I thought I'd never leave it. They had me there for three full months, and I hurt every minute of that time until the last two days."

There are one hundred and fifty-five agricultural holdings in Logan County. One hundred and sixteen of them are classified as farms, and thirty-nine are ranches. Most of the farmers run a few cattle, but their principal crop is grain—feed grain and a little wheat. The farms range in size from around a section (six hundred and forty acres) to about two thousand acres, and (for reasons of soil quality and availability of water) they are confined to a narrow belt along the southern edge of the county. The rest of the county is cattle country. There are a few ranches in Logan County of around three thousand acres, but most of them are larger. Small ranches are impractical in the Sand Hills; it takes about twenty acres of such range to support a cow and her calf. Most of the Logan County ranches are profitable enterprises. In 1969, they marketed a total of fifteen thousand five hundred calves, at an average price of a hundred and twenty dollars a head, and received a gross return of just under two million dollars. The biggest ranch in Logan County is owned by Peter Kiewit & Sons (the family concern that also owns the Omaha *World-Herald*) and totals around thirty thousand acres. The Milldale Ranch Company (whose brand—a sort of gothic "H"—is the oldest registered brand in Nebraska) embraces twenty-nine thousand acres, and other important operations include the Logan County Lake & Cattle Co. ranch (twenty-three thousand acres), the Baskin Diamond-Bar Ranch (fourteen thousand acres), the Santo Land & Cattle Co. (ten thousand acres), and the Wayne Salisbury ranch, with seven thousand acres of uncommonly good range.

The Baskin ranch is the biggest ranch in the neighborhood of Stapleton still owned by the founding family. Its present proprietor is a tall, leathery man of seventy-two named Robert Baskin. The ranch house is just outside town, a bit north of the railroad tracks and the depot. I walked out and called on Baskin there one Saturday afternoon. He led me across a dining room furnished with a Duncan Phyfe table and cabinets full of Haviland china, and into an office hung with family photographs. He put me in a comfortable chair and sat down at a rolltop desk. "Life has treated me all right," he told me. "My dad founded this ranch and got it going, and I've got me a real good son-in-law to carry it on. I mean Dave Jones. Dave more or less runs the Diamond-Bar now, and it couldn't be in better hands. My dad used to say he was planting trees for me. I planted them for my daughter, and now Dave is planting them for their children. I like to think the Diamond-Bar will last. Our brand is an old brand. It's up there close to the Milldale 'H'. My dad bought it off a couple of bachelor brothers from Denmark who homesteaded here in the very early years. He got the money to start this ranch by cutting meat in

North Platte and buying and selling Indian horses in the summer. He started out with twelve hundred acres, and he added to it bit by bit—a section or two at a time. I brought it up to its present size. All the ranches around here are made up of bits and pieces. Nobody's ranch is just right. There are always gaps, so you have to cross your neighbor when you move your cattle. I have some good neighbors and I have some not so good. I can get along with anybody who treats me halfway right. But I sure don't believe in being pushed over and walked the full length of. Western hospitality is practically a thing of the past. One of my neighbors had a branding. I went over to help out, and I brought along a couple of my men. Then, a week or so later, I'm branding, and my neighbor comes over to help. But he only brings *one* hand. That isn't what I call hospitality. Wayne Salisbury is branding today, and Dave and two of our hands are over there helping out. Wayne isn't the neighbor I was talking about. We're branding here next Saturday, and I know Wayne will be here with two of his men to help. Nobody can brand without his neighbors in to help. We sell about nine hundred calves a year, and we'll be branding about six hundred of them next week. Everybody wants to expand his operation. Raising cattle is the world's biggest gambling den, and you can't win unless you've got some size. When I was buying a lot of land, back in the middle thirties, you could get it for two or three dollars an acre. Now it's sky-high. It's sixty, seventy, even eighty dollars an acre. The way prices are today, a man can't make a living ranching unless he's already got his ranch.

It's impossible to start from scratch. It would mean a capital outlay of almost a quarter of a million dollars for even a little ranch—for only three thousand acres. A man couldn't live long enough to get his money back on an investment like that. And that's just for land. We're all of us mechanized now. We don't need but six or eight hands to run the Diamond-Bar in summer, and in winter there's just two hands and Dave and me. We used to have one man did nothing but ride the range and check up on fences and if the windmills and water tanks were working all right. Some people ride the range in a truck these days, or on a motorbike. We do it by plane. Dave has a little Cessna Skylark. He can check on forty windmills in thirty minutes. I don't mean to say that we've given up the horse. You can't haul a bull out of a spring hole with a motorcycle. And you can't brand and notch and inoculate and castrate without some horses and riders to rope your calves. We have about a hundred head of horses. They're mostly quarter horses. We break and sell a lot of them to stables and such back East. To towns and cities everywhere. There's nothing new about country people leaving the farm and moving into town. But now it looks like the horse is following them in."

Baskin drove me back to the Motel in an air-conditioned Cadillac. He raised a hand in greeting to everybody on the street, and everybody waved to him. He let me off in front of the Cafe. Several boys were lounging there, and I knew two of them. They were the Perry boys—Robert, a senior at the high school, and his fifteen-year-old

322

brother, Monty Joe. Monty had a bandage around his forehead.

"What happened to you?" I asked.

Robert laughed. "He got himself kicked by a calf," he said.

"I sure did," Monty said. "I sure guess I did. It was out at the Salisbury branding this morning. One of the riders dragged up a calf, and me and the guy I was working with grabbed him to hold for the brand and the other stuff they do. But he was laying the wrong way. The Salisbury brand goes on the left side. So we made him flip over and I was holding his front legs and one of them broke loose and kicked me. Those calves are only a couple of months old, but they're strong, and when they smell that hot iron coming at them it's like they get stronger. We had a calf one time that strained so hard he actually ruptured himself. And I guess those little hoofs are sharp. One of the cowboys drove me in to the Platte, and the doctor had to take nine stitches. But you know what? On the way in, we were going about ninety miles an hour, and the Highway Patrol stopped us. But when they saw what the trouble was, they waved us right on. They let us get up to almost a hundred."

The pastor of St. John's Church is a young Nebraskan named John Schlaf. Stapleton is his first parish. "I spent last week where I could see nothing but dead concrete and the hurrying footsteps of man," Father Schlaf told me. "I was at a conference in Omaha. When I got home last night, I felt the difference. I felt the expanse, the space, some reflection of God in the countryside. Down there, I felt closed in—uptight. Down in Missouri, when I was in seminary, I used to think of working in Los Angeles. They needed priests there. But then I got more realistic and saw that I was rurally oriented. I grew up a little east of here, in the little town of Spalding. And Omaha isn't even a city in big-city terms. But, of course, I'm a natural celibate. I like privacy. I don't even have a housekeeper here. If I'd wanted a housekeeper, I'd have gotten married. Stapleton is an ideal kind of parish for a priest like me—a little break for rest and study. I'll be moving on. But I could stay here for the rest of my life and love every month of it. It's a real parish, everybody participates, it's a community, it's beautiful. Everybody knows if somebody needs help, and they see that he gets it. We have some poor people here. They're poor by national income standards. But they don't know it—their needs are small. And if you call them poor, they'd be indignant. They'd be insulted. Stapleton is still remote. The war and the riots and the drugs and the pollution—they seem so far away. And race. Mexicans can't belong to the Elks down in North Platte. That bugs a lot of us, but that's the only race problem here. They've got some Jewish people in North Platte, but I never heard a word of anti-Semitism. Everybody here is sympathetic to civil rights. Of course, it's well removed. There aren't any Negroes in western Nebraska. But if a few Negro families moved into town, our people would lean over backward to be friendly. But if more than a few moved in—I don't know. They'd probably begin to feel threatened. I'm sure of one thing. These are good, Christian people, peace-loving people, but if a hippie group showed up here looking for wild marijuana and everything else, I'd be worried. There'd be bloodshed. These people would stomp on them."

My last day in Stapleton was a Saturday. That night, after supper, after packing my bags, after a farewell walk around town (up to the depot and down to the school), I dropped into the Wagon Wheel Tavern for a farewell glass of beer. There was only a handful of people there. I saw James Morey playing the pinball machine, Wayne Salisbury with a group at the bar, Grace Young at a table with her father drinking a Coke and eating a bowl of popcorn. Elwin Miller and his wife, a pretty, red-haired girl, were sitting in a booth, and they called to me to join them. We sat and talked and drank Hamm's beer and listened to two cowboys with crewcuts and long sideburns arguing about Clint Eastwood (his age and origins and whether he could actually ride a horse or if he used a double) until about eleven o'clock. The Millers drove off to a dance at Mullen, some sixty miles away, and I walked back to the Motel. Except for the cars nosed in at the Wagon Wheel, the street was empty, and the only light was the wild green mercury glare of the streetlight at the Corner and a glow behind the barred back window of the post office. The only sound was the wind—the hot, dry, everlasting wind—stirring the cottonwood trees.

From *American Fried: Adventures of a Happy Eater*

CALVIN TRILLIN

Calvin Trillin, born in Kansas City in 1926, is a New Yorker *staff writer and author of a nationally syndicated newspaper column. His adventures as a happy eater enrich the national folklore, according to the* New York Times. *All Americans, seasoned travelers or not, will identify with the search for the "perfect hamburger" he hilariously describes here.*

I know a radical from Texas who holds the stock market in contempt but refuses to give up his seven shares of Dr. Pepper. He says that Dr. Pepper, like the late President Eisenhower, is above politics. I have personally acted as a courier in bringing desperately craved burnt-almond chocolate ice cream from Will Wright's in Los Angeles to a friend who survived a Beverly Hills childhood and now lives in New York—living like a Spanish Civil War refugee who hates the regime but would give his arm for a decent bowl of gazpacho. I have also, in the dark of night, slipped into a sophisticated apartment in upper Manhattan and left an unmarked paper bag containing a powdered substance called Ranch Dressing—available, my client believes, only in certain supermarkets in the state of Oklahoma. I once knew someone from Alabama who, in moments of melancholy or stress or drunkenness, would gain strength merely by staring up at some imaginary storekeeper and saying, in the accent of an Alabama road-gang worker on his five-minute morning break, "Jes gimmie an R.C. and a moon pah."

Because I happened to grow up in Kansas City and now live in New York, there may be, I realize, a temptation to confuse my assessment of Kansas City restaurants with the hallucinations people all over the country suffer when gripped by the fever of Hometown Food Nostalgia. I am aware of the theory held by Bill Vaughan, the humor columnist of the Kansas City *Star*, that millions of pounds of hometown goodies are constantly crisscrossing the country by U.S. mail in search of desperate expatriates—a theory he developed, I believe, while standing in the post office line in Kansas City holding a package of Wolferman's buns that he was about to send off to his son in Virginia. I do not have to be told that there is a tendency among a lot of otherwise sensible adults to believe that the best hamburgers in the world are served in the hamburger stands of their childhood. A friend of mine named William Edgett Smith, after all, a man of good judgment in most matters, clings to the bizarre notion that the best hamburgers in the world are served at Bob's Big Boy—Glendale, California, branch—rather than at Winstead's Drive-in in Kansas City. He has, over the years, stubbornly rejected my acute analysis of

327

the Big Boy as a gimmick burger with a redundant middle bun, a run-of-the-mill tripledecker that is not easily distinguishable from a Howard Johnson's 3-D.

"It has a sesame seed bun," Smith would say, as we sat in some midtown Manhattan bar eating second-rate cheeseburgers at a dollar seventy-five a throw—two expatriates from the land of serious hamburger-eaters.

"Don't talk to me about seeds or buns," I'd say to Smith. "I had a Big Boy in Phoenix and it is not in any way a class burger."

"Phoenix is not Glendale," Smith would say, full of blind stubbornness.

Smith has never been to Winstead's, although he often flies to California to visit his family (in Glendale, it goes without saying) and I have reminded him that he could lay over in Kansas City for a couple of hours for little extra fare. He has never been able to understand the monumental purity of the Winstead's hamburger—no seeds planted on the buns, no strong sauce that might keep the exquisite flavor of the meat from dominating, no showy meat-thickness that is the downfall of most hamburgers. Winstead's has concentrated so hard on hamburgers that for a number of years it served just about nothing else. Its policy is stated plainly on the menu I have framed on the kitchen wall for inspiration: "We grind U.S. Graded Choice Steak daily for the sandwich and broil them on a greaseless grill." That is the only claim Winstead's makes, except "Your drinks are served in sterilized glasses."

I can end any suspicion of hometown bias on

my part by recounting the kind of conversation I used to have with my wife, Alice, an Easterner, before I took her back to Kansas City to meet my family and get her something decent to eat. Imagine that we are sitting at some glossy road stop on the Long Island Expressway, pausing for a bite to eat on our way to a fashionable traffic jam:

ME: Anybody who served a milkshake like this in Kansas City would be put in jail.

ALICE: You promised not to indulge in any of that hometown nostalgia while I'm eating. You know it gives me indigestion.

ME: What nostalgia? Facts are facts. The kind of milkshake that I personally consumed six hundred gallons of at the Country Club Dairy is an historical fact in three flavors. Your indigestion is not from listening to my fair-minded remarks on the food of a particular American city. It's from drinking that gray skim milk this bandit is trying to pass off as a milkshake.

ALICE: I suppose it wasn't you who told me that anybody who didn't think the best hamburger place in the world was in his hometown was a sissy.

ME: But don't you see that one of those places actually *is* the best hamburger place in the world? Somebody has to be telling the truth, and it happens to be me.

Alice has now been to Kansas City many times. If she is asked where the best hamburgers in the world are served, she will unhesitatingly answer, from the results of her own extensive quality testing, that they are served at Winstead's. By the time our first child was three, she had already been to Winstead's a few times, and as an assessor of hamburgers, she is, I'm proud to say, her father's daughter. Once, I asked her what I could bring her from a trip to Kansas City. "Bring me a hamburger," she said. I did. I now realize what kind of satisfaction it must have given my father when I, at about the age of ten, finally agreed with him that *Gunga Din* was the greatest movie ever made.

I once went to Kansas City for the express purpose of making a grand tour of its great restaurants. Almost by coincidence, I found myself on the same plane with Fats Goldberg, the New York pizza baron, who grew up in Kansas City and was going back to visit his family and get something decent to eat. Fats, whose real name is Larry, got his nickname when he weighed about three hundred pounds. Some years ago, he got thin, and he has managed to remain at less than one hundred sixty ever since by subjecting himself to a horrifyingly rigid eating schedule. In New York, Fats eats virtually the same thing every day of his life. But he knows that even a man with his legendary will power—a man who can spend every evening of the week in a Goldberg's Pizzeria without tasting—could never diet in Kansas City, so he lets himself go a couple of times a year while he is within the city limits. For Fats, Kansas City is the DMZ. He currently hold the world's record for getting from the airport to Winstead's.

Fats seemed a bit nervous about what we would

find at Winstead's. For as long as I can remember, everyone in Kansas City has been saying that Winstead's is going downhill. Even in New York, where there has always been obsessive discussion of Winstead's among people from Kansas City, the Cassandras in our ranks have often talked as if the next double-with-everything-and-grilled-onions I order at Winstead's will come out tasting like something a drugstore counterman has produced by peeling some morbid-looking patty from waxed paper and tossing it on some grease-caked grill—a prophecy that has always proved absolutely false. I can hardly blame a Kansas City emigré for being pessimistic. We have all received letters about Winstead's decline for years—in the way people who grew up in other parts of the country receive letters telling them that the fresh trout they used to love to eat now tastes like turpentine because of the lumber mill upstream or that their favorite picnic meadow has become a trailer park. When Winstead's began serving French-fried potatoes several years ago, there was talk of defection in New York. The price of purity is purists. The French fries did turn out to be unspectacular—a lesson, I thought, that craftsmen should stick to their craft. The going-downhill talk was strong a few years later when Winstead's introduced something called an eggburger. My sister has actually eaten an eggburger—she has always had rather exotic tastes—but I found the idea so embarrassing that I avoided William Edgett Smith for days, until I realized he had no way of knowing about it. Fats told me on the plane that there had been a lot of going-downhill talk since Winstead's sold out to a larger company. He seemed personally hurt by the rumors.

"How can people talk that way?" he said, as we were about to land in Kansas City.

"Don't let it bother you, Fats," I said. "People in Paris are probably always going around saying the Louvre doesn't have any decent pictures any more. It's human nature for the locals to badmouth the nearest national monument."

"You'll go to Zarda's Dairy for the banana split, of course," Fats said, apparently trying to cheer himself up by pitching in with some advice for the grand tour. "Also the Toddle House for hash browns. Then you'll have to go to Kresge's for a chili dog."

"Hold it, Fats," I said. "Get control of yourself." He was beginning to look wild. "I'm not sure a grand tour would include Kresge's chili dogs. Naturally, I'll try to get to the Toddle House for the hash browns; they're renowned."

I gave Fats a ride from the airport. As we started out, I told him I was supposed to meet my sister and my grandfather at Mario's—a place that had opened a few years before featuring a special sandwich my sister wanted me to try. Mario cuts off the end of the small Italian loaf, gouges out the bread in the middle, puts in meatballs or sausages and cheese, closes everything in by turning around the end he had cut off and using it as a plug, and bakes the whole thing. He says the patent is applied for.

"Mario's!" Fats says. "What Mario's? When I come into town, I go to Winstead's from the airport."

"My grandfather is waiting, Fats," I said. "He's eighty-eight years old. My sister will scream at me if we're late."

"We could go by the North Kansas City Winstead's branch from here, get a couple to go, and eat them on the *way* to whatzisname's," Fats said. He looked desperate. I realized he had been looking forward to a Winstead's hamburger since his last trip to Kansas City five or six months before—five or six months he had endured without eating anything worth talking about.

That is how Fats and I came to start the grand tour riding toward Mario's clutching Winstead's hamburgers that we would release only long enough to snatch up our Winstead's Frosty Malts ("The Drink You Eat With a Spoon"), and discussing the quality of the top-meat, no-gimmick burger that Winstead's continued to put out. By the time we approached Mario's, I felt nothing could spoil my day, even if my sister screamed at me for being late.

"There's LaMar's Do-Nuts," Fats said, pulling at the steering wheel. "They do a sugar doughnut that's dynamite."

"But my grandfather . . ." I said.

"Just pull over for a second," Fats said. "We'll split a couple.

I can now recount a conversation I would like to have had with the "freelance food and travel writer" who, according to the Kansas City *Star*, spent a few days in town and then called Mario's sandwich "the single best thing I've ever had to eat in Kansas City." I mean no disrespect to Mario, whose sandwich might be good enough to be the single best thing in a lot of cities. I hope he gets his patent.

ME: I guess if that's the best thing you've ever had to eat in Kansas City you must have got lost trying to find Winstead's. Also, I'm surprised at the implication that a fancy free-lance food and travel writer like you was not allowed into Arthur Bryant's Barbecue, which is only the single best restaurant in the world.

FREE-LANCE FOOD AND TRAVEL WRITER : I happen to like Italian food. It's very Continental.

ME: There are no Italians in Kansas City. It's one of the town's few weaknesses.

FLFTW: Of course there are Italians in Kansas City. There's a huge Italian neighborhood on the northeast side.

ME: In my high school we had one guy we called Guinea Gessler, but he kept insisting he was Swiss. I finally decided he really *was* Swiss. Anyway, he's not running any restaurants. He's in the finance business.

FLFTW: Your high school is not the whole city. I can show you statistics.

ME: Don't tell me about this town, buddy. I was born here.

"Actually, there probably *are* a lot of good restaurants there, because of the stockyards," New Yorkers say—swollen with condescension—when I inform them that the best restaurants in the world are in Kansas City. But, as a matter of fact, there are *not* a lot of good steak restaurants in Kansas

City; American restaurants do not automatically take advantage of proximity to the ingredients, as anyone who has ever tried to find a fresh piece of fish on the Florida Coast does not need to be told. The best steak restaurant in the world, Jess & Jim's, does happen to be in Kansas City, but it gets its meat from the stockyards in St. Joe, fifty miles away. The most expensive steak on the menu is Jess & Jim's Kansas City Strip Sirloin. When I arrived on the first evening of my tour, it was selling for $6.50, including salad and the best cottage-fried potatoes in the tri-state area. They are probably also the best cottage-fried potatoes in the world, but I don't have wide enough experience in eating cottage fries to make a definitive judgment.

Jess & Jim's is a sort of roadhouse, decorated simply with bowling trophies and illuminated beer signs. But if the proprietor saw one of his waitresses emerge from the kitchen with a steak that was no better than the kind you pay twelve dollars for in New York—in one of those steak houses that also charge for the parsley and the fork and a couple of dollars extra if you want ice in your water—he would probably close up forever from the shame of it all. I thought I might be unable to manage a Jess & Jim's strip sirloin. Normally, I'm not a ferocious steak-eater—a condition I trace to my memories of constant field trips to the stockyards when I was in grade school. (I distinctly remember having gone to the stockyards so many days in a row that I finally said, "Please, teacher, can we have some arithmetic?" But my sister, who went to the same school at the same time, says we never went to the stockyards—which just goes to show how a person's memory can play tricks on her.) As it turned out, I was able to finish my entire Jess & Jim's Kansas City Strip Sirloin— even though I felt rather full when I sat down at the table. I had eaten a rather large lunch at Winstead's, Mario's and the doughnut place. I had spent the intervening hours listening to my sister tell me about a place on Independence Avenue where the taxi drivers eat breakfast and a place called Laura's Fudge Shop, where you can buy peanut-butter fudge if you're that kind of person, and a place that serves spaghetti in a bucket. My sister has always been interested in that sort of thing—spaghetti in a bucket, chicken in a basket, pig in a blanket. She's really not an eater; she's a container freak.

It has long been acknowledged that the single best restaurant in the world is Arthur Bryant's Barbecue at Eighteenth and Brooklyn in Kansas City— known to practically everybody in town as Charlie Bryant's, after Arthur's brother, who left the business in 1946. The day after my Jess & Jim's Kansas City Strip Sirloin had been consumed, I went to Bryant's with Marvin Rich, an eater I know in Kansas City who practices law on the side. Marvin happens to number among his clients the company that bought Winstead's—the equivalent, in our circle, of a Bronx stickballer having grown up to find himself house counsel to the Yankees. Marvin eats a lot of everything—on the way to Bryant's, for instance, he brought me up-to-date on the local chili-parlor situation with great precision—but I have always thought of him as a barbecue specialist. He even attempts his own barbecue at home—dispatching his wife to buy hickory logs, picking out his own meat, and covering up any mistakes with Arthur Bryant's barbecue sauce, which he keeps in a huge jug in his garage in defiance of the local fire ordinances.

Bryant's specializes in barbecued spareribs and barbecued beef—the beef sliced from briskets of steer that have been cooked over a hickory fire for thirteen hours. When I'm away from Kansas City and depressed, I try to envision someone walking up to the counterman at Bryant's and ordering a beef sandwich to go—for me. The counterman tosses a couple of pieces of bread onto the counter, grabs a half-pound of beef from the pile next to him, slaps it onto the bread, brushes on some sauce in almost the same motion, and then wraps it all up in two thicknesses of butcher paper in a futile attempt to keep the customer's hand dry as he carries off his prize. When I'm *in* Kansas City and depressed, I go to Bryant's. I get a platter full of beef and ham and short ribs. Then I get a plate full of what are undoubtedly the best French-fried potatoes in the world ("I get fresh potatoes and cook them in pure lard," Arthur Bryant has said. "Pure lard is expensive. But if you want to do a job, you do a job.") Then I get a frozen mug full of cold beer—cold enough so that the ice has begun to form on the surface. But all of those are really side dishes to me. The main course of Bryant's, as far as I'm concerned, is something that is given away free—the burned edges of the brisket. The counterman just pushes them over to he side as he slices the beef, and anyone who wants them helps himself. I dream of those burned edges. Sometimes, when I'm in some awful, over-priced restaurant in some strange town—all of my restaurant-finding techniques having failed, so that I'm left to choke down something that costs seven dollars and tastes like a medium-rare sponge—a blank look comes over my face: I have just realized that at that very moment someone in Kansas City is being given those burned edges *free*.

Marvin and I had lunch with a young lawyer in his firm. (I could tell he was a comer: He had spotted a hamburger place at Seventy-fifth and Troost that Marvin thought nobody knew about.) We had a long discussion about a breakfast place called Joe's. "I would have to say that the hash browns at Joe's are the equivalent of the Toddle browns," Marvin said judiciously. "On the other hand, the cream pie at the Toddle House far surpasses Joe's cream pie." I reassured Marvin that I wouldn't think of leaving town without having lunch at Snead's Bar-B-Q. Snead's cuts the burned edges off the brisket with a little more meat attached and puts them on the menu as "brownies." They do the same thing with ham. A mixed plate of ham and beef brownies make a stupendous meal—particularly in conjunction with a coleslaw that is so superior to the soured confetti they serve in the East that Alice, who has been under the impression that she didn't like coleslaw, was forced to admit that she had never really tasted the true article until she showed up, at an advanced age, at Snead's. Marvin, a man who has never been able to rise above a deep and irrational prejudice against chicken, said nothing about Stroud's, although he must have been aware of local reports that the pan-fried chicken there had so moved the New York gourmet Roy Andries de Groot that he could only respond to his dinner by stopping at the cash register and giving Mrs. Stroud a kiss on the forehead.

After an hour or so of eating, the young lawyer went back to the office ("He's a nice guy," Marvin said, "but I think that theory of his about the banana-cream pie at the airport coffee shop is way off base"), and Marvin and I had a talk with Arthur Bryant himself, who is still pretty affable, even after being called Charlie for twenty-five years. When we mentioned that we had been customers since the early Fifties, it occurred to me that when we first started going to Bryant's it must have been the only integrated restaurant in town. It has always been run by black people, and white people had never been able to stay away. Bryant said that was true. In fact, he said, when mixed groups of soldiers came through Kansas City in those days, they were sent to Bryant's to eat. A vision flashed through my mind:

A white soldier and a black soldier become friends at Fort Riley, Kansas. "We'll stick together when we get to Kansas City," the white soldier says. "We're buddies." They arrive in Kansas City, prepared to go with the rest of the platoon to one of the overpriced and underseasoned restaurants that line the downtown streets. But the lady at the U.S.O. tells them they'll have to go to "a little place in colored town." They troop toward Bryant's—the white soldier wondering, as

339

the neighborhood grows less and less like the kind of neighborhood he associates with good restaurants, if what his father told him about not paying any attention to the color of a man's skin was such good advice after all. When they get to Bryant's— a storefront with five huge, dusty jugs of barbecue sauce sitting in the window as the only decoration—the white soldier flirts for a moment with the idea of deserting his friend. But they had promised to stick together. He stiffens his resolve, and walks into Bryant's with his friend. He is in THE SINGLE BEST RESTAURANT IN THE WORLD. All of the other guys in the platoon are at some all-white cafeteria eating tasteless mashed potatoes. For perhaps the only time in the history of the republic, virtue has been rewarded.

Bryant told us that he and his brother learned everything they knew about barbecue from a man named Henry Perry, who originated barbecue in Kansas City. "He was the greatest barbecue man in the world," Bryant said, "but he was a mean outfit." Perry used to enjoy watching his customers take their first bite of a sauce that he made too hot for any human being to eat without eight or ten years of working up to it. What Bryant said about Henry Perry, the master, only corroborated my theory that a good barbecue man is likely to tend toward the sullen—a theory I had felt wilting a bit in the face of Bryant's friendliness. (A man who tends briskets over a hickory fire all night, I figure, is bound to stir up some dark thoughts by morning.) I'm certain, at least, of my theory that a good barbecue man—or a good cook of any kind, for that matter—is not likely to be a promoter or a back-slapper. Once, while my wife and I were waiting to try out the fried clams at a small diner on the Atlantic Coast, I asked the proprietor if he had any lemon. "No, but I'll just make a note of that and I'll have some by the next time you come in," he said, turning on his best smile as he made the note. "You have to keep on your toes in this kind of business." We looked around and noticed, for the first time, a flashy new paint job and a wall plaque signifying some kind of good-citizen award. "Watch it," my wife whispered to me, "we're in for a stinker." We were. The redecoration job must have included reinforcing the tables so they would be able to support the weight of the fried clams.

When Arthur Bryant took over the place that had originally been called Perry's #2, he calmed the sauce down, since the sight that made him happiest was not a customer screaming but a customer returning. He eventually introduced French fries, although the barbecued sweet potatoes that Perry used to serve do not sound as if they were the source of a lot of customer complaints. Arthur Bryant is proud that he was the one who built up the business. But he still uses Perry's basic recipe for the sauce ("Twice a year I make me up about twenty-five hundred gallons of it") and Perry's method of barbecuing, and he acknowledges his debt to the master. "It's all Perry," he says. "Everything I'm doing is his." He keeps jugs of barbecue sauce in the window because that was Henry Perry's trademark. I immediately thought of a conversation I would like to have with the mayor and the city council of Kansas City one of these days:

ME: Have you ever heard of Henry Perry?

MAYOR AND CITY COUNCIL (In unison): Is that Commodore Perry?

ME: No, that is Henry Perry, who brought barbecue to Kansas City from Mississippi and therefore is the man who should be recognized as the one towering figure of our culture.

MAYOR AND CITY COUNCIL: Well, we believe that all our citizens, regardless of their color or natural origin—

ME: What I can't understand is why this town is full of statues of the farmers who came out to steal land from the Indians and full of statues of businessmen who stole the land from the farmers but doesn't even have a three-dollar plaque somewhere for Henry Perry.

MAYOR AND CITY COUNCIL: Well, we certainly think—

ME: As you politicians are always saying, we have *got* to re-order our priorities.

Some time after my grand tour of Kansas City restaurants, I managed to get to the Glendale, California, branch of Bob's for a Big Boy. Since I had to be in Los Angeles anyway, I decided to take the opportunity to end the debate with Smith once and for all, and also to check out a place called Cassell's Patio, which some people in Los Angeles have claimed has the best hamburger in the world. (Mr. Cassell ostentatiously grinds his beef right in front of one's very eyes, but then he uses too much of it for each hamburger patty. I suspect that Cassell's hamburger probably is the

342

best one available in Los Angeles, but among Kansas City specialists it would be considered a very crude hamburger indeed.)

"The game is just about up, Smith," I informed William Edgett Smith before I left for California. "You won't be able to get away with any of that 'Phoenix is not Glendale' stuff any more."

"Be sure to go to the original branch, across from Bob's international headquarters on Colorado," Smith said.

The Big Boy at Bob's on Colorado Avenue tasted like the Big Boy at Bob's in Phoenix—only slightly superior, in other words, to a Mcdonald's Big Mac anywhere. I was not surprised. Smith knows nothing about food. He once dragged us into a kind of Women's Lib restaurant he had thought was glorious, and it only required one course for anyone except Smith to realize that the point of the restaurant was to demonstrate, at enormous damage to the customers, that women are not necessarily good cooks. I have been at family-style dinners in Szechuan Chinese restaurants with Smith when his persistence about including Lobster Cantonese in the order has forced the rest of us to threaten him with exile to a table of his own. I long ago decided that the one perceptive remark he ever made about food—the observation that it is C. C. Brown's in Hollywood rather than Will Wright's that has the best hot fudge sundae in Southern California— was a fluke, an eyes-shut home run by a .200 hitter.

"It's all over, Smith," I said to him when I returned to New York. "I had one and I can tell you that Glendale is Phoenix."

"You went to the original, you're sure, on Colorado?" Smith asked. "Right across from Bob's international headquarters," I said.

"And did you ask for extra sliced tomatoes?" he said.

I paused for a long time, trying to remain calm. "You didn't say anything about extra sliced tomatoes," I said.

"But the whole taste is dependent on extra sliced tomatoes," he said. "The waitress would have been happy to bring you some. Bob prides himself on their friendliness."

"You realize, of course," I said, "that it's only a matter of time before I get back to Glendale and ask for extra sliced tomatoes and call this shameless bluff."

"I'm surprised you didn't ask for sliced tomatoes," Smith said. "It's the sliced tomatoes that really set it off."

WESTERN
UNITED STATES

Big Bend

ROY BONGARTZ

Roy Bongartz: A Rhode Islander, Bongartz has been a travel writer for a quarter century and is the author of a guidebook to the Southwest. In the retelling of his visit to the Big Bend National Park reprinted here, he discovers how easy it is to feel a lone explorer in the wild and primitive landscape of this popular park.

Big Bend National Park is a secret mountain hide-away of cool piney highlands and baking desert valleys, a 1,100-square-mile piece of West Texas lost down here a hundred miles below the Interstate and the nearest towns. All of it is bordered by the mercurial, elusive Rio Grande that forms that deep southerly incursion into the Mexican states of Coahuila and Chihuahua. A quarter-million annual visitors seem to lose themselves in the rough distances of one of our wildest and most primitive national parks. All you need do is to take one of the lesser used hiking trails, or set out on a bumpy dirt road to see the ruins of an early ranch or silver mine, and you may soon believe you are quite alone in the world.

The road into the park leads straight through sagebrush and cactus from the town of Alpine, about 200 miles east of El Paso on U.S. 90 in what the locals call the "Alps of Texas." It is seventy-seven miles to the park boundary and another twenty-four to park headquarters and the visitor center, the road leading past a forlorn tavern called The Camel and a campground with "full hook-ups" advertised on a sign many miles ahead, neither with a sign of any business whatever. About sixty miles down that road a sign reading "School Bus Stop" calls one's attention to a modest ranch nearly hidden back in the underbrush.

Near the border of the national park a broad jumble of coppery mountains arises with fringes of black-green forest on their heights. These are the Chisos Mountains, the name supposedly coming from an Apache word for ghosts, and along their base a paved parkway gives assess to gravel roads and dirt tracks that climb into the secret recesses of valleys and mesas. This tumbled earth reaches south to the Rio Grande, which itself disappears in several long stretches to hide within three canyons that shelter it below 2,000-foot-high cliffs (one cliff-side in Texas, the other in Mexico).

My son Joe, aged eleven, and I decided to set up our tent first of all at Rio Grande Village, a campground in the low-lying riverbank land at the eastern end of the park twenty miles beyond the visitor center. Here venerable cottonwoods make a shady oasis in the sere landscape that rises into the hills and mountains behind it. Four miles beyond we found the head of a half-mile foot trail into the mouth of Boquillas Canyon, which swallows the river as it flows off toward the Gulf of Mexico 600 miles away. The high, narrow walls put the river in shadows up ahead of us as we walked along the shore and then pushed our way through tunnels of thick bamboo to a sandy beach. The hot sun there soon had us splashing into the river, hanging into a rock or an overhanging branch to keep the strong current from taking us along with it.

Later we followed the riverbank path to its end where the flowing river swallowed it, and peered into the shadowy walls of the canyon, which goes on through for twenty-six miles. This and the other canyons may all be explored by raft trips, either with your own craft (you need a park permit for this) or with a group organized by professionals based just outside the park in the ghost town of Terlingua. Joe and I walked back up the riverbank, where the land opens out flat, to a point where a couple of Mexican boys spotted us and rowed across the stiff current in an old rowboat. We climbed aboard and they took us over to their country for a quarter. After securing the boat, they untied a couple of burros from the tree and bade us climb aboard for a dusty half-mile ride into their village of Boquillas, Coahuila.

Small rectangular whitewashed houses gleamed in the glaring light, setting off the duller adobe structures bordering the wide sand main street. Desert flowers grew in coffee cans in windows and doorways. A parrot squawked in a cage. An outdoor table displayed pieces of cut, polished quartz for sale. A starkly simple cafe with a dirt floor had a cooler with iced Carta Blanca beer somehow hauled up here all the way from Monterrey, served on an enameled table embossed with beer advertising. The village was quiet except for the parrot and an occasional child's call. No car or truck moved anywhere. Then there was the sound of hoofbeats as a rider moved off over the beaten earth of the road south. Suddenly a radio blared a *norteña*, a kind of Mexican folk music of the north, plaintive singing with accordion, drum, and guitar.

Alvar Nuñez Cabeza de Vaca, the Spanish explorer who brought home tales of the legendary Seven Golden Cities of Cibola in the New World that resulted in much of Spain's 16th-century expeditions in the Americas, was probably the first European to travel in the Big Bend Country—when he was lost with a remnant of a company of such gold seekers in 1535; it is believed he crossed the Rio Grande at the site of the present village of Lajitas. Nobody from outside came by for another half century, when another Spanish group touched the area, and it was not until 1683 that any European presence was established in Big Bend, when Captain Juan Dominguez de Mendoza established *presidios*—forts—along the river to protect Spanish trade routes. One of these early presidios, in the village of San Vicente on the Mexican side of the river, still exists as a ruin.

Hostile Indians, first Apaches and later Comanches raiding from the north, discouraged settlers until a century ago. A spring in Big Bend, the Aguaje de Dolores, is named for the Day of Sorrows, or Good Friday, in memory of the day in 1787 that a Spanish general, Juan de Ugalde, attacked and defeated a large band of Apaches at their water source.

By 1821 Mexico had taken over sovereignty of Big Bend, and in an attempt to make the area safe for settlers the military commander of Chihuahua offered a bounty to American mercenaries at the rate of $100 for the scalp of an Apache warrior, $50 for a squaw's, and $25 for a child's. The deal was called off when one zealous Texan brought in several scores of scalps that were suspected of being those of local Mexican ranchers instead of Indians.

The first American settler in the Big Bend area was a rancher named Ben Leaton, who took over the remains of the Los Julimas Mission, dating from 1683, as a private fortress in the mid 1800's. (The fort, now restored, is a historic site today at Presidio, Texas, seventy-five miles upriver from the national park.) He enclosed his enclave with adobe walls that were three feet thick, eighteen feet high, and had room to shelter a whole village. His house had a fireplace big enough to roast a whole beef. Leaton is remembered for having invited the warlike Apaches to a great feast at his house. He treated them to a roasted beef and plenty of mescal, and they promised everlasting friendship, but nevertheless made off with all his cattle on their way home. Leaton then proposed another dinner for the Indians. Trusting Leaton, they accepted and showed up to seat themselves around the great table in his main room. When they were all in place, Leaton, instead of severing the roast on the spit, drew aside a screen, revealing a cannon which he fired at his guests like sitting ducks, killing most of them.

Our second campsite in the park was at the Basin, the central area, which has a restaurant, a lodge, motel rooms, a general store, and a post office. Nearby is an amphitheater where on our first night the talk was about a fire that had raged the previous spring at the heights of Laguna Meadows, set by a careless backpacker. Although scores of firefighters were flown in to douse the blaze, the ranger informed us that natural fires—those set by lightning, for example—now are left to burn unless they threaten people or their property. This policy has caused considerable controversy in the West when large tracts of woodland have been destroyed, but the official plan is "to restore fire to its role in a natural ecosystem, integrate fire into the management of resources." The reasoning is that when a forest burns it makes space for other plants that will eventually renew the land—grass, to begin with. A scientist was painstakingly photographing certain swatches of burned-over ground, week after week, to record which plants came through first, then what next, and so on, over many months.

It is a steep climb up the winding road to the Basin, at a much cooler altitude of some 5,000 feet than that of the river we have left below us. Horseback trails lead out from stables here, including the popular half-day Window Trail and the day-long South Rim trip. The former leads downhill alongside a stream bed through clumps of piñon, oak, and juniper that are bordered by desert country just a short way beyond the stream. At the end of the trail the horses are tethered as riders walk up to a wide smooth stone, polished by the boots and shoes of generations of sourdoughs and tourists, for a great view through the huge notch cut into the side of the rock wall of the Basin down here. Through it you look out on a spectacular chaos of mountain slope and tumbled rock stretching off, interspersed with buttes and peaks and chimneys all the way down into Mexico thirty miles south.

The next day Joe and I packed lunches for a trip to the South Rim, 7,200 feet above sea level and one of the outstanding spots in the park. It was hot down in the Basin on the morning we started out on our horses; our guide was a high school senior from Fort Worth, slouched movie-cowboy style in his saddle. Coolness touched us lightly as we rose bit-by-bit to higher levels along the switchbacks of the trail. "Whoa!" our guide shouted suddenly, his horse rearing, as a pack of skittering javelinas—nearsighted wild boars native to the mountains—clattered under and around us on their way up the mountain.

Mexican jays made an electric buzzing around us as we steadily made our way upward, the camp-sites and buildings down at the Basin looking small in the distance and finally disappearing in the foliage. We left the horses a couple of hundred yards from the top and walked to the South Rim for a long lunch and rapt viewing of the twisting river far below and the hazy reaches of Mexico eighty miles out over the Chihuahua desert. Our guide tossed a stone over the rim and waited for it to resound as it finally hit bottom half a mile straight down; it seemed to take a long, long time. "That's just how long you'd have to live if you fell over," our young Texan said with relish.

Somewhere below us the river was hidden by the most inaccessible of the three canyons,

Mariscal. Also down there is what is left of a ghost town, Glenn Springs, which is reachable on another trail leading off the main parkway. The town originated as a center for making candelilla wax out of a cactus that looks something like asparagus and coats its long stems with wax to preserve moisture inside. The wax is boiled away in water with sulphuric acid, skimmed off, and sold for various industrial and consumer uses. Though Glenn Springs is gone, wax *smuggling* is still known, because there is a Mexican government monopoly on wax gathering and sale, across the river. But prices for it are higher on the United States side.

Glenn Springs was the scene of a raid by Mexican bandits, or revolutionaries, on May 5, 1916, at a time that nine United States calvary troops were stationed there to protect the locals. The Mexicans, reported as numbering from between 65 to 400 "bandits," looted the store and left four dead, which soon brought out the National Guard to Big Bend and the establishment at the Springs of a permanent cavalry station, which remained until 1920. By then the price of wax had dropped and the town was being abandoned.

Peering over that South Rim into the mysterious canyons and mesas reaching away in untroubled wilderness you see no sign of man, no plane or road or structure of any kind. There is no sign along the distant river that anybody ever set foot there in all of history. There were cave men living here six to eight thousand years ago, according to archaeologists, evidently a migratory people who left few traces—there are indeed some petroglyphs to be seen on rockfaces in the park, marks resembling deer prints and simple geometric designs in red cinnabar paint, the ore that produces mercury and brought in commercial cinnabar mining up to recent times.

About 1,0000 A.D. a different civilization came to Big Bend, the pueblo culture of the Jumano who came down from present-day Mexico to farm the floodplain along the Rio Grande. The descendants of those early cave dwellers, also known as the "Archaic Indians," lived on in Big Bend to become the Chisos bands known to the earliest Spaniards. But then they mysteriously disappeared. It is intriguing to stare down into Mexico and wonder where they went, whether possibly they're still alive somewhere in the distant reaches of the desert, maybe down in isolated Copper Canyon, where Indians—an estimated 50,000 of them—called Tarahumaras live with little contact with the rest of Mexico and the outside world. Many of those Tarahumara families are, incidentally, still living today in caves, where the smoke-blackened walls look exactly as they must have done a millennium ago.

Big Bend has birds found nowhere else in the United States, including the Mexican jay, and the gray vireo, the Colima warbler, the varied bunting, and the Lucifer hummingbird. The desert silence is perfect for catching sight of a bird or an animal—there is the whisper of the wind around a cactus and then just the tiny rattle of a pebble dislodged by a gopher. An eagle circling and circling just off our high cliff up here on the Rim seems completely unaware of us, although some Big Bend birds make visitors very much a part of their routine, mainly the buzzards, who hang around the campgrounds for scraps of food and maybe to have a little fun. One of them swooped in and whipped Joe's cap off his head and was flying off with it until Joe's yells (or something) got to him and he dropped it.

Off in the distance to the west we see the vast wine-glass outline—narrow stem widening out above broadly—of Santa Elena Canyon where the walls are so narrow down on the river that boatmen can at places reach out and touch the United States and Mexico at the same time. Driving along the endless hot highway, the land seemed moonlike and empty of all life, but I knew there were many species of wildlife out there, a hundred kinds of birds who breed here and hundreds of other species who visit; seventy-five kinds of mammals, fifty-five species of reptiles, and ten amphibians also live in these mostly arid, secret, rocky expanses. Many bats live in the park, including those with such winningly descriptive names as the ghost-faced bat, the long-nosed bat, the big-eared bat, and the pallid bat. Jackrabbits and cottontails are seen along the roads all the time, almost as often as the wonderfully funny road runners, who like to race cars. Tarantulas, scorpions, and rattlesnakes also live here, but in daylight generally give people a wide berth. (At night, however, one is told to step carefully everywhere outdoors, especially where the ground is wet.)

The so-called "father" of the national park was a longtime Texas Ranger in these parts named E. E. Townsend, who in a letter to a friend once recalled the first time he had laid eyes on the Big

356

Bend country back in 1894: "With Deputy Marshal Bufe Cline, I was on the trail of some mules that had been stolen in Mexico and smuggled to this side of the Rio Bravo [Mexican name for Rio Grande]. We suddenly came to the southwestern edge of Bandera Mesa, that vast uplift which forms a mighty bulwark as the western wall of Green Valley and stands more than 1,000 feet above that misnamed basin. It was a vision of such magnitude as to stir the sluggish soul of a Gila Monster. The memory of it will persist until the mind is cleared by more thrilling adventures in a new and better world. The expansive desert basin, checkerboarded by intermingling colors as if daubed by the playful hands of careless children, extended for miles. I was too busy chasing men to visit it at the time, but a few months later I penetrated its deepest canyons and strange forests. Its immensity has grown on me with the passing years."

Thanks to Townsend's efforts, the state of Texas made Big Bend a state park in 1933, and a few years later, with the help of Amon G. Carter, publisher of the Fort Worth *Star-Telegram*, a million dollars was raised from public gifts to buy more land to make the whole area a national park, eventually established in 1944. More and more, the vast area has gradually been opened to visitors who want to backpack into remote areas or who have four-wheel-drive vehicles that can negotiate the rough, primitive back roads. Ordinary cars can manage a number of the dirt and gravel roads as well, but drivers should check at a ranger station for information about current conditions. Flash flooding follows the often spectacular thunderstorms in Big Bend, causing washouts.

Among hiking trails there are eight self-guiding ones marked for interesting examples of flora and fauna; the park, besides all those animals, has a counted 850 species of plant life. There are ten regular hiking trails in addition to the complex of trails in the high Chisos that you can hike or ride horses on to reach the South Rim, East Rim, and other points up there in the high country. And another seventeen hiking routes are designated as "primitive," meaning usually that they follow old ranch or mine roads and must be negotiated with the help of a topographic map (available at the visitor center). The hikes are specified as being "easy," "medium difficulty," "strenuous," and "backpackers only," the latter meaning that a map, water and food supply, compass, and experience are all prerequisites.

From the Basin, Joe and I drove the forty miles down to the parkway and below the Chisos Mountains along to the river village of Castolon, an old trading-post center where the Park Service has restored some early structures. The store remains just as it has been for half a century, with its long, dark counter, creaking board floor, old fashioned coffee mill, and shelves of canned goods, camping gear, blue jeans, and bottled soda. Its proprietor, Magdaleno Garcia, sells staple supplies mostly to Mexicans who come over by rowboat ferry from the village of Santa Elena. A campground nearby is little frequented but an occasional tenter or trailer dweller also turns up in the old store. On a hot day, the dim light and the air moved by the slowly turning overhead fan provide a welcome haven from the sun outside.

We continued for eight miles along the bank of the Rio Grande to the end of the road at the mouth of the starkly imposing Santa Elena Canyon, and found our way right into the canyon itself along a footpath into a scene somehow very lonely, with an odd sense of abandonment. Maybe the feeling comes from the darkness, everything in shade from the steep walls rising up sharply above us. There is a strong sense of end-of-the-world here in Santa Elena Canyon, and though I knew that the rafters made regular two- and three-day trips all the way through it, it still seemed mysteriously unknowable, the river flowing out of it as if from some enchanted and somehow malevolent source back in there.

I recalled a story of a natural passageway said to tunnel under the river from one country to another, accessible from the United States side through a cave three miles from the river bank—except that nobody knows where the cave is any more. The Indians were said to have used this as a secret route. That kind of a yarn goes over easily here at the canyon mouth, where the atmosphere is strange, unreachable. If there is a menace in the atmosphere at the mouth of Santa Elena Canyon it is a generalized one, reaching out to the world at large, not to any individual—but whatever it is, it is great as a backdrop to ghosts. Suddenly I recalled that diffused glowing light people claim to see down in the Big Bend country on spring evenings just after sunset, visible all the way from the highway between Alpine and Marfa, maybe fifty or seventy-five miles away. Nobody has measured it; nobody has found it, got to it, explained it. It is said, for one thing, not to be visible at all from an airplane, and again that it might be some sort of reflection from mica beds. Another legend is that it is the campfire of Apache ghosts.

Up at Persimmon Gap, on the other road into the park, the one that comes down from the town of Marathon, are supposed to be traces of the war trail of the Comanches, who raided this country on terrifying horseback campaigns from their plains homelands to the north. In the 18th century they went after horses deep into Mexico, but in the 19th century, when the buffalo was being killed off on their familiar plains, they raided for cattle, too.

They raided Apaches and Mexicans and Americans until the last Indian was captured and packed off to a reservation in 1890—not yet a whole hundred years ago. The surviving Comanches now mostly live around Lawton, Oklahoma. As for the Apaches, they are in Arizona and New Mexico; none are supposed to be in Big Bend any more. But Alsate comes back here still, they say, to steal campers' food and to leave moccasin prints in the dust. Alsate was one of the great Apache warriors, and a profile visible in the skyline at the western edge of the park in Maverick Mountain seems to be that of a man: It is called Alsate's Face. There is a strong feeling, at sunset at the entrance to Santa Elena Canyon, that the Indians are still here somewhere in Big Bend. Maybe they are daring us to come on into the shadows of the canyon and find out.

A Woman's Trip across the Plains in 1849

CATHERINE HAUN

Catherine Haun was a young bride when she and her husband, a lawyer, decided to follow the path of the gold rush. Old debts and hopes for a better life in a better climate prompted their move from Iowa. Their buoyant spirits are typical of the emigrants of the flush years of gold rush travel. Her account, moreover, is a reminiscence, dictated to her daughters in later years. Like many emigrants, she remembered details of the road vividly and softened the hardships of the journey in the retelling. Even her story of the woman who escaped from the Indians has the color of romance about it. Catherine Haun and her husband were educated and from middle-class families. Her wagon train was large, well equipped, and experienced.

Early in January of 1849 we first thought of emigrating to California. It was a period of National hard times and we being financially involved in our business interests near Clinton, Iowa, longed to go to the new El Dorado and "pick up" gold enough with which to return and pay off our debts.*

Our discontent and restlessness were enhanced by the fact that my health was not good. Fear of my sister's having died while young of consumption, I had reason to be apprehensive on that score. The physician advised an entire change of climate thus to avoid the intense cold of Iowa, and recommended a sea voyage, but finally approved of our contemplated trip across the plains in a "prairie schooner," for even in those days an out-of-door life was advocated as a cure for this disease. In any case, as in that of many others, my health was restored long before the end of our journey.

Full of the energy and enthusiasm of youth, the prospects of so hazardous an undertaking had no terror for us, indeed, as we had been married but a few months, it appealed to us as a romantic wedding tour.

The territory bordering upon the Mississippi River was, in those days, called "the west" and its people were accustomed to the privations and hardships of frontier life. It was mostly from their ranks that were formed the many companies of emigrants who traveled across the plains, while those who came to California from the Eastern states usually chose the less strenuous ocean voyage by way of the Isthmas of Panama or around the Horn.

*The Panic of 1837 was followed by prolonged economic depression. The region of the Mississippi valley suffered depressed farm prices well into the next decade.

At that time the "gold fever" was contagious and few, old or young, escaped the malady. On the streets, in the fields, in the workshops and by the fireside, golden California was the chief topic of conversation. Who were going? How was best to "fix up" the "outfit"? What to take as food and clothing? Who would stay at home to care for the farm and womenfolks? Who would take wives and children along? Advice was handed out quite free of charge and often quite free of common sense. However, as two heads are better than one, all proffered ideas helped as a means to the end. The intended adventurers dilligently collected their belongings and after exchanging such articles as were not needed for others more suitable for the trip, begging, buying or borrowing what they could, with buoyant spirits started off.

Some half dozen families of our neighborhood joined us and probably about twenty-five persons constituted our little band.

Our own party consisted of six men and two women. Mr. Haun, my brother Derrick, Mr. Brown, three young men to act as drivers, a woman cook and myself. Mr. Haun was chosen Major of the company, and as was the custom in those days, his fellow travelers ever afterwards knew him by this title. Derrick was to look after the packing and unpacking coincident to camping at night, keep tab on the commissary department and, when occasion demanded, lend a "helping hand." The latter service was expected of us all—men and women alike, was very indefinite and might mean anything from building campfires and washing dishes to fighting Indians, holding back a loaded wagon on a down grade or lifting it over bowlders when climbing a mountain.

Mr. Bowen furnished his own saddle horse, and for his services was brought free of expense to himself. His business was to provide the wood or fuel for the campfire, hunt wild game and ride ahead with other horsemen to select a camping ground or in search of water. He proved himself invaluable and much of the time we had either buffalo antelope or deer meat, wild turkey, rabbits, prairie chickens, grouse, fish or small birds.

Eight strong oxen and four of the best horses on the farm were selected to draw our four wagons—two of the horses were for the saddle.

Two wagons were filled with merchandise which we hoped to sell at fabulous prices when we should arrive in the "land of gold." The theory of this was good but the practice—well, we never got the goods across the first mountain. Flour ground at our own grist mill and bacon of home-curing filled the large, four-ox wagon while another was loaded with barrels of alcohol. The third wagon contained our household effects and provisions. The former consisted of cooking utensils, two boards nailed together, which was to serve as our dining table, some bedding and a small tent. We had a very generous supply of provisions. All meats were either dried or salted, and vegetables and fruit were dried, as canned goods were not common sixty years or more ago. For luxuries we carried a gallon each of wild plum and crabapple preserves and blackberry jam. Our groceries were wrapped in India rubber covers and we did not lose any of them—in fact still had some when we reached Sacramento.

The two-horse spring wagon was our bed-room and was driven by the Major—on good stretches of road by myself. A hair mattress, topped off with one of feathers and layed on the floor of the wagon with plenty of bedding made a very comfortable bed after a hard day's travel.

In this wagon we had our trunk of wearing apparel, which consisted of underclothing, a couple of blue checked gingham dresses, several large stout aprons for general wear, one light colored for Sundays, a pink calico sunbonnet and a white one intended for "dress up" days. My feminine vanity had also prompted me to include, in this quasi wedding trouseau, a white cotton dress, a black silk manteaux trimmed very fetchingly with velvet bands and fringe, also a lace scuttle-shaped bonnet having a face wreath of tiny pink rosebuds, and on the side of the crown nestled a cluster of the same flowers. With this marvelous costume I had hoped to "astonish the natives" when I should make my first appearance upon the golden streets of the mining town in which we might locate. Should our dreams of great wealth, acquired over night come true it might be embarrassing not to be prepared with a suitable wardrobe for the wife of a very rich man!

When we started from Iowa I wore a dark woolen dress which served me almost constantly during the whole trip. Never without an apron and a three-cornered kerchief, similar to those worn in those days, I presented a comfortable, neat appearance. The wool protected me from the sun's

365

rays and penetrating prairie winds. Besides it econ-
omized in laundrying which was a matter of no
small importance when one considers how limited,
and often utterly wanting were our "wash day"
conveniences. The chief requisite, water, being
sometimes brought from miles away.

In the trunk were also a few treasures; a bible,
medicines, such as quinine, bluemass, opium,
whiskey and hartshorn for snake bites and citric
acid—an antidote for scurvey. A little of the acid
mixed with sugar and water and a few drops of
essence of lemon made a fine substitute for lemon-
ade. Our matches, in a large-mouthed bottle were
carefully guarded in this trunk.

The pockets of the canvas walls of the wagon
held every day needs and toilet articles, as well as
small fire arms. The ready shotgun was suspended
from the hickory bows of the wagon camp. A ball
of twine an awl and buckskin strings for mending
harness, shoes etc. were invaluable. It was more
than three months before we were thoroughly
equipped and on April 24th, 1849 we left our
comparatively comfortable homes—and the uncomfortable creditors—for the uncertain and dangerous trip, beyond which loomed up, in our
mind's eye, castles of shining gold.

There was still snow upon the ground and the
roads were bad, but in our eagerness to be off we
ventured forth. This was a mistake as had we
delayed for a couple of weeks the weather would
have been more settled, the roads better and much

Bluemass was a quinine derivative.

of the discouragement and hardship of the first days of travel might have been avoided.

Owing partly to the new order of things and partly to the saturated soil, travel was slow for our heavy laden wagons and untried animals. We covered only ten miles the first day and both man and beast were greatly fatigued. As I look back now it seems the most tiresome day of the entire trip.

That night we stopped at a farm and I slept in the farm house. When I woke the next morning a strange feeling of fear at the thought of our venturesome undertaking crept over me. I was almost dazed with dread. I hurried out into the yard to be cheered by the bright sunshine, but old Sol's very brightness lent such a glamor to the peaceful, happy, restful home that my faint heartedness was only intensified. . . . It was a restful scene—a contrast to our previous day of toil and discomfort and caused me to brake completely down with genuine homesickness and I burst out into a flood of tears. . . . I remember particularly the flock of domesticated wild geese. They craned their necks at me and seemed to encourage me to "take to the woods." Thus construing their senseless clatter I paused in my grief to recall the intense cold of the previous winter and the reputed perpetual sunshine and wealth of the promised land. Then wiping away my tears, lest they betray me to my husband, I prepared to continue my trip. I have often thought that had I confided in him he would certainly have turned back, for he, as well as the other men of the party, was disheartened and was struggling not to betray it. . . .

In the morning our first domestic annoyance

occurred. The woman cook refused point blank to go any further. Evidently she had not been encouraged by any wild geese for she allowed her tears to be seen and furthermore her Romeo had followed her and it did not require much persuading on his part to induce her to return. Here was a dilemma! Had this episode happened on the previous morning when my stock of courage was so low and the men were all so busy with their own thoughts—our trip would have ended there.

Our first impulse was that we should have to return, but after a day's delay during [which] our disappointment knew no bounds, I surprised all by proposing to do the cooking, if everybody else would help. My self-reliance and the encouragement of our fellow travelers won the day and our party kept on. Having been reared in a slave state my culinary education had been neglected and I had yet to make my first cup of coffee. My offer was, however, accepted, and as quantity rather than quality was the chief requisite to satisfy our good appetites I got along very well, even though I never became an expert at turning pancakes (slapjacks) by tossing them into the air; a peculiarly scientific feat universally acquired by the pioneer miners of '49.

At the end of a month we reached Council Bluffs, having only travelled across the state of Iowa, a distance of about 350 miles every mile of which was beautifully green and well watered. We also had the advantage of camping near farmhouses and the generous supply of bread, butter, eggs and poultry greatly facilitated the cooking. Eggs were 2½ cents a dozen—at our journey's end we paid $1 apiece, that is when we had the dollar. Chickens were worth eight and ten cents a piece. When we reached Sacramento $10 was the ruling price and few to be had at that.

As Council Bluffs was the last settlement on the route we made ready for the final plunge into the wilderness by looking over our wagons and disposing of whatever we could spare. . . .

For the common good each party was "sized up" as it were. People insufficiently provisioned or not supplied with guns and ammunition were not desirable but, on the other hand, wagons too heavily loaded might be a hindrance. Such luxuries as rocking chairs, mirrors, washstands and corner what-nots were generally frowned down upon and when their owners insisted upon carrying them they had to be abandoned before long on the roadside and were appropriated by the Indians who were always eager to get anything that might be discarded.

The canvas covered schooners were supposed to be, as nearly as possible, constructed upon the principle of the "wonderful one-horse shay." It was very essential that the animals be sturdy, whether oxen, mules or horses. Oxen were preferred as they were less liable to stampede or be stolen by Indians and for long hauls held out better and though slower they were steady and in the long run performed the journey in an equally brief time. Besides, in an emergency they could be used as beef. When possible the provisions and ammunition were protected from water and dust by heavy canvas or rubber sheets.

Good health, and above all, not too large a

proportion of women and children was also taken into consideration. The morning starts had to be made early—always before six o'clock—and it would be hard to get children ready by that hour. Later on experience taught the mothers that in order not to delay the trains it was best to allow the smaller children to sleep in the wagons until after several hours of travel when they were taken up for the day.

Our caravan had a good many women and children and although we were probably longer on the journey owing to their presence—they exerted a good influence, as the men did not take such risks with Indians and thereby avoided conflict; were more alert about the care of the teams and seldom had accidents; more attention was paid to cleanliness and sanitation and, lastly but not of less importance, the meals were more regular and better cooked thus preventing much sickness and there was less waste of food.

Among those who formed the personnel of our train were the following families—a wonderful collection of many people with as many different dispositions and characteristics, all recognizing their mutual dependence upon each other and bound together by the single aim of "getting to California."

A regulation "prairie schooner" drawn by four oxen and well filled with suitable supplies, with two pack mules following on behind was the equipment of the Kenna family. There were two men, two women, a lad of fifteen years, a daughter thirteen and their half brother six weeks of age.

This baby was our mascot and the youngest member of the company.

.) . .

One family by the name of Lemore, from Canada, consisted of man, wife and two little girls. They had only a large express wagon drawn by four mules and a meager but well chosen, supply of food and feed. A tent was strapped to one side of the wagon, a roll of bedding to the other side, baggage, bundles, pots, pans and bags of horse feed hung on behind; the effect was really grotesque. As they had already traveled half across the continent, seemed in good shape and were experienced emigrants they passed muster and were accepted. Not encumbered with useless luggage and Mr. Lamore [sic] being an expert driver his wagon did not sink into the mud or sand and got over grades and through creeks with comparative ease. He required but little help thus being a desirable member of the train.

Mr. West from Peoria, Ill. had another man, his wife, a son Clay about 20 years of age and his daughter, America, eighteen. Unfortunately Mr. West had gone to the extreme of providing himself with such a heavy wagon and load that they were deemed objectionable as fellow argonauts. After disposing of some of their supplies they were allowed to join us. They had four fine oxen. This wagon often got stalled in bad roads much to the annoyance of all, but as he was a wagon maker and his companion a blacksmith by trade and both were accommodating there were always ready hands to "pry the wheel out of mire."

. . .

A mule team from Washington, D.C. was very insufficiently provisioned . . . [by] a Southern gentleman "unused to work. . . ." They deserted the train at Salt Lake as they could not proceed with their equipment and it was easier to embrace Mormonism than to brave the "American Desert."

Much in contrast to these men were four batchelors Messers Wilson, Goodall, Fifield and Martin, who had a wagon drawn by four oxen and two milch cows following behind. The latter gave milk all the way to the sink of the Humboldt where they died, having acted as draught animals for several weeks after the oxen had perished. Many a cup of milk was given to the children of the train and the mothers tried in every way possible to express their gratitude. When these men lost all their stock and had to abandon their wagon they found that through their generosity they had made many friends. Having cast their bread, or milk, upon the waters it returned, double fold. I remember the evenings' milking was used for supper, but that milked in the morning was put into a high tin churn and the constant jostling that it got all day formed butter and delicious butter-milk by night. We all were glad to swap some of our food for a portion of these delicacies.

After a sufficient number of wagons and people were collected at this rendezvous we proceeded to draw up and agree upon a code of general regulations for train government and mutual protection— a necessary precaution when so many were to travel together. Each family was to be independent yet a part of the grand unit and every man was expected to do his individual share of general work and picket duty.

John Brophy was selected as Colonel. He was particularly eligible having served in the Black Hawk War and as much of his life had been spent along the frontier his experience with Indians was quite exceptional.

Each week seven Captains were appointed to serve on "Grand Duty." They were to protect the camps and animals at night. One served each night and in case of danger gave the alarm.

When going into camp the "leader wagon" was turned from the road to the right, the next wagon turned to the left, the others following close after and always alternating to right and left. In this way a large circle, or corral, was formed within which the tents were pitched and the oxen herded. The horses were picketed near by until bed time when they were tethered to the tongues of the wagons.

While the stock and wagons were being cared for, the tents erected and camp fires started by the side of the wagons outside the corral, the cooks busied themselves preparing the evening meal for the hungry, tired, impatient travelers.

When the camp ground was desirable enough to warrant it we did not travel on the Sabbath.

Although the men were generally busy mending wagons, harness, yokes, shoeing the animals etc., and the women washed clothes, boiled a big mess of beans, to be warmed over for several meals, or perhaps mended clothes or did other household straightening up, all felt somewhat rested on Monday morning, for the change of occupation had been refreshing.

If we had devotional service the minister—protem—stood in the center of the corral while we all kept on with our work. There was no disrespect intended but there was little time for leisure or that the weary pilgrim could call his own.

When possible we rested the stock an hour at noon each day; allowing them to graze, if there was anything to graze upon, or in any case they could lie down, which the fagged beasts often preferred to do as they were too tired to eat what we could give them. During the noon hour we refreshed ourselves with cold coffee and a crust of bread. Also a halt of ten minutes each hour was appreciated by all and was never a loss of time.

However, these respites could not always be indulged in as often the toil had to be kept up almost all day and much of the night—because of lack of water. Night work told very seriously upon the stock—they were more worn with one night's travel than they would have been by several day's work, indeed, invariably one or more poor beasts fell by the wayside—a victim of thirst and exhaustion.

It took us four days to organize our company of 70 wagons and 120 persons; bringing our wagons and animals to the highest possible standard of preparedness; wash our clothes; soak several days' supply of food—and say good bye to civilization at Council Bluffs. Owing to the cheapness of eggs and chickens we reveled in their luxuries, carrying a big supply, ready cooked with us.

On May 26th we started to cross the Missouri

River and our first real work affronted us. The wheels of the wagon had to be taken off and the bodies carried onto the flat-boats. They were then piled with goods and covered with heavy canvas or rubber sheets to protect the provisions from water. Sometimes two or three small wagons were taken at the same time.

The flat-boats were attached by a pully to a rope stretched across the river to prevent its being carried down stream, and even so row as best the men could, it landed very far down the opposite shore and had to be towed up stream to the landing before the load could be taken off. Ropes were tied to the horns of the oxen and around the necks of the mules and horses to assist them in stemming the current as they swam the river. The women and children sat tailor fashion on the bottom of the raft. Much time and strength was thus consumed and owing to the great size of our caravan we were a week in getting across—as long a time as it takes now to go from the Pacific Coast to Chicago and return.

This was naturally annoying to those safely over, but we were as patient as possible under the circumstances—being fresh and good natured when we started out—but nevertheless we were convinced that our train was too large to admit of much speed even though it might be a safeguard against Indian attacks—a dread always uppermost in our minds. However, on the road some of the more slothful fell behind to augment the following company, since often only a short distance separated its different trains—a few impatient ones caught up with the caravan ahead of us, and during the first few weeks we met emigrants who had become discouraged almost before they were fairly started and were returning homeward. Indeed very few companies "stuck together" the whole trip. When we reached Sacramento not more than a dozen of our original train of 120 were with us.

Finally we were all safely landed upon the west side of the river, on the site of the City of Omaha, Nebraska, but there wasn't no sign of a town there then—only beautiful trees and grass. Several days' travel brought us to the Elkhorn River. . . . The bed of the river was quicksand. . . . Having once entered the water, wagons had to be rushed across to avoid sinking into the quicksand.

The Indians were the first that we had met and, being a novelty to most of us, we eyed them with a good deal of curiosity. One Indian girl of about fourteen years of age wept loud and incessantly for an hour or more until we women sympathizing with her in her apparent grief, gave her a few trinkets and clothes and were astonished at the efficacy of the cure.

The squaws carried their pappooses in queer little canopied baskets suspended upon their backs by a band around their heads and across their foreheads. The infant was snugly bound, mummy-fashion with only its head free. It was here that I first saw a bit of remarkable maternal discipline, peculiar to most of the Indian tribes. The child cried whereupon the mother took it, basket and all, from her back and nursed it. It still fretted and whimpered apparently uncomfortable or ill. The other then stood it up against a tree and dashed water in the poor little creature's face. By the time that it recovered its breath it stopped crying. No pampered, restless urchin for the Indian household, no indeed.

The bucks with their bows and arrows, beaded buckskin garments and feather head gears were much in evidence and though these prairie redmen were generally friendly they were insistent beggars, often following us for miles and at mealtime disgustingly stood around and solicited food.* They seldom molested us, however, but it was a case of the Indian, as well as the poor, "Ye have always with ye."

During the entire trip Indians were a source of anxiety, we being never sure of their friendship. Secret dread and alert watchfulness seemed always necessary for after we left the prairies they were more treacherous and numerous being in the language of the pioneer trapper: "They wus the most onsartainest vermints alive."

One night after we had retired, some sleeping in blankets upon the ground, some in tents, a few under the wagons and others in the wagons, Colonel Brophy gave the men a practice drill. It was impromptu and a surprise. He called: "Indians, Indians!" We were thrown into great confusion and excitement but he was gratified at the promptness and courage with which the men responded. Each immediately seized his gun and made ready

*Among Indian tribes the sharing of food was a traditional sign of amity and friendship. Haun's response is typical of most emigrants and illustrates the degree to which the travelers often misread and misunderstood the Indians' customs.

for the attack. The women had been instructed to seek shelter in the wagons at such times of danger, but some screamed, others fainted, a few crawled under the wagons and those sleeping in wagons generally followed their husbands out and all of us were nearly paralized with fear. Fortunately, we never had occasion to put into actual use this maneuver, but the drill was quite reassuring and certainly we womenfolk would have acted braver had the alarm ever again been sounded. . . .

The following night brother Derrick and Mr. Bowen were sleeping as was their custom, under a wagon next to ours and it being very warm they turned their comforters down to the foot of their couch. Behold, next morning the covering was missing! It could hardly have been taken by an animal else some trace of their foot-prints and that of the dragging bedding would have been seen. The Indians with their soft moccasins and the light rapid steps and springing, long strides they take when in retreat seldom left evidence upon the ground.

This unwelcome call, so soon after the former theft, was anything but reassuring. It was not pleasant to know how shy, steathy and treacherous even these *friendly* Indians were and that they kept such close watch upon our every movement both day and night.

The next night when we retired I had a nervous attack was really so timid that I saw that the canvas of our wagon was snugly together; all strings and fastenings securely tied and—yes, womanlike I added pins here and there, leaving no peekholes: for I just couldn't go to sleep knowing that some bold, prying savage eye might look in at me during the night. Of course I had shut out all ventilation and during the night my husband opened the wagon cover wide enough for not only the savage eye but the whole savage himself to enter! Probably this was done as soon as I had gone to sleep.

Carl West was inclined to sonambulism and these annoying visits from the Indians so worked upon his mind that that night he dreamed that he was attacked by Indians and ran screaming from his wagon. He was bear footed and half clad but he ran so fast that it was all that two of his companions could do to overtake him.

The emigrants were often sorely tried and inconvenienced by losses more or less serious for in spite of the most alert guard it was almost impossible to see the advancing thief crawling, like a snake, on the ground up to his intended prey. . . .

Finally after a couple of weeks' travel the distant mountains of the west came into view.

This was the land of the buffalo. One day a herd came in our direction like a great black cloud, a threatening moving mountain, advancing towards us very swiftly and with wild snorts, noses almost to the ground and tails flying in midair. I haven't any idea how many there were but they seemed to be innumerable and made a deafening terrible noise. As is their habit, when stampeding, they did not turn out of their course for anything. Some of our wagons were within their line of advance and in consequence one was completely demolished and two were overturned. Several persons were hurt, one child's shoulder being dislocated, but fortunately no one was killed.

Two of these buffaloes were shot and the humps and tongues furnished us with fine fresh meat. They happened to be buffalo cows and, in consequence, the meat was particularly good flavor and tender. It is believed that the cow can run faster than the bull. The large bone of the hind leg, after being stripped of the flesh, was buried in coals of buffalo chips and in an hour the baked marrow was served. I have never tasted such a rich, delicious food!

One family "jerked" some of the hump. After being cut into strips about an inch wide it was strung on ropes on the outside of the wagon cover and in two or three days was thoroughly cured. It was then packed in a bag and in the Humboldt Sink, when rations were low it came in very handy. Spite of having hung in the Alkali dust and being rather shrivelled looking, it was relished for when hunger stares one in the face one isn't particular about trifles like that.

. . .

Buffalo chips, when dry, were very useful to us as fuel. On the barren plains when we were without wood we carried empty bags and each pedestrian "picked up chips" as he, or she, walked along. Indeed we could have hardly got along without thus useful animal, were always appropriating either his hump, tongue, marrowbone, tallow, skin or chips! . . .

The Indian is a financier of no mean ability and invariably comes out A1 in a bargain. Though you may, for the time, congratulate yourself upon your own sagacity, you'll be apt to realize a little later on that you were not quite equal to the shrewd redman—had got the "short end of the deal." One of their "business tricks" was to sell horses or other necessities which were their booty acquired during an attack upon a preceding train. When we were well along in our journey—in the Humboldt Sink—we overtook emigrants one of whom had swapped his watch with the Indians for a yoke of oxen. A few hours afterwards he found that they had been stolen when left to rest while the owners had gone in search of water. The rightful owners established their claim and after a compromise the oxen were joint property. The watch being the profit of the middleman.

Trudging along within the sight of the Platte, whose waters were now almost useless to us on account of the Alkali, we one day found a post with a cross board pointing to a branch road which seemed better than the one we were on. . . . We decided to take it but before many miles suddenly found ourselves in a desolate, rough country that proved to be the edge of the "Bad Lands". I shudder yet at the thought of the ugliness and danger of the territory. Entirely destitute of vegetation the unsightly barren sandstonehills, often very high and close together formed of great bowlders piled one on top of the other like glaciers, with ravines and gulches between and mighty full of crouching, treacherous Indians, they fairly swarmed and we feared that we had been purposely misled in order that they might do us harm. This, however, could not have been the case for the road often was between precipitous walls hundreds of feet high and had they cared to attack us from the heights above we could have made no effective defense. After the possible massacre had been accomplished their booty would have been our money, clothing, food and traveling paraphernalia—and worse still those of our women who had been unfortunate enough to have escaped death.*

Unlike the Indians of the prairies and plains these mountain inhabitants did not have horses and were expert in concealing themselves, and during our entire trip we were never so apprehensive and terrified. We pushed almost recklessly forward in our endeavor to get back to the road along the river. The unevenness of the surface seemed almost like a maze, and being without a single landmark you can imagine our almost frenzied fear that we might be traveling in a circle. We made our resting stops as brief as possible and the days' work from early dawn until dark.

We saw nothing living but Indians, lizards and snakes. Trying, indeed, to feminine nerves. Surely Inferno can be no more horrible in formation. The pelting sun's rays reflected from the parched ground seemed a furnace heat by day and our campfires, as well as those of the Indians cast grotesque glares and terrifying shadows by night. The demen needed only horns and cloven feet to complete the soul stirring picture!

To add to the horrors of the surroundings one man was bitten on the ankle by a venomous snake. Although every available remedy was tried upon the wound, his limb had to be amputated with the

*Haun's allusion is to the common fear among emigrant women that they would be raped if captured by Indians.

aid of a common handsaw. Fortunately for him, he had a good, brave wife along who helped and cheered him into health and usefulness; for it was not long before he found much that he could do and was not considered a burden, although the woman had to do a man's work as they were alone. He was of a mechanical turn, and later on helped mend wagons, yokes and harness; and when the train was "on the move" sat in the wagon, gun by his side, and repaired boots and shoes. He was one of the most cheery members of the company and told good stories and sang at the campfire, putting to shame some of the most able bodied who were given to complaining or selfishness. . . .

Finally after several days we got back onto the road and were entering the Black Hills Country. . . .

Here we also found fragments of a women's cotton dress tied to bushes and small pieces were scattered along the road. Whether this had been intended as a decoy to lead some of our men into a trap should they essay a possible rescue we did not know and the risk was too great to be taken.

We had not traveled many miles in the Black Hills—the beginning of the Rocky Mountains—before we realized that our loads would have to be lightened as the animals were not able to draw the heavily laden wagons over the slippery steep roads. We were obliged to sacrifice most of our merchandise that was intended for our stock in trade in California and left it by the wayside; burying the barrels of alcohol least the Indians should drink it and frenzied therby might follow and attack us. . . .

The roads were rocky and often very steep from this on to the Great Salt Lake—the distance across the Rocky Mountains. Sometimes to keep the wagons from pressing upon the animals in going down grade young pine trees were cut down and after stripping them of all but the top branches they were tied to the front and under the rear axle. The branches dragging upon the ground, or often solid rock, formed a reliable brake. Then again a rope or chain would be tied to the rear of the wagon and every one, man, woman and child would be pressed into service to hold the wagon back. At other times a chain or rope would be fastened to the front axle and we climbed up impossible bowlders and pulled with might and main while the men pushed with herculanian strength to get the loaded wagons over some barrier. The animals owing to cramped quarters, were often led around the obstacle. Many times the greater part of the day would be consumed in this strenuous and altogether unladylike labor.

And oh, such pulling, pushing, tugging it was! I used to pity the drivers as well as the oxen and horses—and the rest of us. The drivers of our ox teams were sturdy young men, all about twenty-two years of age who were driving for their passage to California. They were of good family connections and all became prominent citizens. One a law student, Charles Wheeler, studied all his leisure time, and often could be seen with his open book as he walked beside his team. One, the whistler, Chester Fall, had been intended for the Ministry and the third Ralph Cushing had run away from college.

The latter was the life of our party and a general favorite with the entire train. I see him now, in my mind's eye, trudging along; his bright countenance and carefree air, an inspiration. The familiar tunes that he played upon his harmonica seemed to soften the groaning and creaking of the wagons and to shorten the long miles of the mountain road.

"Home Sweet Home," "Old Kentucky Home," "Maryland, My Maryland," "The Girl I left Behind Me," "One More Ribber to Cross," seemed particularly appropriate and touched many a pensive heart. The strains of his ballads went straight to America West's heart even as her sweet voice as she sang at the campfire Cupid used as an arrow with which to pierce Ralph Cushing's manly breast. When the clumsy, heavy wagon of America's father got mired Ralph was among the first to render assistance and towards the end of the journey when we were all enduring great hardships our young couple lent a ray of romance by their evident regard for each other, for "All the world loves a lover." . . .

During the day we womenfolk visited from wagon to wagon or congenial friends spent an hour walking, ever westward, and talking over our home life back in "the states" telling of the loved ones left behind; voicing our hopes for the future in the far west and even whispering a little friendly gossip of emigrant life.

High teas were not popular but tatting, knitting, crocheting, exchanging recepes for cooking beans or dried apples or swapping food for the sake of variety kept us in practice of feminine occupations and diversions.

We did not keep late hours but when not too engrossed with fear of the red enemy or dread of impending danger we enjoyed the hour around the campfire. The menfolk lolling and smoking their pipes and guessing or maybe betting how many miles we had covered the day. We listened to readings, story telling, music and songs and the day often ended in laughter and merrymaking.

It was the fourth of July when we reached the beautiful Laramie River. Its sparkling, pure waters were full of myriads of fish that could be caught with scarcely an effort. It was necessary to build barges to cross the river and during the enforced delay our animals rested and we had one of our periodical "house cleanings." This general systematic re-adjustment always freshened up our wagon train very much, for after a few weeks of travel things got mixed up and untidy and often wagons had to be abandoned if too worn for repairs, and generally one or more animals had died or been stolen.

After dinner that night it was proposed that we celebrate the day and we all heartily join[ed] in. America West was the Goddess of Liberty, Charles Wheeler was orator and Ralph Cushing acted as master of ceremonies. We sang patriotic songs, repeated what little we could of the Declaration of Independence, fired off a gun or two, and gave three cheers for the United States and California Territory in particular!

The young folks decorated themselves in all manner of fanciful and grotesque costumes—Indian characters being most popular. To the rollicking music of violin and Jew's harp we danced until midnight. There were Indian spectators, all bewildered by the (to them) weird war dance of the Pale Face and possibly they deemed it advisable to sharpen up their arrow heads. During the frolic when the sport was at its height a strange white woman with a little girl in her sheltering embrace rushed into the corral. She was trembling with terror, tottering with hunger. Her clothing was badly torn and her face disheveled. The child crouched with fear and hid her face within the folds of her mother's tattered skirt. The woman could give no account of her forlorn condition but was only able to sob: "Indians," and "I have nobody nor place to go to." After she had partaken of food and was refreshed by a safe night's rest she recovered and the next day told us that her husband and sister had contracted cholera on account of which her family consisting of husband, brother, sister, herself and two children had stayed behind their train. The sick ones' died and while burying the sister the survivors were attacked by Indians, who, as she supposed, killed her brother and little son. She was obliged to flee for her life dragging with her the little five year old daughter.

She had been three days walking back to meet a train. It had been necessary, in order to avoid Indians, to conceal herself behind trees or bowlders much of the time and although she had seen a train in the distance before ours she feared passing the Indians that were between the emigrants and herself. She had been obliged to go miles up the

Laramie to find a place where she could get across by wading from rock to rock and the swift current had lamed her and bruised her body.

Raw fish that she had caught with her hands and a squirrel that she killed with a stone had been their only food. Our noise and campfire had attracted her and in desperation she braved the Indians around us and trusting to the darkness ventured to enter our camp. Martha, for that was her name, had emigrated from Wisconsin and pleaded with us to send her home; but we had now gone too far on the road to meet returning emigrants so there was no alternative for her but to accept our protection and continue on to California. When she became calmed and somewhat reconciled to so long and uncertain a journey with strangers she made herself useful and loyally cast her lot with us. She assisted me with the cooking for her board; found lodgings with the woman whose husband was a cripple and in return helped the brave woman drive the ox team. Mr. & Mrs. Lamore kept her little girl with their own. . . .

Upon the second day of our resumed travel, still following up the North Platte, Martha spied a deserted wagon some little distance off the road which she recognized as her own. Mr. Bowen went with her to investigate, hoping to find her brother and son. The grave of her sister was still open and her clothing as well as that of her husband, who was in the wagon where he had died, were missing. The grewsome sight drove her almost mad. Mr. Bowen and she did not bury the bodies lest they might bring contagion back to us. No trace of either brother or son could be found.

All supplies and the horses had been stolen by the Indians.

Cholera was prevalent on the plains at this time; the train preceding as well as the one following ours had one or more deaths, but fortunately we had not a single case of the disease. Often several graves together stood as silent proof of smallpox or cholera epidemic. The Indians spread the disease among themselves by digging up the bodies of the victims for the clothing. The majority of the Indians were pock-marked. . . .

Turning in a southwesterly direction we came to Fort Bridger, named for the celebrated scout. It was simply a trading post for the white and Indian fur trappers. We saw a renegade white man here who having lived for years among the Indians had forgotten his native language and dressing and eating as they did, his long unkept hair and uncouth appearance was loathsome in the extreme; it being hard to distinguish him from his brother Indians. We regarded him with more fear and abhorance than we did a manly buck, and his squaw and family of half-breeds as unfortunates.

It was with considerable apprehension that we started to traverse the treeless, alkali region of the Great Basin or Sink of the Humboldt. Our wagons were badly worn, the animals much the worse for wear, food and stock feed was getting low with no chance of replenishing the supply. During the month of transit we, like other trains, experienced the greatest privations of the whole trip. It was no unusual sight to see graves, carcasses of animals and abandoned wagons. In fact that latter furnished us with wood for the campfires as the sagebrush was scarce and unsatisfactory and buffalo chips were not as plentiful as on the plains east of the Rocky Mountains.

The alkali dust of this territory was suffocating, irritating our throats and clouds of it often blinded us. The mirages tantalized us; the water was unfit to drink or to use in any way; animals often perished or were so overcome by heat and exhaustion that they had to be abandoned, or in cases of human hunger, the poor jaded creatures were killed and eaten. . . .

One of our dogs was so emaciated and exhausted that we were obliged to leave him on this desert and it was said that the train following us used him for food.

Before leaving Bear River, knowing of the utter lack of fresh water, we cooked large quantities of bread to be used on the desert. We gave a half loaf each day to each horse until the flour gave out. This was a substitute for grain.

Across this drear country I used to ride horseback several hours of the day which was a great relief from the continual jolting of even our spring wagon. I also walked a great deal and this lightened the wagon. One day I walked fourteen miles and was not very fatigued.

. . . The men seemed more tired and hungry than were the women. Our only death on the journey occurred in this desert. The Canadian woman, Mrs. Lamore, suddenly sickened and died, leaving her two little girls and grief stricken husband. We halted a day to bury her and the infant that had lived but an hour, in this weird, lonely spot on God's footstool away apparently from everywhere and everybody.*

The bodies were wrapped together in a bed-comforter and wound, quite mummyfied with a few yards of string that we made by tying together torn strips of a cotton dress skirt. A passage of the Bible (my own) was read; a prayer was offerred and "Nearer, My God to Thee" sung. Owing to the unusual surroundings the ceremony was very impressive. Every heart was touched and eyes full of tears as we lowered the body, coffinless, into the grave. There was no tombstone—why should there be—the poor husband and orphans could never hope to revisit the grave and to the world it was just one of the many hundreds that marked the trail of the argonaut.

This burial and one I witnessed at sea some years later made a lasting impression upon me and I always think of them when I attend a funeral; such a grewsome sensation was caused by the desolation. The immense, lonesome plain; the great fathomless ocean—how insignificant seems the human body when consigned to their cold embrace! . . . Martha and the lamented Canadian wife had formed a fast friendship while on the plains and the former was a faithful nurse during the latter's illness. What more natural than that the dying mother should ask her friend to continue to care

*Haun's account of the death of Mrs. Lamore and of the newborn infant does not mention that the death occurred after childbirth. Her phrase "suddenly sickened and died" is typical of the taboos that shrouded the facts of pregnancy and birth among emigrant women.

for her orphan girls and to make [them] the sisters of her own daughter?

Years afterward when prosperity crowned Mr. Lamore's efforts the three girls were sent "back to the states" to school and Martha's daughter became the wife of a prominent United States Congressman. [Martha's little son was soon reunited with his mother. He had been traded by the Indians to some passing emigrants for a horse. In fact, the child was traveling but a few days' journey behind her in another emigrant train.]

. . . we reached Sacramento on November 4, 1849, just six months and ten days after leaving Clinton, Iowa, we were all in pretty good condition. . . .

Although very tired of tent life many of us spent Thanksgiving and Christmas in our canvas houses. I do not remember ever having had happier holiday times. For Christmas dinner we had a grizzly bear steak for which we paid $2.50, one cabbage for $1.00 and—oh horrors—some *more* dried apples! And for a Christmas present the Sacramento river rose very high and flooded the whole town! . . . It was past the middle of January before we . . . reached Marysville—there were only a half dozen houses; all occupied at exorbitant prices. Some one was calling for the services of a lawyer to draw up a will and my husband offered to do it for which he charged $150.00.

This seemed a happy omen for success and he hung out his shingle, abandoning all thought of going to the mines. As we had lived in a tent and had been on the move for nine months, traveling

2400 miles we were glad to settle down and go housekeeping in a shed that was built in a day of lumber purchased with the first fee. The ground was given us by some gamblers who lived next door and upon the other side, for neighbors, we had a real live saloon. I never had received more respectful attention than I did from these neighbors.

Upon the whole I enjoyed the trip, spite of its hardships and dangers and the fear and dread that hangs as a pall over every hour. Although not so thrilling as were the experiences of many who suffered in reality what we feared, but escaped, I like every other pioneer, love to live over again, in memory those romantic months, and revisit, in fancy, the scenes of the journey.

Welcome to the L.A. Freeway

TOM HUTH

Tom Huth is a contributor to California *magazine and other publications. His hair-raising account of life on the Los Angeles Freeway will hit familiar panic buttons for many travelers to Southern California.*

It is late in the afternoon (any afternoon, it could have been) and I am flying out the Ventura Freeway in tight configuration with a Catholic nun. Her Toyota is holding steady in the right lane and I'm alongside in the number three, doing an effortless sixty-five. Then suddenly, inexplicably, the semi ahead of us throws a rear tire. It pops off, whole, in a yellowish cloud of dust . . . arcs tantalizingly through the air . . . hangs suspended over the white line before our eyes. For a moment, that lifetime, the nun and I are joined in horrified communion, watching the tire falling back to earth. If it bounces left it will probably crash through my windshield; if right, then the nun will be chosen. There is no time to react, to think, to pray. But the good Lord is with us today, because the tire bounces neither left nor right, but true—straight into the air—and flies between our two capsules like a meteoroid. The drama is over in a couple of seconds, and we hurtle on (the trucker included) toward our destinations, catching just a glimpse in our rearview mirrors of the fresh panic behind.

This is the freeway: life as we know it, every lane the fast lane.

The Los Angeles freeway system is built upon an extraordinary set of assumptions upon which depend the lives of approximately five million people every day. A driver must take for granted that the brake lights of the cars in front of him are in good working order; that the driver behind him has nimble reflexes; that the vehicles on either side will not bust a kingpin or a steering rod; that the truck up ahead will not drop an I-beam in his path; that all parties to this scheme are awake, attentive, fairly sober and reasonably desirous of going on living. In fact, the driver's belief must be so absolute that he cannot allow himself to think about these things at all, or he'll have to pull over, drop out.

A highway patrolman recalls: "This lady she stopped in the number one [the left] lane on the northbound Hollywood at Mulholland, so they called me for a traffic hazard. I got there and, sure enough, all these cars are coming up and screeching their tires and moving around her. So I go up and say, 'What's the matter with your car?' and she goes, 'Nothing.' She's all shaking and everything. She says, 'I can't drive.' I say, 'What do you mean you can't drive?' She says, 'Because I'm scared.' So I made a traffic break and got her over to the right shoulder, and I says, 'You okay now?'

and she goes, 'No.' And I says, 'Okay, I'll follow you off . . . and we'll call for help.' "

That lady wasn't crazy, she merely was seeing through the illusion.

Freeway aficionado Paul (Panther) Pierce, in his book *Take an Alternate Route*, remembers a man he found one afternoon cowering on the center divider alongside his disabled car. He was a farmer who'd never taken the freeways before, and this was his sorry tale: he had entered into traffic in the left lane that morning with a full tank of gas—had been swept up helplessly into the race, been boxed in place by the other drivers, been afraid even to change lanes—had driven on in terror like this, always keeping to the left, being shuttled from freeway to freeway, for six hours—until finally he ran out of gas and coasted to a merciful stop against the fence.

A psychiatrist in Houston had studied this phenomenon and duly classified it as a new type of phobia, and yet what's more interesting, actually, is how few drivers fall victim to it. The illusion of well-being at sixty miles an hour (the cars close enough that their occupants could reach out and shake hands) is so convincing that Angelenos can log a cumulative eighty-six million miles each day on their freeway—with less than one accident of any kind for every million miles driven. And in the process they have made an engrossing sport out of the ordinary act of commuting.

Picture it as a Parker Brothers board game, the players deftly shuttling their tokens between lanes, from one freeway to another, trying to find the quickest route to the buried treasure and back home again. If a player lives in Azusa and has to meet his agent in Westwood and then make a lunch date in Costa Mesa, it's easy—he just grabs the Foothill to the 605 to the westbound San Bernardino to the Santa Monica, then he jumps on the southbound San Diego down to the Newport, then he catches the Santa Ana up to the Orange to the westbound Foothill again and he's back at Go. If he's a heads-up player, he'll stay tuned into the radio traffic alerts—the Chance cards of the L.A. Freeway Game—and plan his strategies accordingly.

Of course, this same spirit might apply to negotiating any modern urban road network. But if you'll look at the divided-highway maps of other cities, you'll see only the most anemic of skeletons—a few east-west and north-south arteries, a scenic low-tech parkway, perhaps a tidy little beltway running around the perimeter—the routes named after the unremembered dead: Dan Ryan, Wilbur Cross, John C. Lodge, Henry Watterson. There's no grandeur at all to the chase, no complexity, no ingenuity required. Only L.A., with its twenty-six freeways covering some 700 miles between Ventura, San Bernardino and Laguna—freeways fabled in movie and song—provides an arena, a challenge to body and mind, worthy of the serious metropolitan driver. It was just a few years ago that everybody was babbling about the amazing dexterity that teenagers exhibited at the controls of video games. We kept exclaiming: "Why, their eye-to-hand coordination is simply out of this world!" But, all along, Angelenos by the millions have been out there on the freeways playing the game for keeps. It's not as brazenly heroic as hang gliding or skydiving or scaling El Capitan by the tips of one's fingers, but a sport for the masses, instead: Everyman taking his life into his own hands, as it should be.

At ten minutes past midnight the world's busiest roadway, the Ventura as it approaches the San Diego, is at peace with its city. A three-quarter moon is rising over the Valley Federal Savings sign and only a few taillights stretch out ahead of me to pinpoints in the backlit sky. The city looks extremely kind at night from the freeway, its detail softened by fog. I swing south on the Hollywood toward downtown and then north through the four-level to the Pasadena, the grandfather of them all, finished in '41.

Running with the freeways at night encourages dreaming, and I remember now when I was a boy, sitting in the backseat of the family Buick and watching over my dad's shoulder as he piloted us through the streets of Detroit, both hands clamped firmly on the wheel, always making tiny corrections in our course, apparently keeping us alive from one moment to the next. The city traffic seemed to annoy him, the stupidity of other drivers, and he'd snap at me if, in my eagerness to get his view of the road, I'd kick the back of his seat.

At 1:30 A.M. the Foothill is an abandoned airport runway, as empty as the playgrounds in *West Side Story* in the lull before violence. The freeways are so smooth that one can lose all sense of motion, the curves so graceful that the steering wheel seems to move of its own accord. My father, I'm sure, would have enjoyed this sort of driving if he'd lived to know it—cruising alone through the concrete canyons, letting his mind drift away to the strains of Vivaldi, the cellos swooning along with the sweeps of the great interchanges—the Glendale to the Golden State to the eastbound 101 then peeling off to the Long Beach and looping around to the Pomona—trumpets heralding a power plant blazing past on the right, a woodwind quartet trilling in at the Paramount on-ramp.

The people who created our freeways certainly never intended them to be driven by motorists using only ten percent of their brain cells, with the other ninety percent off in space. But this is the result of such peerless design—raceways stripped of all activity but the performance of nonstop driving, whole hillsides blasted away to ensure uneventful passage—a total autopian environment in which monotony leads ineluctably to hallucination. Only the raised Botts dots between each lane (named after the Caltrans engineer who invented them) keeping the voyager's consciousness from straying too far.

At 4:30 on the Riverside the smell of orange blossoms mingles with the aroma of yesterday's exhaust, and at five the dawn begins to show through a stand of eucalyptus trees in the outside world. A happy yellow Denny's sign looms to the east like the sun itself. Even now, an hour before the morning rush officially begins at monitoring stations throughout the metropolis, the inbound traffic on the San Bernardino is getting thick.

At 5:45 the first slowdown, brake lights flashing on. The radio chimes in:

On the Harbor Freeway northbound at the Artesia they've rolled an ambulance . . . on the Pomona northbound at Wilcox a couple of cars got together—they're prying them apart right now . . . on the southbound Glendale at Fletcher there's a workbench in the fast lane . . . and on the southbound Hollywood a quarter of a mile north of the four-level, a dead dog in the number one lane. . . .

Drivers dance from lane to lane, settling into their favorite slots. A VW dives into traffic from the right and skips across three lanes in one Nureyevian flourish. At 5:55 the traffic jams up and I kick off the San Bernardino onto the Foothill, but they're still chasing me—the pack, bearing down from behind.

At about this time, Michael Mathias is arriving for work at the California Highway Patrol's central L.A. station, which squats in the shadows beneath one gargantuan arm of the Harbor-Santa Monica interchange. He runs through an equipment check on his cruiser—the siren, the flashers, the Remington shotgun loaded and mounted at arm's reach—and as the radio dispatcher calls "Move 'em out!" he rolls onto the streets and heads for his beat—those six miles of the Hollywood Freeway between Alameda and Lankershim.

"So far as procedures," he advises me casually enough, "whenever I make a stop, all I ask is that you get out of the car and stand behind the door and watch traffic. If you see a car coming, just yell at me and jump—that's the best I can tell you. It's safer outside the car than inside. If I get run over or something, all you have to do is turn on the radio . . . push this button down . . . just tell 'em. 'Officer down,' or something like that, and give 'em the location."

Mathias is young and bouncy, square jawed, enthusiastic about being a highway patrolman—has been doing it for a year, goes strictly by the book, and the fun hasn't begun to wear off. "I just get on the Hollywood and go up and down," he says of his eight-hour day. "Basically, what we try to do is just keep a high visual horizon and look for violators and people doing things out of the ordinary. Just scan everything. . . . And if there's nothin' going on—if everybody's pretty much following the program—we catch up to the next bunch of traffic . . . check that out."

He notices a woman driver pulled over on the right shoulder and stops to offer help. I stand outside, as I'm told, the traffic roaring in my ears, the jet stream whipping at my hair, seeming to singe my eyebrows. Back in the car a few minutes later Mathias explains that if the driver had been a man, he wouldn't have stopped. "If they're close to a call box a man can usually handle himself," he says. "Females, we've found, you know, they get frightened easily. People try to molest 'em, things like that. So I just go up and tell her to lock all the doors and windows and not let anybody in except AAA."

Mathias issues his share of tickets, but for the most part he keeps order on the freeways in subtler ways—by merely making his enlightened presence known to people who aren't following the program. "Like that Monte Carlo in the number two lane," he says now, "he's following too close. I'll go up there, get alongside him, let him see me . . . like this. He'll back off and slow down." A moment later something amuses him. "That guy in the number one lane knows I can't get to him right now," he explains, "so he's speeding. People play games with me. See? He's up there in the number two lane now, going in and out of traffic." The cop laughs. He enjoys this hide-and-seek, playing with his power, relieving the boredom. "If I wanted him," he assures me, "I could get him."

While the freeway patrolman is on the lookout for reckless drivers, his wide-angle vision is taking in much more than that—more than we civilians realize. As I sit there staring at the head of the driver in front of us, Mathias is noticing out-of-date registration stickers, illegally tinted windows, babies without car seats, outlawed axle modifications, open beer containers, drivers wearing stereo headsets ("That's a no-no, too"). Now he spies a green van without a rear license. He slides past it and reads the number off the front plate, calls it in to the dispatcher to check for outstanding warrants, and then falls back in traffic unobtrusively, keeping the suspect under observation until the dispatcher returns with a negative.

So the freeway driver, often unbeknownst, is continually being watched, followed, scrutinized by a higher consciousness. "It takes awhile," says Mathias, "but pretty soon your eyes are scanning everything . . . your eyes constantly going back and forth." There's a robotic quality to it, those eyes searching only for the x factors.

Still, the human element works its way into the game. He spots a Mustang with a year-old registration sticker and he knows this deserves a citation, but he hesitates. "This is a hard one," he admits. "I don't like stopping girls like that because when she went by I looked at her and she looked at me—and smiled real big. And if I stop her right now she'll think I'm trying to make her or something—and that's one of our big no-nos." While the young cop ponders such interdisciplinary delicacies, another violator catches his eye, and the pretty lady gets off free today.

On the Orange Freeway southbound approaching Lambert, a vehicle has gone off the roadway and over the side . . . on the Golden State southbound transition to the Pasadena, a vehicle fire reported . . .

The occasional foul-ups claim the attention of Skywatch Control, but in fact the morning rush hour is known in the freeway business as the easy one. The drivers are rested, refreshed, on their toes. In the words of Stan Buckmaster, supervisor of the Caltrans L.A. Traffic Operations Center, "The A.M. traffic is ninety percent regulars. These are the commuters—they're pros. They're familiar with the roadway, and they probably recognize the vehicles in their proximity because they all go in at the same time." They know where they're getting on, where they're exiting, when to make their moves—the pros.

At 7:25 this morning back on the eastbound Ventura the roadbed is a mass of shimmering sheet metal and yet the cars, locked into fighter-plane formation, still rocket ahead at fifty miles an hour. This is the time on the freeways—just one brake light short of congestion, one car length short of sanity—when we're taken to the edge. It requires acute concentration, a pianist's touch on the foot pedals, a sixth sense—"a strange and exhilarating mixture," says Reyner Banham, "of long-range confidence and close-range wariness." If a driver leaves too much space in front of him, the pack will jump in and destroy his momentum; if he leaves too little, he might end up with his head through the windshield. He has scant time to use his turn signals—if he sees an opening, he just goes for it. He forgets about his horn—that's a defensive measure. This sport is all offense, guts. And yet somehow the new players surging in from the right always find enough room to join in.

Gary Bork, Chief of the Caltrans's Traffic Operations Branch refers to the attitude of the L.A. driver as "aggressive but polite." He says, "Recently I was in Oregon and we flew over in a helicopter . . .and their problem was that nobody on that freeway let anybody in from the ramps. And another thing—the people on the ramps were not aggressive. But, you know, you come up to a ramp *here,* and those guys are going to get *on!* And the people *let* 'em on." Not because they're just wonderful human beings, but because "they want the system to work!" Whatever legends have been handed down about the looniness of Los Angeles motorists, they don't describe the overwhelming reality. Only when this morning's traffic finally slows to a creep around Tarzana do the commuters snap out of their supercharged trances and begin to look around at their neighbors, take out their newspapers, their hairbrushes, their battery-powered shavers, their knitting, their famous little distractions.

On the San Diego southbound at 8:15 our progress is herky-jerky over Sepulveda Pass. A daredevil motorcyclist (wearing a camouflage jacket) tears by between lanes, nearly amputating my left arm. We speed up around Wilshire and now a semi is on my tail, fifty tons of brute intimidation grinning in the mirror, its air horn bellowing, *"Move over, jackass!"*

Los Angeles, the city stuck on fast forward, is a miracle of synchronicity. Even the casual stroller on the boardwalk gets used to hearing urgent voices over his shoulder—demon bicyclists warning *"On your left!"* as they fly past, or simply *"Left!"* or *"Right!"* or *"Behind you!"* We have taken to wheels and developed out of daily habit the culture of the near-miss, which has been elevated to its purest form on the freeways.

On the eastbound 210 west of Lake, a chemical spill . . . on the Pasadena in the vicinity of the Golden State, a solo spin out. . . .

For many people, commuting is the only chance they have to be alone, a time to reflect (even while maneuvering to stay alive) on great and devilish schemes. The patterns of movement lend themselves to reenacting the morning's domestic squabble or rehearsing a confrontation with the boss. David Brodsly writes, "Perhaps no aspect of the freeway experience is more characteristic than the sudden realization that you have no memory of the past ten minutes of your trip." It's a situation, says John Lilly, having "all the characteristics of the most esoteric and far-out discipline that you could find in the Far East"—a place, says Banham where many Angelenos "spend the two calmest and most rewarding hours of their daily lives." It would not even be an exaggeration to say that some people enjoy playing the freeway game because, after all, it's the best thing they're able to do on this planet.

The San Diego to the Laguna to the Santa Ana, the Orange to the Artesia to the Newport to the Garden Grove—we're doing Orange County now, eating up the mileage like Pac-Man, doubling back to catch the northbound Harbor, checking them off on the map one by one, more than 550 miles covered by noon.

When I get off for gas, the surface world is not a welcome relief but an aggravation. The interruptions to train of thought are less predictable—cars jerking out from the curb, trucks double parked, pedestrians darting through traffic with paper sacks in their arms. No rhythm, no hum, no flow. We have to stop at red lights, wait our turn, go where the arrows tell us to go. We have to obey a visible higher authority, whereas motion is all we want and need—motion, or at least the promise of motion any second now.

According to the latest (1984) figures, there are

seventy-four accidents a day on the urban freeways of Los Angeles, Orange, and Ventura counties. There are 29.5 people injured each day in those collisions, and for every three days that pass two people are killed. A carnage, you might say, and yet the odds for any one gambler are very, very attractive:

- The average motorist, if he commuted ten miles in each direction five days a week, would have an accident of some sort only once in approximately one hundred years.

- A company with one thousand employees, each commuting twenty miles a day, would go about twenty-three years before it lost even one of them to a fatality.

At Caltrans's downtown headquarters, engineers study traffic behavior and come up with new technologies such as ramp meters and message boards to try to accommodate the freeway animal—safely—in ever-larger numbers. The design standard is 1,800 vehicles per lane per hour—one every two seconds—but the engineers know that downgrades, for example, will carry more traffic than upgrades because drivers can see further. Curves can reduce a road's capacity (although expert landscaping can diminish the effect). The weather, the angle of the sun, the width of the lanes—all play their roles. Friday brings the heaviest traffic and the most accidents. The engineers know that in the summer the morning load is lighter because students are out of school, the afternoon load heavier because hundreds of thousands of tourists are in the area. The weekend recreational driver is less mindful and more accident prone than the same person commuting on weekdays. The right lane, according to one study, has more accidents than the left; the afternoons considerably more than the mornings.

Caltrans knows—because it has counted—the number of emergency call boxes on its system (3,335), the number of Botts dots (5,752,810), the precise number of trees (170,048.83). Caltrans has a traffic monitoring and strategy center—"the war room," one official calls it—to which highway planners come and gawk from all over the free and unfree worlds.

Nevertheless, no one at Caltrans seems willing to predict how much longer the system can work the way it does. The freeway grid is nearly completed, and yet every month more drivers enter the competition. It helps that industries keep spreading out over the Southland so that traffic increasingly flows in all directions at all times. It would help if more companies staggered their working hours, as they did during the Olympics. So perhaps the ultimate limit, theorizes senior transportation engineer Don Juge, is "1,800 vehicles per lane per hour for twenty-four hours."

However, it's just possible that imagination is the only constraint. Maybe the L.A. motorist will continue to sharpen his skills, intensify his focus, condition his synapses, deepen his belief, learn the program better and better. Maybe a new evolutionary species is emerging—a driver becoming one with his machine and its mission: a bionic pilot with the high-rise scanning capabilities of a highway patrolman, the reaction time of a Caltech computer, and the psychic preawareness of a Jedi saint—your basic twenty-first-century internal-combustion yogi, a Californian if ever there was one.

The rush hour never ends. The thundering herd keeps charging up from behind (like those younger men at the office), and all a driver can do is snap off his rearview mirror. And keep driving. At one in the afternoon—two, three, it's all the same—unswervingly it's a men's game we're playing here, perpetual motion passing for relationship.

After fourteen hours on the freeways, the body begins faltering, the brain misfiring. The eyes burn from unblinking concentration; the heel of the accelerator foot goes numb. The mind reads danger on all sides now, a photochemical wasteland, and after 688 miles I finally abandon true faith, hypothetical as it was, and buckle the seat belt.

The afternoon rush hour is the sloppy one. People are tired from working, sluggish from lunchtime indulgences, hot, cranky, impatient to get home. Thrown in with the regular commuters now are the shoppers, the museum goers, the beach and ballpark and early theater crowds, the visiting cousins from Iowa, the luckless pensioners trying to fight their way back from the Social Security office.

Plenty of action out here . . . a collision involving a school bus and a tanker truck . . . a vehicle fire with a tie-up all the way back to the East L.A. interchange . . . a pedestrian stranded up on the center divider. . . .

On the Long Beach outbound, the last leg, 6:30 P.M., there are billboards for Smirnoff Vodka, Cuervo Tequilla, Haagen-Dazs Cream Liqueur, Las Vegas, 93 on Your Dial—Traffic Reports Every Ten Minutes, and Peace in Ireland. The afternoon's blinding metallic haze has given way to evening again and the first intimations of fog. Finally, at 6:40, after 855 miles and almost nineteen hours of headlong pursuit, I am able to report that it's possible to drive the entire Los Angeles freeway network in one day without getting killed or caught. But barely. The hard-charging night has a million eyes now—the retreating red taillights of the homebound warriors, the onrushing headlights of the counterinsurgents—and a big harvest Shell sign is coming up full over the South Compton offramp.

The Encircled River

JOHN MCPHEE

John McPhee, born in Princeton, New Jersey, in 1931, was a playwright and Time *magazine editor before becoming a* New Yorker *staffer in 1965. His numerous books include* Oranges *and* The Pine Barrens, *as well as* The Survival of the Bark Canoe *and the* Deltoid Pumpkin Seed *(about a strange aircraft). This extract is from* Coming into the Country *(his critically acclaimed travelogue through Alaska).*

In the morning—cool in the forties and the river calm—we strike the tents, pack the gear, and move down toward Kiana. Gradually, the village spreads out in perspective. Its most prominent structure is the sheet-metal high school on the edge of town. Dirt-and-gravel streets climb the hill above the bluff. Houses are low, frame. Some are made of logs. Behind the town, a navigational beacon flashes. Drawing closer, we can see caribou antlers over doorways—testimony of need and respect. There are basketball backboards. We are closing a circuit, a hundred water miles from the upper Salmon, where a helicopter took us, from Kiana, at the start. Under the bluff, we touch the shore. Kiana is now high above us, and mostly out of sight. The barge is here that brings up supplies from Kotzebue. The river's edge for the moment is all but unpopulated. Fish racks up and down the beach are covered with split drying salmon—ruddy and pink. We disassemble the Kleppers, removing their prefabricated bones, folding their skins, making them disappear into canvas bags. I go up the hill for a carton, and return to the beach. Into envelopes of cardboard I tape the tines of the caribou antler that I have carried from the mountains. Protecting the antler takes longer than the dismantling and packing of the kayaks, but there is enough time before the flight to Kotzebue at midday. In the sky, there has as yet been no sound of the airplane—a Twin Otter, of Wien Air Alaska, the plane that brought us here to meet the chopper. Stell Newman has gone up the beach and found some people at work around their fish racks. He now has with him a slab of dried salmon, and we share it like candy.

Children were fishing when we were here before. They yanked whitefish out of the river and then pelted one another with the living fish as if they were snowballs. Women with tubs were gutting salmon. It was a warmer day then. The sun was so fierce you looked away; you looked north. Up at the airstrip behind the town—a gravel strip, where we go now with our gear—was the Grumman canoe. It had been flown in, and cached there, long before. The helicopter, chartered by the government and coming in from who knows where, was a new five-seat twin-engine Messerschmitt with a bubble front. On its shining fuselage, yellow-and-black heraldry identified it as the property of Petroleum Helicopters, Inc. The pilot removed a couple of fibre-glass cargo doors, took out a seat, and we shoved the canoe into an opening at the rear of the cabin. It went in halfway. The Grumman was too much for the Messerschmitt. The canoe was cantilevered, protruding to the rear. We tied it in place. It was right side up, and we filled it with gear. Leaving the rest of us to wait for a second trip, Pourchot and the pilot took off for the Salmon River. With so much canoe coming out of its body, the helicopter, even in flight, seemed to be nearing the final moment of an amazing pregnancy. It went over the mountains northeast.

There was a wooden sign behind the airstrip: "WELCOME TO THE CITY OF KIANA. 2nd Class City. Population 300 . . . Establish 1902 . . . Main Sources: Bear, Caribou, Moose, Geese, Salmon, Shee, Whitefish, Trout." The burning sun was uncomfortable. I walked behind the sign. In its shadow, the air was chill. I dragged the helicopter seat out of the sun and into the shade of a storage hut, sat down, leaned back, and went to sleep. When I woke up, I was shivering. The temperature a few feet away, in the sunlight, was above seventy degrees.

What awakened me were the voices of children. Three small girls had followed us up from the Kobuk, where we had watched them fish. They had crossed the runway and picked blueberries, and now were offering them from their hands. The berries were intensely sweet, having grown in the long northern light. The little girls also held out pieces of hard candy. Wouldn't we like some?

They asked for nothing. They were not shy. They were totally unself-conscious. I showed them an imitating game, where you clear your throat—hrrum—and then draw with a stick a figure on the ground. "Here. Try to do that." They drew the figure but did not clear their throats. "No. That's not quite right. Hrrum. Here now. Try it again." They tried twice more. They didn't get it. I sat down again on the chopper seat. Stell Newman let them take pictures with his camera. When they noticed my monocular, on a lanyard around my neck, they got down beside me, picked it off my chest, and spied on the town. They leaned over, one at a time, and put their noses down against mine, draping around my head their soft black hair. They stared into my eyes. Their eyes were dark and northern, in beautiful almond faces, aripple with smiles. Amy. Katherine. Rose Ann. Ages nine and eleven. Eskimo girls. They looked up. They had heard the helicopter, and before long it appeared.

I sat in the co-pilot's seat, others in the seat I had been napping on. We lifted off, and headed out to join Pourchot, who was waiting on a gravel bar in the upper Salmon. The rotor noise was above conversation, but the pilot handed me a pair of earphones and a microphone. He showed me on a panel between us the mechanics of communicating. I couldn't think of much to say. I was awed, I suppose, in the presence of a bush pilot (mustache akimbo) and in the presence of the bush itself—the land and the approaching mountains. I didn't want to distract him, or myself. He kept urging me to talk, though. He seemed to want the company. His name was Gene Parrish, and he was a big man who had eaten well. He smoked a cigar, and on the intercom was garrulous and friendly.

Before us now was the first ridgeline. Flying close to ground, close to the mountainside, we climbed rapidly toward the crest, and then—crossing over it—seemed to plunge into a void of air. The ground ahead, which had been so near, was suddenly far below. We soon reached another mountainside, and again we climbed closely above its slope, skimmed the outcropping rocks at the top, and jumped into a gulf of sky.

Parrish said, "Y'all ever seen these mountains before?"

Some of the others had, I said, but I had not.

"Me, neither," he said. "Aren't they fabulous? Alaska is amazing, isn't it? Wherever you go, everything is different. These mountains sure are fabulous."

Indeed they were something like it—engaging, upsweeping tundra fells. They were not sharp and knife-edged like the peaks of the central Brooks. They were less dramatic but more inviting. They looked negotiable. They were, as it happened, the last mountains of the range, the end of the line, the end of the cordillera. They were, after four thousand miles, the last statement of the Rocky Mountains before they disappeared into the Chukchi Sea.

Parrish went up the side of a still higher mountain and skimmed the ridge, to reveal, suddenly, a drainage system far below.

"Is that the Salmon River?" I said.

"Oh, my, no," he said. "It's a ways yet. Where y'all from?"

"I'm from New Jersey. And you?"

"Louisiana."

He said he had come to Alaska on a kind of working vacation. At home, where his job was to fly back and forth between the Louisiana mainland and oil rigs in the Gulf of Mexico, he seldom flew over anything much higher than a wave. Because the Messerschmitt had two engines, he said, he would not have to autorotate down if one were to fail. In fact, he could even climb on one engine. So it was safe to fly this way, low and close—and more interesting.

We flew up the sides of mountain after mountain, raked the ridges, fluttered high over valleys. In each new valley was a stream, large or small. With distance, they looked much alike. Parrish checked his airspeed, the time, the heading; finally, he made a sharp southward turn and began to follow a stream course in the direction of its current, looking for a gravel bar, a man, a canoe. Confidently, he gave up altitude and searched the bending river. He found a great deal of gravel. For thirty, forty miles, he kept searching, until the hills around the river began to diminish in anticipation of—as we could see ahead—the wet-tundra Kobuk plain. If the river was the Salmon, Pourchot was not there. If Pourchot was on the Salmon, Parrish was somewhere else.

The Salmon had to be farther east, he guessed, shaking his head in surprise and wonder. We rollercoasted the sides of additional mountains and came upon another significant drainage. It appeared to Parrish to be the right one. This time, we flew north, low over the river, upstream, looking for the glint of the canoe. We had as much luck as before. The river narrowed as we went farther and farther, until it became a brook and then a rill, with steep-rising mountains on either side. "I don't believe it. I just *can't* believe it," Parrish said. There was nothing much below us now but the kind of streak a tear might make crossing a pilot's face. "This just ain't right," he said. "This is not working out. I was sure of the heading. I was sure this was the river. But nothing ever is guaranteed. Nothing—nothing—is guaranteed."

He turned one-eighty and headed downstream. Spread over his knees was a Nome Sectional Aeronautical Chart, and he puzzled over it for a while, then he handed it to me. Maybe I could help figure where we were. The map was quite wonderful at drawing straight lines between distant airstrips, but its picture of the mountains looked like calves' brains over bone china, and the scale was such that the whole of the Salmon River was only six inches long. The chopper plowed on to the south. I held the map a little closer to my eyes, studying the blue veiny lines among the mountains. The ludicrousness of the situation washed over me. I looked back at Kauffmann and the others, who seemed somewhat confused. And small wonder. A map was being handed back and forth between a man from New Jersey and a pilot from Louisiana who were amiss in—of all places—the Brooks Range. In a sense—in the technical

sense that we had next to no idea where we were—
we were lost.

There are no geographical requirements for pilots in the United States. Anyone who is certified
as a pilot can fly anywhere, and that, of course,
includes anywhere in Alaska. New pilots arrive
steadily from all over the Lower Forty-eight. Some
are attracted by the romance of Alaska, some by
the money around the pipeline. The Alyeska Pipeline Service Company, soon after it began its construction operations, set up its own standards for
charter pilots who would fly its personnel—standards somewhat stiffer than those of the Federal
Aviation Administration. Among other things,
Alyeska insisted that applicants without flying experience in Alaska had to have fifty hours of docu-
mented training there, including a line check above
the terrain they would be flying.

One effect of the pipeline charters has been to
siphon off pilots from elsewhere in the Alaskan
bush. These pilots are often replaced by pilots
inexperienced in Alaska. Say a mail pilot quits and
goes off to fly the pipeline. His replacement might
be three days out of Teterboro. The mail must go
through. Passengers in such planes (passengers ride
with bush mail) sometimes intuit that they and the
pilot are each seeing the landscape in a novel way.
Once, for example, in the eastern-Alaska interior,
I rode in a mail plane that took off from Fairbanks
to fly a couple of hundred miles across mountains
to Eagle, a village on the upper Yukon. It was a
blustery, wet morning, and clouds were lower by
far than summits. As rain whipped against the
windshield, visibility forward was zero. Looking

down to the side, the pilot watched the ground below—trying to identify various drainages and pick his way through the mountains. He frequently referred to a map. The plane was a single-engine Cessna 207 Skywagon, bumping hard on the wind. We went up a small tributary and over a pass, where we picked up another river and followed it downstream. After a time, the pilot turned around and went many miles back in the direction which he had come. He explored another tributary. Then, abruptly, he turned again. The weather was not improving. Soon his confidence in his reading of the land seemed to run out altogether. He asked in what direction the stream below was flowing. He could not tell by the set of the rapids. He handed the map to a passenger who had apparently visited the region once or twice before. The passenger read the map for a while and then counselled the pilot to stay with the principal stream in sight. He indicated to the pilot which direction was downhill. At length, the Yukon came into view. I, who love rivers, had never felt such affection for a river. One would not have to be Marco Polo to figure out now which way to go. I had been chewing gum so vigorously that the hinges of my jaws would ache for two days. We flew up the Yukon to Eagle. When we landed, a young woman with a pickup was waiting to collect the mail. As the pilot stepped out she came up to him and said, "Hello. You're new, aren't you? My name is Anna."

That was a scheduled flight on an American domestic airline. The company was Air North, which serves many bush communities, and its advertising slogan was "Experience Counts." An-other Air North pilot told me once that he liked being a bush pilot in Alaska—he had arrived from New York several months before—but he was having a hard time living on his pay. He said there was better money to be made operating bulldozers on the pipeline than operating planes for Air North. As a result, experienced, able pilots had not only been drawn away to fly pipeline charters; experi-enced, able pilots were also flying bulldozers on the tundra.

Some people I know in the National Park Ser-vice who were studying a region near the upper Yukon chartered a helicopter in an attempt to find the headwaters of a certain tributary stream. When they had been in flight for some time and had not seen anything remotely resembling the terrain they were looking for, they grew uneasy. When they looked ahead and saw the bright-white high-rising Wrangells, mountain peaks two hundred miles from where they were going, they realized they were lost. The pilot, new in Alaska, was from Alabama. "This is different, unique, tough coun-try," a pilot from Sitka once told me. "A guy has to know what he's doing. Flying is a way of life up here, and you have to get used to it. You can't drive. You can't walk. You can't swim."

In Anchorage, John Kauffmann had introduced me to his friend Charlie Allen, a general free-lance bush pilot with a wide reputation for having no betters and few peers. From the Southeastern Ar-chipelago to Arctic Alaska, Allen had been flying for twenty-five years. He was dismayed by the incompetence of some people in his profession, and was not at all shy to say so. "Alaska is the land of the bush pilot," he said. "You have to think highly of this bush pilot, because he's dirty, he has a ratty airplane, and he's alive. It's a myth, the bush-pilot thing. It's 'Smilin' Jack.' The myth affects pilots. Some of them, in this magic Eddie Rickenbacker fraternity, are more afraid of being embarrassed than they are of death. Suppose they're low on gas. They're so afraid of being embarrassed they keep going until they have no recourse but to crash. They drive their aircraft until they cough and quit. Kamikaze pilots. That's what we've got up here—kamikaze pilots from New Jersey. Do you think one of them would ever decide the weather's too tough? His champion-aviator's manhood would be impugned. Meanwhile, he's a hero if he gets through. A while ago, some guy ran out of gas at night on the ice pack. He had been chartered for a polar-bear hunt. He chopped off his fuel tanks with an axe and used the fuel tanks as boats. He and the hunters paddled out. He was then regarded as a hero. He was regarded as Eddie Rickenbacker *and* Smilin' Jack. But he was guilty of outrageous technical behavior. He was the fool who got them into the situation in the first place.

"Aircraft-salvage operations have a backlog of planes waiting to be salvaged in Alaska. Helicopters go out for them. In the past year and a half, I have helped salvage six planes that have been wrecked by *one* pilot. Don't identify him. Just call him 'a government employee.' Why do passengers *go* with such pilots? Would they go to the moon with an astronaut who did not have round-trip fuel? If you were in San Francisco and the boat to Maui was leaking and the rats were leaving, even if you had a ticket you *would not go*. Safety in the air is where you find it. Proper navigation helps, but proper judgment takes care of all conditions. You say to yourself, 'I ain't going to go today. The situation is too much for me.' And you resist all pressure to the contrary."

Allen paused a moment. Then he said, "You don't have to run into a mountain. Only a pilot is needed to wreck an airplane."

Of reported accidents, there have lately been something like two hundred a year in Alaska. Upwards of twenty-five a year produce fatal injuries, killing various numbers of people. Another fifteen crashes or so produce injuries rated "serious." The figures seem to compliment the fliers in a state where a higher percentage of people fly—and fly more often—than they do anywhere else in the United States. Merrill Field, a lightplane airfield in Anchorage, handles fifty-four thousand more flights per year than Newark International. On the other hand, if you get into an airplane in Alaska your chances of not coming back are greater by far than they would be in any other part of the country. Only Texas and California, with their vastly larger populations, consistently exceed Alaska in aircraft accidents. Government employees in Alaska speak of colleagues who have been lost "in line of duty." In air accidents during the past two years, the Bureau of Land Management has lost four, Alaska Fish and Game has lost one, U.S. Fish and Wildlife has lost three, the U.S. Forest Service has lost five, and the National Park Service has lost seven (in a single crash). A gallery of thirteen of the great bush pilots in the history of Alaska was presented in an Alaska newspaper not long ago. Of the thirteen, ten—among them Carl Eielson, Russ Merrill, Haakon Christensen, Big Money Monsen—died flying. I dropped in at a bar one day, in a small Alaskan town, where a bush pilot had one end of a plastic swizzlestick clamped between his teeth and was attempting to stretch it by pulling the other end. He had apparently been there some time, and he was challenging all comers to see who could stretch a swizzlestick the farthest. Jay Hammond, governor of Alaska, was himself a bush pilot for twenty-eight years, and a conspicuously good one. In an interview with him, I mentioned the sorts of things that cause disgust in pilots like Charlie Allen, and Hammond said, "There is nothing you can do by statute to assure competence." I wondered if that was altogether true—if, at the very least, regulations such as Alyeska's regarding pilots who come in from outside could not be extended to the state at large.

All this applies, of course, only to bush pilots and not to the big jetflying commercial carriers, whose accidents are extremely rare and are not outstanding in national statistics. As we flew from Fairbanks to Kotzebue to begin the trip to the Salmon River, we were in a Boeing 737 of Wien Air Alaska. One Captain Clayton came on the horn and said he would be pleased to play the harmonica for us as soon as he had finished a Fig Newton. A while later, he announced that his mouth was now solvent—and, above the clouds, he began to play. He played beautifully. The speaker system in that particular aircraft seemed to have been wired especially to meet his talent. He played three selections, and he found Kotzebue.

"This is not right. This just is *not* right," Gene Parrish said again, giving up on still another river and moving (west this time) to try again. Apparently, one of the streams he had passed over was, in fact, the Salmon. "I do my best," he said. "I do my best. I had the right heading—I'm certain of that. I do my best, but there ain't no guarangoddamntee." Of the next river he looked over perhaps twenty miles, without success. Then he began to mention fuel. He thought we should go back to Kiana and tap a drum. So he continued west, and crossed another mountain. Now he flew above a stream with a tributary coming into it that had a pair of sharp right-angled bends that formed the shape of a staple. Pictured on the Nome Sectional Aeronautical Chart was a staple-shaped pair of bends in a tributary of the Salmon River. The stream on the map and the stream on the earth appeared to be the same, but there was no guarangoddamntee. Forgetting Kiana for the time being, Parrish headed up the river. Down near the spruce, swinging around the bends, we hunted the gravel bars, looking for the shine of metal. There was much gravel but no aluminum. He turned once more for Kiana. There had been a hill on our left, and according to the map there should have been another tributary coming in on the far side of the hill. If the smaller stream was there, this was surely—so it seemed—the Salmon. Parrish could not resist having a look. He turned again, and flew north of the hill, which sloped down to the right bank of a tributary stream. We went on up the river. "This *must* be the Salmon, but it sure don't look right," Parrish said, and in the same instant Pourchot and the Grumman came into view. The chopper set down so near Pourchot it almost blew him over. We pulled out our gear, and wished Parrish well in his continuing tour of Alaska. In a whirling dust storm, the Messerschmitt took off, spattering us with sand and flying bits of dry debris. The dust would take a lot longer to settle than the laws of physics would suggest. Now we were alone between fringes of spruce by a clear stream where tundra went up the sides of mountains. This was, in all likelihood, the most isolated wilderness I would ever see, and that is how we got there.

Colorado

CHRISTIAN MILLER

Christian Miller, born in Scotland in 1920, says she made her cross-country bicycle trip because of a "keen interest in all things American, combined with my realization that I would never really get to know America if I only traveled there on a rather high financial level." As her tour through Colorado confirms, she "really got to know America."

It just wasn't going to be possible. I knew it. I sat at the foot of the Rockies and gazed hopelessly at the steep iron-grey road that wound upwards, following the course of a river, until it was lost from sight among the towering, threatening crags.

After only a few miles of bicycling, my mountain sickness had come back; I felt dizzy and weak, and in the pit of my stomach a demoralising feeling was lurking, like the dull weight that, as a child, I had experienced on my way to the dentist. There was absolutely no way, I realised, that I could force my shaking legs up that forbidding road; disconsolately, I flopped face-downwards on the grass of a roadside meadow and tried to think what to do next.

Suddenly I heard a sound in the air above me—something half way between the hiss of a taut sail and the rustle of windblown leaves. I rolled on to my back and looked up. A vast bird, like Sinbad's roc, was swooping down on me.

"Sorry if I frightened you," apologised the thin young man, panting slightly as he stumbled to a halt. Above and behind him, the multi-coloured triangle of his hang-glider framed him like half-folded wings, giving him the look of a stained-glass saint in a cathedral window. "Thought I'd get clean over you, but I guess I ran out of sky." Deftly, he unbuckled himself and laid the glider on the grass. "Jeese, that was a hairy ride."

Sitting down beside me, he pulled out a packet of cigarettes.

"Care for a smoke?"

I shook my head. "Hairy?"

"Thermals kinda haywire." He turned over on to his back and smoked silently for a few minutes. Then he glanced at Daisy. "Which way you going?"

"I was meaning to cross the pass, but it doesn't look as if I'll make it."

"How so?"

"I think the altitude's got me."

"Could give you a lift part of the way, if you like. My recovery team should be down soon, and we'll be heading back that way."

Half an hour later I was riding up towards the pass in the front seat of an enormous car, Daisy tucked into what I would have called the boot but which the driver referred to as his trunk. The other occupants of the car were talking animatedly in hang-glider language, and behind us, as the car ground up the precipitous inclines, swayed an elongated trailer packed with gliders, their huge triangle-shapes as neatly folded as the wings of sleeping bats.

Somehow, I had always imagined the Rockies to be picturesque tree-clad mountains, decorated in almost equal parts by clear rushing streams, leaping trout, amiable bears, and singing film-stars, and I was completely unprepared for the reality, which was precipitous, bleak, and very forbidding. I hadn't even the slightest urge to do any part of the climb on my own, and when the driver pulled off the road at a point which was obviously not the top of the pass I felt distinctly glum.

Everyone but me piled out of the car and peered—over what seemed to be a terrifying drop—towards the plain behind us. I was selfishly glad when they came back to the car.

"Hey—doesn't look as if we'll fly again till evening. Would you like us to run you right up to the top? Got loads of time on our hands."

The pass was deep in snow, the road winding over it like a dribble of dirty oil. A large notice stood outlined against some miserable-looking fir trees; it announced that the elevation was 11,307 feet and that the pass was a watershed between the Atlantic and the Pacific. I had hoped for a cheery café, of the kind that one finds at the top of Alpine ski-lifts, but as the glider boys reversed their trailer-car and set off down the road we had just climbed I found myself completely alone. There was just the snow, the trees, the lowering sky—and the sinister-looking grey road, snaking away downwards towards the distant Pacific; I rode a few yards down it, and then I got off again.

I might as well, I thought, take a photograph, just to remember what the Continental Divide looked like.

Lacking a human companion to decorate the foreground of photographs, I had by now taken literally dozens of snaps of Daisy, posed beside everything from Yorktown's George II cannons to Mississippi paddleboats. Now, on top of the Rockies, I leant her against a post at the side of the road, and stepped back to immortalise her against a panorama of snow and sky.

I fumbled with the little slide-thing that was supposed to adjust the distance on my camera, and peered through the viewfinder. Yes, there was the post—outlined against the sky. But where was Daisy? I took the camera away from my eye and gazed unbelievingly. Daisy had completely vanished. I hastened, slipping on the icy tarmac, back to the post; a flurry of snow in the ravine that lay behind it told me how idiotic I'd been not to test the firmness of the patch of snow on which I had left her—it had given way, and Daisy, with all my gear lashed to her, had fallen about 60 feet down the ravine.

It took three trips down the ravine to get everything up—two for the gear and one for Daisy herself—and on the third ascent I didn't know whether I was crying from exasperation, exhaustion, or just simple pain. The pain was because somewhere on the second descent—which I'd done by sitting on my heels and tobogganing down— the soles had ripped completely off my shoes. They were still attached at the back, but from my insteps forward they just flapped, like the lower jaws of a pair of paranoiac crocodiles. I tried putting my socks on outside my shoes; this held the soles in their right position until the socks themselves gave out, after which it was simply Every Toe for Itself—and the unlucky ones went straight down on to below-zero rock.

Gibbering with misery, I finally got everything back on to the road, and, tying the soles of my socks to my insteps with two guy-lines off my tent, started off down the far side of the pass.

At first the road wasn't particularly steep, but then it suddenly turned into an imitation of the Cresta Run. The wheels of the bicycle were going round so fast that the spokes—cutting through the freezing air—made a noise like a swarm of bees. Worse than that, the brake-pads started to melt, giving off a smell like burnt toast.

I slithered to a stop, and stood shivering at the roadside while the brakes cooled; the rims of the wheels, as well as the actual pads, were too hot to touch. In fact, just about the only thing that didn't seem in danger of melting was me—I was not only half-frozen, but also soaking wet; the snow that had collected in the folds of my clothes as I struggled up and down the ravine had melted into an icy mush that had penetrated right through to my skin.

I coasted downhill, stopping every few minutes to allow the wheels to cool, and also to glance anxiously at the sun, which was edging its usual inexorable way towards the savage-looking horizon. I had become, by now, fairly adept at judging the time of day by the angle of the sun, and when it got to about 45 degrees above the western horizon I would usually start looking for a campsite. But that day, although the sun was already obviously sinking, I didn't dare halt; or, to be more exact, there wasn't much point in halting, because the country was scaringly wild and the temperature equally scaringly low, and I had a horrid conviction that if I camped I would die either of fright or hypothermia, or quite possibly both. I really had to find somewhere warm and dry to sleep, and when I reached a tiny town to the west of the watershed, I booked into the first motel and tottered straight from a hot bath into bed.

When I woke up the next morning a revving and roaring and spluttering of motor-bicycles was shaking the wooden walls of my motel, causing the twin tooth-glasses in the bathroom to judder on their plastic shelf and the wire coat-hangers to shimmy along the metal rod of the wardrobe. I slipped out of bed and, pulling on my T-shirt, drew back the curtains; not more than a couple of yards away from my window a posse of leather-clad motor-bicyclists was vrmm-vrmming their machines, as if in preparation for a take-off into outer space. Their helmets, domed like those of astronauts but sharing, because of their raised visors, a curiously anachronistic kinship with the headgear of crusading knights, were decorated with the painted emblems of yet a third culture—the feathers and tomahawks of American Indians. Suddenly, as if to confuse both time and culture still further, they formed a line astern that might have been modelled on the battle-order of some Napoleonic sea-fight, and roared off down the wide street.

In the silence that followed their departure, I began to hear the small domestic sounds of a town awakening—the whirr of an electric razor, the clatter of a frying-pan, the slam of a refrigerator door. I pushed the window up and leant out, elbows on sill.

My motel consisted of a row of huts, standing along the unpaved verge of what seemed to be the town's only street. I was beginning to get used to the width of American streets, but this one—which was large enough to swallow a four-lane highway—was the most extravagant waste of land I'd yet seen.

But then, what would have been the point of saving land, when there was so much of it going spare? With an average of only 60 people per square mile—compared with nearly 600 per square mile in the British Isles—the main streets of most American towns could have been made as wide as football-grounds without anyone noticing the loss of land. Indeed, it might have given people a welcome excuse to use their cars to cross the road; they seemed to use them for just about every other errand—apart from in city centres, it was rare to see an American walking.

This particular wide street had only one car on it and, in the distance, one bicycle, carrying a small boy who, riding perilously along the bumpy grass verge, was throwing newspapers on to the porches of the houses. The houses were all of wood, and mostly only one-storey; as usual, they had no gardens, but were surrounded, inside their picket fences, by worn, patchy grass, the dusty monotony of which was relieved only by garden furniture and an occasional swing or climbing frame. One front yard was decorated by a sort of monstrous Christmas-tree made entirely from the antlers of dead deer; several hundred of these, bleached grey-white by sun and wind, were intertwined with all the precision of a formal arrangement of flowers. They towered high above my head, a grisly monument to somebody's addiction to the chase.

The whole town, in fact, had a greyish-whitish look. Only the advertisement signs proclaiming—in brilliant scarlet, vermilion, emerald green, gold, or electric blue—the rival virtues of cigarettes, petrol, soft drinks, cafés or motels, added colour to the scene; the signs, often higher than the houses, gave the town something of an air of a minute elf village, built under the shade of a patch of gaudy flowers.

But the sky—the sky had a blue so deep that it seemed to have actual thickness, so that I felt that if I could rise into it I would have to swim rather than fly; cloudless, featureless, it flowed from horizon to horizon like a curving azure sea, illuminated by a light so crystal-clear that there might not have been a single mote suspended in the millions of miles that lay between my eyes and the sun.

Miraculously—for I was still about 7,000 feet above sea-level—my mountain sickness had vanished; I felt ravenously hungry, and finding a vacant stool at the bar of a workmen's café, recklessly ordered orange juice, cornflakes, coffee, and waffles with bacon and maple syrup.

Pouring the sticky syrup lavishly over the buttery bacon-decorated waffles it struck me that, apart from when I was feeling ill, the amount I was eating was getting a bit out of hand. Breakfast like the one I was eating today, midmorning snacks of buns and Cokes, picnic lunches of hunks of ham and half loaves of fresh bread, nibbles of apples and chocolate bars, suppers of anything and everything I could lay my hands on—I'd never guessed that bicycling would make me so hungry. I kidded myself that all the exercise I was taking would burn up the calories, but I had a sneaking feeling that I wasn't exactly getting thinner.

An old man on the next stool at the breakfast bar eyed my order with interest; he was wearing an oil-stained denim boiler suit and the pores of his heavily-lined face were pitted with grime.

"Travelling far?" he asked, as if hazarding a guess at the reason for my hunger.

"I'm on a bike trip."

He thought about this for a few moments, silently reaching for sugar to put into his coffee. The chrome cover of the glass sugar-jar had a sliding section that moved back to release the grains; his large, broken-nailed thumb fumbled clumsily at the slide, giving him, unexpectedly, the pathetic air of a backward child struggling to unwrap a piece of candy. Then—

"Where'd you start from?"

"Virginia."

"Thought you must have been raised out east." And he smiled shyly, as if gratified that his guess had been proved right but at the same time reluctant to show pride in his own sagacity.

I was on the point of saying that I wasn't actually *from* Virginia, when it dawned on me that I was by now so far from the Atlantic that it was quite possible that the inhabitants of this isolated little town might find a Virginian accent as foreign as an English one. It seemed more polite to let him go on thinking I was a Virginian rather than to tell him that he was wrong, so I just went on eating.

Finally mastering the slide of the sugar-jar, the old man directed a small avalanche of white grains into a cup of milky coffee; as he stirred the now-glutinous liquid, a button detached itself from the cuff of his boiler suit, and fell, with a small plop! of a rising minnow, into the beige depths.

"Gosh darn," said the old man, mildly, fishing about with a small plastic spoon. Then, as if to excuse the behaviour of the button, he went on, "My wife died, six months past."

I made a small noise of commiseration.

"Yup," he said, as if agreeing to something that I had not, in fact, said. "Sure do miss her. Forty years, and never a night apart. Except when I had to go to hospital—hernia, that was."

Locating the button, he scooped it out of the coffee, and put it down on the throw-away plastic plate that had, until a few minutes before, supported his breakfast doughnut. A drop of coffee, spreading outwards from the tuft of thread attached to the shank of the button, marked the white polystyrene with a star-shaped pattern that might almost have been a tear.

Hastily I said, "What do you do, here?"

"Got my own engineering works, right next

door. Care to come and visit, when you've finished your feed?"

I had an instant vision of unpacking my kit, to find a needle and thread. I hardened my heart; it was still, after all, a long way to the Pacific.

As I bicycled out of the town, heading, at this part of the journey, almost due north, I saw my breakfast companion standing—looking distressingly lonely—at the door of his "engineering works." It was a small corrugated-iron hut, almost hidden among a jumble of rusty machinery parts and tractors so old that I doubted if they would ever run again. He raised his hand in a farewell gesture; I wished—too late—that I had made time to sew on that button.

If you ever want to be enchanted by skylarks the place to go is not Shelley's English countryside but the wild, watery plains that separate the mountain ranges of western Colorado. Around me as I bicycled along the rolling land on the far side of the Rockies lay miles of deserted scrub-land, intersected by marshy-looking streams; ragged barbed-wire fences outlined enclosures so enormous that I could only just make out where they began and ended, the white-faced Hereford cattle that wandered through them so far from the road that they showed up only as reddish-brown dots, outlined indistinctly against distant, tufty patches of wind-stunted trees. Along each horizon, to my right and left, lay mountain ranges, at first blue and then—on their higher peaks—white and majestic under their still-unmelted winter snow. Occasionally I could see the outlines of wooden farm buildings, grouped as tightly as chickens round their red-roofed mother-hen farmhouses.

The farms were all set back a mile or so from the road, joined to it by rough tracks guarded, at their junction with the tarmac, by metal cattle-grids. Over the entrance to each track a simple arch—usually two stripped tree-trunks joined by a wooden crossbar—carried a board on which was carved the name of the farm. Silver Sage Ranch, Lazy S Ranch (the S carved horizontally, to show exactly how lazy it was), Dry Creek Ranch (why did anyone choose to build a ranch *there?*), Tumbleweed Ranch (easy to see how that one got its name—great balls of tumbleweed, looking like giant pot-scrubbers, were bowling about all over the place), and occasionally one that must surely have perpetuated the name of some wife or sweet-heart—Mary-Lou Ranch, Abigail Ranch,—or, poignantly, Last Resting-place.

The spring growth had not yet begun, and everything—the scrubby fields, the verges of the road, the sedgy outlines of the creeks, the low rolling mounds of the distant foothills—was a uniform dun brown, broken only by paler beige patches of dried-up grass and the vertical brownish bristles of the leafless, dwarfish trees. It would have been a distinctly bleak and depressing place, but for the incredible blue of the sky—reflected all around in the water of the creeks and marshes, so that the entire plain seemed to be scattered with a mosaic of lapis lazuli—and, of course, the larks. Hovering so high as to be out of sight, they poured down a cascade of glittering song, and as I passed from the territory of one bird to the next, the changing patterns of melody seemed to carry me effortlessly along the road; I felt dancer-light, totally free, and outrageously happy.

"Oh, pardon," said the fat woman sitting on the side of the road. Coasting recklessly around a blind corner, I had nearly run over her feet. They were encased in a pair of old baseball boots; the rest of her was wrapped in a pink-and-white spotted housedress, against which her heavy breasts strained like two over-inflated footballs. "Pardon— we shouldn't have parked right here. But the kids had to go to the bathroom—you know how it is with kids." And she laughed merrily, the black curls of her untidy hair bouncing like springs on her plump polka-dotted shoulders.

Bathroom? I looked around, wondering if I'd unexpectedly reached some roadside motel. But for miles in every direction there was nothing to be seen but the burnt-up wasteland. Oh yes, of course—bathroom. By now I really should have grown used to the American euphemism. With what I hoped was an acceptable degree of tact, I feigned interest in Daisy's handlebars while, one, two, three, four and then a fifth child popped out from behind the tussocks of grass, zipping up jeans or pulling up knickers according to sex. Finally, from behind a small hillock, the father of the family appeared; he was very tall, with the loose-jointed look of the cowboy heroes of almost any early Western, and his eyes seemed to match exactly the blue of the sky.

We all moved further down the road, to a safer parking place; the family station-waggon, which at first refused to start, responded to the combined pushes of the four bigger children and, steered on to the verge, proved to be a positive cornucopia of chocolate-chip cookies, apples and Cokes. I contributed some imitation butterscotch—the packet stamped Wee Glen Genuine Scottish Candy—and we all sat munching in the sunshine. The inevitable question wasn't long in coming.

"Where'you headin' for?"

By now I had fallen into a subterfuge—rather than say that I was aiming for the Pacific, I would name as my destination some relatively near point without—unless absolutely cornered—disclosing that it would only be a stopping-off place on a much longer journey. This was not only because people in the eastern states had, when I had said openly that I was planning to cross the continent on my bicycle, simply thought I was joking, but also because, as I neared the centre of America, they sometimes seemed to think that I was saying that I was going to the Pacific in order to conceal my true destination.

"Go on, quit kidding," they would say. "Tell us where you're *really* going." And if I insisted that I really was heading for Oregon, I occasionally sensed a slight atmosphere of disquiet, as if I puzzled them—and they didn't enjoy being puzzled. So, I now said that I was thinking of having a look at Old Faithful. The geyser was, in fact, something I very much wanted to see, and lay only about a hundred miles to the north.

"Keep meanin' to take the kids up there. Mebbe we will, some summer."

The children squirmed, and yelled approval;

they all seemed to be roughly the same age, which I found puzzling.

"Any of you twins?" I asked, rescuing my bicycle-pump from the marginally smallest boy, who was trying to fit its nozzle into the ear of his younger sister. A chorus of negation, overlaid with howls of laughter, smothered this apparently preposterous suggestion.

"Naw, naw—I'm the eldest, then there's Gary, then David, and then. . . ."

Already I'd lost track of who was who, so I plunged in hastily with another question.

"And where are you going?"

"To git the groceries. And mebbe some shoes for Mary Sue."

Mary Sue, who looked about four, flopped over on to her back and held her feet in the air, exhibiting rather a lot of grubby knicker.

"My feet just grows and grows," she announced proudly.

"Where d'you go for groceries, round here?" I'd wondered how families in these sparsely-populated areas did their shopping. The mother named a town that I hadn't been planning to reach for another two days.

"But isn't that awfully far?"

"Lordy, no. Only about 70 miles."

Seventy miles? Just to do a bit of shopping? She laughed at what must have been my obvious amazement.

"Why, that's nothing. Henry here," and she poked a loving finger into her husband's stomach, "Henry here, he'll drive a hundred miles easy on a Saturday, just to git a bit of fishing."

Henry grinned happily. "Lovely fishing up in the mountains," he volunteered. "Trout as big as this." And he made the traditional gesture, hands held mendaciously far apart.

The children fell about, shrieking with glee. "Bigger'n that, Pa. Big as this." And they stretched their arms even wider, measuring fish the size of sharks.

"No, kids, that's enough. Don't you go teasing your Pa. Bad enough, spilling his night crawlers."

Night crawlers? I'd seen advertisements for them tacked up in many rural shop-windows. Night crawlers—so much a dozen. They sounded so unspeakably horrible that even my insatiable curiosity to see everything hadn't given me the courage to find out exactly what they were. Dimly, I imagined a cross between a leech and a wire-worm, humping its way with incandescent eyes through darkness unilluminated by either moon or stars. Tentatively, I asked, "Have you got any? Night crawlers? I'd love to see them." Liar, I told myself, under my breath.

"Nope. Sorry. Did have some, all ready for fishing." So that's what they were—some sort of bait. "But the kids spilt 'em. Have to git some more, Saturday." Thank heavens, I thought, reprieved from a confrontation that I secretly dreaded.

With much laughing and wriggling and shoving for places, the family piled back into their station-waggon. But they hadn't driven more than a hundred yards before they stopped and reversed to where I was standing—one foot on a pedal—preparing to bicycle after them.

"Jes' thought—would you like a ride?"

The station-waggon wasn't the usual huge American affair, but a compact, European-sized one, already wildly over-filled. Pa and the two bigger boys were on the front seat, while Ma sat in the back with the two smaller boys and Mary Sue who, cradled on her mother's lap, had already fallen into a thumbsucking doze. But the idea of covering, in maybe two hours, a distance that I had expected would take two days, was irresistible. Wedged between the two boys on the front seat, Daisy tied to the roof-rack with a scaringly frayed piece of string, I peered out though the dust-hazed windscreen. Two mangy bison, penned in a roadside stockade, peered morosely back. Roadside notices flashed past, warning of OPEN RANGE—LOOSE STOCK. A jagged board, slung like an inn-sign, announced that we were LEAVING COLORFUL COLORADO, and was followed swiftly by one which told us we were WELCOME TO BIG WONDERFUL WYOMING. Signposts reeled by, pointing to places familiar—if only by name—to a whole generation of European film-goers and television watchers. Saratoga. Laramie.

Why had I always thought of cowboy country as being dry and rocky? Could it have been because it was easier—and more picturesque—to film in craggy locations than it would have been to struggle in this boggy, comparatively featureless desert? Later, I was also to confess to a Montana friend that many Britons still thought that the American west was peopled with cowboys and Indians wearing nineteenth-century clothes. "Don't worry," she told me consolingly, "there's plenty of east-coast Americans who think so too."

The shopping town, when we finally reached it, seemed much the same as the town where I had spent the previous night, except that it had two wide streets instead of one. They were on different levels, joined by steep, dusty sidestreets on which stood the usual assortment of parked cars and rubbish-bins. It must have been garbage-collection day, for round the bins lay items that the owners hadn't been able to push inside; it didn't look a rich town, but the inhabitants were evidently well-off enough to throw away a stout kitchen chair, whose only fault seemed to be that someone had painted it a particularly vivid shade of puce, an apparently perfect—if slightly old-fashioned—refrigerator, and shoes that I would happily have walked away in, if I hadn't already replaced the ones I had ruined in the Rockies.

Some dark-eyed, straight-haired Indian children were queueing outside a battered iron door; it opened and, curious, I followed them inside. Beyond the door there was a ticket-kiosk and beyond again a small concrete-floored roller-skating rink. The children, although noticeably poorly dressed, appeared to be quite happy to pay out what seemed to me a lot of money to skate round and round the shabby, airless rink. They circled apathetically, seeming almost mesmerised by their own rotating motion; above them four loudspeakers, suspended from the iron girders of the roof, belched out deafening pop music.

I came out of the skating-rink just in time to see a swarthy-looking man ride away down the street on Daisy. Normally I never left her for even a minute without padlocking her, but I hadn't planned to follow the children, and had forgotten. The man was already several hundred yards away—I'd never catch him now.

But what was this? He was turning back—he was riding straight back towards me, grinning all over his face. And who were these other swarthy men, who seemed to have materialised out of the pavement? They were clapping and shouting as if the man on Daisy was doing a circus turn; as he drew near he took both hands off the handlebars and rode triumphantly up to the group, showing all the happy pride of a small boy who has managed to complete his first lap without stabilisers. I reached Daisy just as the second man leapt on and made ready to pedal off.

Now, Daisy had a great many good points—she was extremely light, totally rust-proof, and folded easily. But she also had some disadvantages—she was individualistic, temperamental, and easily damaged. All the way across the continent I had had to discourage people from trying her out, and one thing she absolutely did not need now, if she was going to live to finish the trip, was a buzz round the block under what appeared to be a sixteen-stone gorilla.

"Stop!" I yelled, seizing the back of her seat. The man simply stood on the pedals.

"No! No!" I yelled, dragged along on my heels as he started to get up speed. The group on the pavement was now laughing uproariously, as if the rider and I were some sort of comedy act.

"Stop thief!" I howled, throwing myself forward and clasping the rider round his waist. My compass, which I wore on a cord round my neck, fell forward, the cord entangling in the spokes of the rear wheel. We skidded to a halt.

"Aargh!" I gasped, clutching at the wheel in a desperate attempt to avoid strangulation. All the men started talking at once in a language that I didn't at first recognize. Then it dawned on me that they were speaking Spanish. Mexican immigrants, I thought, wildly searching my mind for the Hispanic equivalent of Cut the String, You Damn Fool. Then someone produced a murderous-looking knife and started sawing at the cord at a point exactly over my jugular vein.

"Calmese, calmese," another Mexican murmured soothingly, stroking my face with fingers that appeared to have had recent intimate contact with a chihuahua's lunch. Someone else imprisoned my hands while the cord was cut; I lay back in the gutter and thankfully breathed in gulps of cold Wyoming air.

Later, like birds on a telegraph wire, the Mexicans and I sat in a row along a brick wall, munching slices of a spicy, gristly sausage and trying to find some language in which we could communicate.

We drew primitive maps in the dust of the gutter. "England," I said. "Inglaterra. Londres." "Ah si!" they answered, cheerfully outlining a representation of the skyline of Manhattan. "No," I said, replying with a sketch of Buckingham Palace and what I felt was a staggeringly gifted portrait of the Queen, complete with a crown. "Ah ha!" they cried, pointing to the crown and making circling

445

motions over my head. "No, I'm positively no relation," I protested, pulling my pockets inside out to emphasise not only my non-regal status but also my even less regal resources.

Somebody cut up another sausage, even spicier and more gristly than the first. I had heard a rumour that Mexican sausages were made of a mixture of donkey and rabbit, in the proportion of one donkey to one rabbit; looking at my slice, I wondered if I'd got one of the hooves. Someone else peeled a shrivelled orange—splitting the skin with nails like the tines of a rusty harrow—and, placing it on a grimy handkerchief, offered it to me with all the panache of a ballet-dancer presenting a rose. The man who had cut my compass cord tried to splice the severed ends and, failing, sliced a strip from his own belt and fashioned me a leather thong, on which the compass swung far better than it had on the cord.

I got away fairly smartly after lunch, but once clear of the town I stopped and sat down to work out where I would go next. One of the beauties of this journey was that I didn't have to stick to any set route—provided that I hit the Pacific somewhere north of San Francisco, and that I reached Portland before the expiry-date of my return ticket, I could go anywhere I wanted. And Portland, according to my calculations, was exactly 1,008 miles away from where I was now sitting.

One thousand and eight miles—why, if my original estimate of 4,200 miles for the entire trip had been more or less right, I'd covered more than three-quarters of it already, in well under three-quarters of the available time. Perhaps, I thought,

I could allow myself the luxury of a little side-trip. I got out all my remaining maps and spread them round me.

As well as a small-scale map that showed me my position relative to the rest of the world, I had started the trip with twenty large-scale automobile-type maps of the United States, covering a sweep from the Atlantic to the Pacific, and I say "remaining" because, so as to keep weight down to a minimum, I had been filling an envelope each week with the sections that I had passed through, and posting them home. Into the envelope—which had to be the very largest I could find—I also tucked used guidebooks, picture postcards, addresses of people who had befriended me, and any other bits of paper that I didn't actually want to lug along with me but which I wanted to keep. Exposed photo-films I posted straight to an English processing firm, telling them to send the prints to my home address; it would have been hopeless to try to get them developed as I travelled, for I was never in one place long enough.

The automobile maps covered a lot of country to both north and south of my most direct route, and sitting in the sunshine, my back against a warm rock, I mulled over the rival merits of the roads that I could take, feeling again the sense of exhilarating freedom that came from being able to do exactly as I pleased. There I was, completely alone; nobody knew where I was; I could go wherever I wanted without consulting anyone else, without making any concession to anyone else's personality or wishes; it was a type of freedom unknown in my past life, where almost every action had been conditioned by the needs—either physical or psychological—of somebody else. Perhaps eventually such total freedom might pall, but at that instant it was wonderful.

In spite of the warmth of the spring sun, the land around me still had a barren, wintry look, and no matter how hard I listened, I could hear no sound of any kind. Far back down the road, the town showed only as a pimple-like rash, breaking out from the tanned stubble of the sage. Then, down the railway track that, at this point, ran parallel to the road, an engine hooted mournfully, as if enquiring if there was anyone alive in the world. Slowly, a train snaked into sight—a hundred or so goods wagons stencilled with UNION PACIFIC AND SANTA FE. The names held for me all the magic of another age; it was as if history was rolling past me and I wouldn't have been surprised, at that moment, to have seen the Deadwood Stage rumble down the road, or glimpse a rider of the Pony Express galloping past, his leather chaps blackened with the sweat of his lathered horse.

The train ground away, clanking wearily, and when it had gone the silence seemed so complete as to be almost supernatural. Then I heard a car approaching; as usual in this sort of rolling terrain, it was audible while still invisible. I looked forward down the tarmac, and then backward the way I had come, finally spotting what looked like a small red lady-bird dipping in and out of sight as it negotiated the humps and hollows of the road. After it had passed me I could, for long minutes, still hear it as it buzzed away; in the still air, the sound lingered pervasively, so that had I not known that the car had just passed me I wouldn't have been able to decide if it was coming or going.

A duck hawk landed on a fence-post not four yards from where I was sitting, regarded me arrogantly from yellow, wide-irised eyes, then, with its menacingly curved beak, nonchalantly set about grooming its tail feathers. Suddenly it swivelled its head, rose on decisive wings, banked steeply, and dived talons-first into the brush. There was a brief shrill squeak, like chalk drawn across a blackboard, and the hawk rose again, bearing in its talons the still-struggling body of a Whitetail prairie dog.

I turned my attention back to my maps. Just where was I going next? The most obvious way to head would have been north-west, towards Portland, at an angle that would—if I pursued it for about 3,000 miles—take me into Alaska. But as I was making such good time, I decided to travel instead almost due west, and then veer south-west into Utah. This would give me a chance to see Salt Lake City, even though it would mean that later on, so as to reach Yellowstone Park, I would have almost to retrace my steps by bicycling due north.

I jumped on to Daisy and set off towards the land of the Mormons. Everything in the world seemed quite remarkably cheerful—not only was the weather staying fine but on that very open road I was getting more than my usual ration of whistles.

Weeks of non-stop exercise had done wonders for my legs, and constant exposure to the sun had lighted my normally mouse-coloured hair so that, seen from the back, I must have exuded something of the irresistible allure of a centre-forward from a reform-school hockey team. At any rate, grossly sex-starved men, overtaking my bicycle from behind in cars or lorries, would let out suggestive cries of unbridled lust, which turned, after they had passed me and had realised—too late—that I was quite literally old enough to be their mother, to such expressions of disappointment that I was tempted to tie a notice to the small of my back, saying "Don't Bother."

But, if I ignored the sad looks on their departing faces, the initial wolf-whistles were rather cheering; besides, I had just passed a signpost that proclaimed that it was only 108 miles to the next town. I had no idea what the town would be like, but it had a most attractive name.

Walking Blind

Enos A. Mills

When Enos Abijah Mills died in 1922—exhausted and brokenhearted, some said, in the struggle to preserve the Rocky Mountain wilderness he loved—his eulogists compared him with John Muir and John Burroughs. Less felicitous than these patriarchs, he was nevertheless an energetic popularizer of the mountains, and was recognized as the moving force behind the creation of Rocky Mountain National Park in Colorado. Enos Mills had come from Kansas around the turn of the century to homestead at the base of Long's Peak; from his isolated outpost, he made many solitary journeys into the mountains. His most memorable adventure follows—snowblind on the summit.

As I climbed out of the dwarfed woods at timberline in the Rocky Mountains, and started across the treeless white summit, the terrific sun glare on the snow warned me of the danger of snowblindness. I had lost my snow glasses. But the wild attractions of the heights caused me to forget the care of my eyes and I lingered to look down into cañons and to examine magnificent snow cornices. A number of mountain sheep also interested me. Then for half an hour I circled a confiding flock of ptarmigan and took picture after picture.

451

Through the clear air the sunlight poured with burning intensity. I was 12,000 feet above the sea. Around me there was not a dark crag nor even a tree to absorb the excess of light. A wilderness of high, rugged peaks stood about—splendid sunlit mountains of snow. To east and west they faced winter's noonday sun with great shadow mantles flowing from their shoulders.

As I started to hurry on across the pass I began to experience the scorching pains that go with seared, sunburnt eyes—snow-blindness. Unfortunately, I had failed to take even the precaution of blackening my face, which would have dulled the glare. At the summit my eyes became so painful that I could endure the light only a few seconds at a time. Occasionally I sat down and closed them for a minute or two. Finally, while doing this, the lids adhered to the balls and the eyes swelled so that I could not open them.

Blind on the summit of the Continental Divide! I made a grab for my useful staff which I had left standing beside me in the snow. In the fraction of a second that elapsed between thinking of the staff and finding it my brain woke up to the seriousness of the situation. To the nearest trees it was more than a mile, and the nearest house was many miles away across ridges of rough mountains. I had matches and a hatchet, but no provisions. Still, while well aware of my peril, I was only moderately excited, feeling no terror. Less startling incidents have shocked me more, narrow escapes from street automobiles have terrified me.

It had been a wondrous morning. The day cleared after a heavy fall of fluffy snow. I had snowshoed up the slope toward a ragged, snow-carpeted spruce forest, whose shadows wrought splendid black-and-white effects upon the shining floor. There were thousands of towering, slender spruces, each brilliantly laden with snow flowers, standing soft, white, and motionless in the sunlight. While I was looking at one of these artistically decorated trees, a mass of snow dropped upon me from its top, throwing me headlong and causing me to lose my precious eye-protecting snow glasses. But now I was blind.

With staff in hand, I stood for a minute or two planning the best manner to get along without eyes. My faculties were intensely awake. Serious situations in the wilds had more than once before this stimulated them to do their best. Temporary blindness is a good stimulus for the imagination and memory—in fact, is good educational training for all the senses. However perilous my predicament during a mountain trip, the possibility of a fatal ending never even occurred to me. Looking back now, I cannot but wonder at my matter-of fact attitude concerning the perils in which that snow blindness placed me.

I had planned to cross the pass and descend into a trail at timberline. The appearance of the slope down which I was to travel was distinctly in my mind from my impressions just before darkness settled over me.

Off I slowly started. I guided myself with information from feet and staff, feeling my way with the staff so as not to step off a cliff or walk overboard into a cañon. In imagination I pictured myself following the shadow of a staff-bearing and slouch-hatted form. Did mountain sheep, curious and slightly suspicious, linger on crags to watch my slow and hesitating advance? Across the snow did the shadow of a soaring eagle coast and circle?

I must have wandered far from the direct course to timberline. Again and again I swung my staff to right and left hoping to strike a tree. I had travelled more than twice as long as it should have taken to reach timberline before I stood face to face with a low-growing tree that bristled up through the deep snow. But had I come out at the point for which I aimed—at the trail? This was the vital question.

The deep snow buried all trail blazes. Making my way from tree to tree I thrust an arm deep into the snow and felt of the bark, searching for a trail blaze. At last I found a blaze and going on a few steps I dug down again in the snow and examined a tree which I felt should mark the trail. This, too, was blazed.

Feeling certain that I was on the trail I went down the mountain through the forest for some minutes without searching for another blaze. When I did examine a number of trees not another blaze could I find. The topography since entering the forest and the size and character of the trees were such that I felt I was on familiar ground. But going on a few steps I came out on the edge of an unknown rocky cliff. I was now lost as well as blind.

During the hours I had wandered in reaching timberline I had had a vague feeling that I might be travelling in a circle, and might return to trees on the western slope of the Divide up which I had climbed. When I walked out on the edge of the cliff the feeling that I had doubled to the western slope became insistent. If true, this was most serious. To reach the nearest house on the west side of the range would be extremely difficult, even though I should discover just where I was. But I believed I was somewhere on the eastern slope.

I tried to figure out the course I had taken. Had I, in descending from the heights, gone too far to the right or to the left? Though fairly well acquainted with the country along this timberline, I was unable to recall a rocky cliff at this point. My staff found no bottom and warned me that I was at a jumping-off place.

Increasing coolness indicated that night was upon me. But darkness did not matter, my light had failed at noon. Going back along my trail a short distance I avoided the cliff and started on through the night down a rocky, forested, and snow-covered slope. I planned to get into the bottom of a cañon and follow downstream. Every few steps I shouted, hoping to attract the attention of a possible prospector, miner, or woodchopper. No voice answered. The many echoes, however, gave me an idea of the topography—of the mountain ridges and cañons before me. I listened intently after each shout and noticed the direction from which the reply came, its intensity, and the cross echoes, and concluded that I was going down into the head of a deep, forest-walled cañon, and, I hoped, travelling eastward.

For points of the compass I appealed to the trees, hoping through my knowledge of woodcraft to orient myself. In the study of tree distribution I had learned that the altitude might often be approximated and the points of the compass determined by noting the characteristic kinds of trees.

Cañons of east and west trend in this locality carried mostly limber pines on the wall that faces south and mostly Engelmann spruces on the wall that faces the north. Believing that I was travelling eastward I turned to my right, climbing out of the cañon, and examined a number of trees along the slope. Most of these were Engelmann spruces. The slope probably faced north. Turning about I descended this slope and ascended the opposite one. The trees on this were mostly limber pines. Hurrah! Limber pines are abundant only on southern slopes. With limber pines on my left and Engelmann spruces on my right, I was now satisfied that I was travelling eastward and must be on the eastern side of the range.

To put a final check on this—for a blind or lost man sometimes manages to do exactly the opposite of what he thinks he is doing—I examined lichen growths on the rocks and moss growths on the trees. In the deep cañon I dug down into the snow and examined the faces of low-lying boulders. With the greatest care I felt the lichen growth on the rocks. These verified the information that I had from the trees—but none too well. Then I felt over the moss growth, both long and short, on the trunks and lower limbs of trees, but this testimony was not absolutely convincing. The moss growth was so nearly even all the way around the trunk that I concluded that the surrounding topography must be such as to admit the light freely from all quarters, and also that the wall or slope on my right must be either a gentle one or else a low one and somewhat broken. I climbed to make sure. In a few minutes I was on a terrace—as I expected. Possibly back on the right lay a basin that might be tributary to this cañon. The reports made by the echoes of my shoutings said that this was true. A few minutes of travel down the cañon and I came to the expected incoming stream, which made its swift presence heard beneath its cover of ice and snow.

A short distance farther down the cañon I examined a number of trees that stood in thick growth on the lower part of what I thought was the southern slope. Here the character of the moss and lichens and their abundant growth on the northerly sides of the trees verified the testimony of the tree distribution and of previous moss and lichen growths. I was satisfied as to the points of the compass. I was on the eastern side of the Continental Divide travelling eastward.

After three or four hours of slow descending I reached the bottom. Steep walls rose on both right and left. The enormous rock masses and the entanglements of fallen and leaning trees made progress difficult. Feeling that if I continued in the bottom of the cañon I might come to a precipitous place down which I would be unable to descend, I tried to walk along one of the side walls, and thus keep above the bottom. But the walls were too steep and I got into trouble.

Out on a narrow, snow-corniced ledge I walked. The snow gave way beneath me and down I went over the ledge. As I struck, feet foremost, one snowshoe sank deeply. I wondered, as I wiggled out, if I had landed on another ledge. I had. Not desiring to have more tumbles, I tried to climb back up on the ledge from which I had fallen, but I could not do it. The ledge was broad and short and there appeared to be no safe way off. As I explored again my staff encountered the top of a dead tree that leaned against the ledge. Breaking a number of dead limbs off I threw them overboard. Listening as they struck the snow below I concluded that it could not be more than thirty feet to the bottom.

I let go my staff and dropped it after the limbs. Then, without taking off snowshoes, I let myself down the limbless trunk. I could hear water running beneath the ice and snow. I recovered my staff and resumed the journey.

In time the cañon widened a little and travelling became easier. I had just paused to give a shout when a rumbling and crashing high up in the righthand slope told me that a snowslide was plunging down. Whether it would land in the cañon before me or behind me or on top of me could not be guessed. The awful smashing and crashing and roar proclaimed it of enormous size and indicated that trees and rocky debris were being swept onward with it. During the few seconds that I stood awaiting my fate, thought after thought raced through my brain as I recorded the ever-varying crashes and thunders of the wild, irresistible slide.

With terrific crash and roar the snowslide swept into the cañon a short distance in front of me. I was knocked down by the outrush or concussion of air and for several minutes was nearly smothered with the whirling, settling snow-dust and rock powder which fell thickly all around. The air cleared and I went on.

I had gone only a dozen steps when I came upon the enormous wreckage brought down by the slide. Snow, earthy matter, rocks, and splintered trees were flung in fierce confusion together. For three or four hundred feet this accumulation filled the cañon from wall to wall and was fifty or sixty feet high. The slide wreckage smashed the ice and dammed the stream. As I started to climb across this snowy debris a shattered place in the ice beneath gave way and dropped me into the water, but my long staff caught and by clinging to it I saved myself from going in above my hips. My snowshoes caught in the shattered ice and while I tried to get my feet free a mass of snow fell upon me and nearly broke my hold. Shaking off the snow I put forth all my strength and finally pushed my feet free of the ice and crawled out upon the debris. This was a close call and at last I was thoroughly, briefly, frightened.

As the wreckage was a mixture of broken trees, stones, and compacted snow I could not use my snowshoes, so I took them off to carry them till over the debris. Once across I planned to pause and build a fire to dry my icy clothes.

With difficulty I worked my way up and across. Much of the snow was compressed almost to ice by the force of contact, and in this icy cement many kinds of wreckage were set in wild disorder. While descending a steep place in this mass, carrying snowshoes under one arm, the footing gave way and I fell. I suffered no injury but lost one of the snowshoes. For an hour or longer I searched, without finding it.

The night was intensely cold and in the search my feet became almost frozen. In order to rub them I was about to take off my shoes when I came upon something warm. It proved to be a dead mountain sheep with one horn smashed off. As I sat with my feet beneath its warm carcass and my hands upon it, I thought how but a few minutes before the animal had been alive on the heights will all its ever wide-awake senses vigilant for its preservation; yet I, wandering blindly, had escaped with my life when the snowslide swept into the cañon. The night was calm, but of zero temperature or lower. It probably was crystal clear. As I sat warming my hands and feet on the proud master of the crags I imagined the bright, clear sky crowded thick with stars. I pictured to myself the dark slope down which the slide had come. It appeared to reach up close to the frosty stars.

But the lost snowshoe must be found, wallowing through the deep mountain snow with only one snowshoe would be almost hopeless. I had vainly searched the surface and lower wreckage projections but made one more search. This proved successful. The shoe had slid for a short distance, struck an obstacle, bounced upward over smashed logs, and lay about four feet above the general surface. A few moments more and I was beyond the snowslide wreckage. Again on snowshoes, staff in hand, I continued feeling my way down the mountain.

My ice-stiffened trousers and chilled limbs were not good travelling companions, and at the first cliff that I encountered I stopped to make a fire. I gathered two or three armfuls of dead limbs, with the aid of my hatchet, and soon had a lively blaze going. But the heat increased the pain in my eyes, so with clothes only partly dried, I went on. Repeatedly through the night I applied snow to my eyes trying to subdue the fiery torment.

From timberline I had travelled downward through a green forest mostly of Engelmann spruce with a scattering of fir and limber pine. I frequently felt of the tree trunks. But a short time after leaving my camp-fire I came to the edge of an extensive region that had been burned over. For more than an hour I travelled through dead standing trees, on many of which only the bark had been burned away; on others the fire had burned more deeply.

Pausing on the way down, I thrust my staff into the snow and leaned against a tree to hold snow against my burning eyes. While I was doing this two owls hooted happily to each other and I listened to their contented calls with satisfaction.

Hearing the pleasant, low call of a chickadee I listened. Apparently he was dreaming and talking in his sleep. The dream must have been a happy one, for every note was cheerful. Realizing that he probably was in an abandoned woodpecker nesting hole, I tapped on the dead tree against which I was leaning. This was followed by a chorus of lively, surprised chirpings, and one, two, three!— then several—chickadees flew out of a hole a few inches above my head. Sorry to have disturbed them I went on down the slope.

As last I felt the morning sun in my face. With

increased light my eyes became extremely painful. For a time I relaxed upon the snow, finding it difficult to believe that I had been travelling all night in complete darkness. While lying here I caught the scent of smoke. There was no mistaking it. It was the smoke of burning aspen, a wood much burned in the cook-stoves of mountain people. Eagerly I rose to find it. I shouted again and again but there was no response. Under favourable conditions, keen nostrils may detect aspen-wood smoke for a distance of two or three miles.

The compensation of this accident was an intense stimulus to my imagination—perhaps our most useful intellectual faculty. My eyes, always keen and swift, had ever supplied me with almost an excess of information. But with them suddenly closed my imagination became the guiding faculty. I did creative thinking. With pleasure I restored the views and scenes of the morning before. Any one seeking to develop the imagination would find a little excursion afield, with eyes voluntarily blindfolded, a most telling experience.

Down the mountainside I went, hour after hour. My ears caught the chirps of birds and the fall of icicles which ordinarily I would hardly have heard. My nose was constantly and keenly analyzing the air. With touch and clasp I kept in contact with the trees. Again my nostrils picked up aspen smoke. This time it was much stronger. Perhaps I was near a house! But the whirling air currents gave me no clue as to the direction from which the smoke came, and only echoes responded to my call.

All my senses worked willingly in seeking wireless news to substitute for the eyes. My nose readily detected odours and smoke. My ears were more vigilant and more sensitive than usual. My fingers, too, were responsive from the instant that my ears failed. Delightfully eager they were, as I felt the snow-buried trees, hoping with touch to discover possible trail blazes. My feet also were quickly, steadily alert to translate the topography.

Occasionally a cloud shadow passed over. In imagination I often pictured the appearance of these clouds against the blue sky and tried to estimate the size of each by the number of seconds its shadow took to drift across me.

Mid-afternoon, or later, my nose suddenly detected the odour of an ancient corral. This was a sign of civilization. A few minutes later my staff came in contact with the corner of a cabin. I shouted "Hello!" but heard no answer. I continued feeling until I came to the door and found that a board was nailed across it. The cabin was locked and deserted! I broke in the door.

In the cabin I found a stove and wood. As soon as I had a fire going I dropped snow upon the stove and steamed my painful eyes. After two hours or more of this steaming they became more comfortable. Two strenuous days and one toilsome night had made me extremely drowsy. Sitting upon the floor near the stove I leaned against the wall and fell asleep. But the fire burned itself out. In the night I awoke nearly frozen and unable to rise. Fortunately, I had on my mittens, otherwise my fingers probably would have frozen. By rubbing my hands together, then rubbing my arms and legs, I finally managed to limber myself, and though unable to rise, I succeeded in starting a new fire. It was more than an hour before I ceased shivering; then, as the room began to warm, my legs came back to life and again I could walk.

I was hungry. This was my first thought of food since becoming blind. If there was anything to eat in the cabin, I failed to find it. Searching my pockets I found a dozen or more raisins and with these I broke my sixty-hour fast. Then I had another sleep, and it must have been near noon when I awakened. Again I steamed the eye pain into partial submission.

Going to the door I stood and listened. A camp-bird only a few feet away spoke gently and confidingly. Then a crested jay called impatiently. The camp-bird alighted on my shoulder. I tried to explain to the birds that there was nothing to eat. The prospector who had lived in this cabin evidently had been friendly with the bird neighbours. I wished that I might know him.

Again I could smell the smoke of aspen wood. Several shouts evoked echoes—nothing more. I stood listening and wondering whether to stay in the cabin or to venture forth and try to follow the snow-filled roadway that must lead down through the woods from the cabin. Wherever this open way led I could follow. But of course I must take care not to lose it.

In the nature of things I felt that I must be three or four miles to the south of the trail which I had planned to follow down the mountain. I wished I might see my long and crooked line of footmarks in the snow from the summit to timberline.

Hearing the open water in rapids close to the cabin, I went out to try for a drink. I advanced slowly, blind-man fashion, feeling the way with my long staff. As I neared the rapids, a water ouzel, which probably had lunched in the open water, sang with all his might. I stood still as he repeated his liquid, hopeful song. On the spot I shook off procrastination and decided to try to find a place where someone lived.

After writing a note explaining why I had smashed in the door and used so much wood, I readjusted my snowshoes and started down through the woods. I suppose it must have been late afternoon.

I found an open way that had been made into a road. The woods were thick and the open roadway really guided me. Feeling and thrusting with my staff, I walked for some time at normal pace. Then I missed the way. I searched carefully, right, left, and before me for the utterly lost road. It had forked, and I had continued on the short stretch that come to an end in the woods by an abandoned prospect hole. As I approached close to this the snow caved in, nearly carrying me along with it. Confused by blinded eyes and the thought of oncoming night, perhaps, I had not used my wits. When at last I stopped to think I figured out the situation. Then I followed my snowshoe tracks back to the main road and turned into it.

For a short distance the road ran through dense woods. Several times I paused to touch the trees each side with my hands. When I emerged from the woods, the pungent aspen smoke said that I must at last be near a human habitation. In fear of passing it I stopped to use my ears. As I stood listening, a little girl gently, curiously, asked: "Are you going to stay here to-night?"

The publishers hope that this
Large Print Book has brought
you pleasurable reading.
Each title is designed to make
the text as easy to see as possible.
G.K. Hall Large Print Books
are available from your library and
your local bookstore. Or, you can
receive information by mail on
upcoming and current Large Print Books
and order directly from the publishers.
Just send your name and address to:

G.K. Hall & Co.
70 Lincoln Street
Boston, Mass. 02111

or call, toll-free:

1-800-343-2806

A note on the text
Large print edition designed by
Bernadette Montalvo.
Composed in 16 pt Plantin
on a Xyvision 300/Linotron 202N
by Genevieve Connell
of G.K. Hall & Co.